LIKE A SPLINTER IN YOUR MIND

To Jacoby, Jeremy, and Keenan

LIKE A SPLINTER IN YOUR MIND

THE PHILOSOPHY BEHIND THE *MATRIX* TRILOGY

MATT LAWRENCE

Blackwell
Publishing

BLACKWELL PUBLISHING

350 Main Street, Malden, MA 02148-5020, USA

108 Cowley Road, Oxford OX4 1JF, UK

550 Swanston Street, Carlton, Victoria 3053, Australia

First published 2004 by Blackwell Publishing Ltd.
Reprinted 2004, 2005

Library of Congress Cataloging-in-Publication Data

Lawrence, Matt.
  Like a splinter in your mind : the philosophy behind the Matrix trilogy / Matt Lawrence.
     p. cm.
  ISBN 1-4051-2523-3 (hardcover : alk. paper) — ISBN 1-4051-2524-1
(pbk. : alk. paper)
  1. Matrix (Motion picture) 2. Matrix reloaded. 3. Matrix revolutions. I. Title.

PN1997.M395L38 2004
791.43'72—dc22

                                                    2004005405

A catalogue record for this title is available from the British Library.

Set in 9.5/14 pt Bell Gothic Light
by Graphicraft Ltd, Hong Kong
Printed and bound in the United Kingdom
by MPG Books, Bodmin Ltd, Cornwall

The publisher's policy is to use permanent paper from mills that operate a sustainable forestry policy, and which has been manufactured from pulp processed using acid-free and elementary chlorine-free practices. Furthermore, the publisher ensures that the text paper and cover board used have met acceptable environmental accreditation standards.

For further information on
Blackwell Publishing, visit our website:
www.blackwellpublishing.com

CONTENTS

110440

ACKNOWLEDGMENTS

When René Descartes said *I think therefore I am*, he had stumbled across a profound philosophical truth. But, of course, it was not the whole truth, and when taken alone it rings of self-sufficiency and individualism. For a more complete understanding of the self I draw on the wisdom of an African proverb: *I am because we are*. The emphasis here is on our interdependence and connectedness. Our very existence depends upon those around us, and the people in our lives shape who we become. This idea of interdependence applies equally well to the creation of this book. This book would not be what it is without those who have helped me along the way; and without the help of some, this book would never have existed at all. So I would like to express my appreciation to everyone who contributed in one way or another.

I'm especially grateful to my wife Lisa for her constant support and valuable feedback. Without her help in so many aspects of my life this book would simply not have been possible. Also crucial were Jacoby Lawrence and Randy Firestone, who provided me with the first feedback on most chapters: I am grateful for their innumerable comments and valuable suggestions. I'm also indebted to Randy for researching and writing the initial draft of the "Cast of Philosophers" appendix, and Suzanne Lawrence for help with proofreading and indexing.

Thanks also to all the philosophers who commented on the various chapters, including James McGrath, David Shoemaker, Celia Sepulveda, Lawrence Fike, Scott Tidwell, Rachel Hollenberg, Gabe Trafas, June Yang, and the anonymous reviewers at Blackwell. Their suggestions improved the book immensely. Thanks also to Lee Bravo and Alex Grzesik, who, along with my Introduction to Philosophy students, researched entries for the Matrix Glossary and Cast of Philosophers. And I am forever grateful to my philosophy students at Long Beach City College, who have been my primary audience over the last six years. Their feedback has been invaluable.

I'd also like to thank Larry and Andy Wachowski for their incredible films and for the permission to quote the *Matrix* scripts. Also thanks to Scott Mayhew for the use of his illustrative talents, and to the production team at Blackwell – especially my editor Nick Bellorini. Nick's strong commitment to the project from very early on was most helpful, and his suggestions greatly improved several of the chapters.

And last, but certainly not least, thanks to my parents for their love and support all of these years.

Matt Lawrence can be found in cyberspace at:
http://home.lbcc.cc.ca.us/~mlawrence

The following illustrations were provided by Scott Mayhew:

Figure 1 (in the Introduction): Plato's Cave: the original Matrix circa 400 BCE.
Figure 8 (chapter 14): The Wachowskis' vision of a computer-generated matrix.
Figure 9 (chapter 14): Kant's vision of a mind-generated matrix.

ACKNOWLEDGMENTS

MATRIX
QUOTATIONS
LEGEND

The *Matrix* sources used in quotations throughout the book can be identified by the following symbols:

†   *The Matrix*
††   *The Matrix Reloaded*
†††   *The Matrix Revolutions*
E   *Enter the Matrix*
SS   *The Matrix – Shooting Script*

INTRODUCTION
JACKING INTO THE PHILOSOPHY BEHIND THE MATRIX

What is the Matrix?

You've felt it your entire life. That there's something wrong with the world. You don't know what it is, but it's there, like a splinter in your mind, driving you mad.

The Matrix is everywhere. It is all around us, even now in this very room. You can see it when you look out your window, or when you turn on your television. You can feel it when you go to work, when you go to church, when you pay your taxes. It is the world that has been pulled over your eyes to blind you from the truth . . . a prison that you cannot smell, or taste, or touch. A prison for your mind.

– Morpheus[†]

What is Philosophy?

The man who has no tincture for philosophy goes through life imprisoned in the prejudices derived from common sense . . . and from convictions which have grown up in his mind without the cooperation or consent of his deliberate reason. To such a man the world tends to become definite, finite, obvious; common objects rouse no questions, and unfamiliar possibilities are contemptuously rejected.

As soon as we begin to philosophize, on the contrary, we find . . . that even the most everyday things lead to problems to which only very incomplete answers can be given.

Philosophy, though unable to tell us with certainty what is the true answer to the doubts which it raises, is able to suggest many possibilities which enlarge our thoughts and free them from the tyranny of custom.

– Bertrand Russell

If to live in the Matrix is to sleep, unwittingly accepting the appearances that are given to you, then to engage in philosophy is to wake up. Philosophy calls on us to question everything – especially those things that seem most obvious. If I were to try to describe what philosophy is in just a few words, I would say that it is to ask the most basic and puzzling questions that life has to offer. To think philosophically is to ask the *deep* questions. But by "deep" I don't mean profound (though philosophical questions often are); rather, I mean that philosophy deals with the questions that sit "at the bottom" of all human thought and action – the most *basic* questions of life. Most of the time we involve ourselves with the more specific nonphilosophical questions: "Do you know about the *Matrix* films?" "Have you seen them all?" "Were they good?" Even the question "What is the Matrix?" is not itself very philosophical. But the intriguing thing about these films is that one cannot really understand the "what the Matrix is" without asking most of the deep questions of human existence. You cannot fully understand the Matrix without first asking: "What is *Real*?" "How do we *know* what is Real?" "*Can* we know what is Real?" And these are some of the great philosophical questions.

It's the Questions that Drive Us

It is always frustrating to hear someone say that the *Matrix* films are just about Kung Fu and special effects. Rather, I'd say that these films are about knowledge, reality, consciousness, freedom, fate, foreknowledge, faith, good, evil, enlightenment, and the very meaning of existence. In short, they are about philosophy – with some pretty cool special effects on the side. The *Matrix* films invite us to explore an incredibly wide range of philosophical questions. We can divide them by subject-matter as follows:

Metaphysics: the study or theory of the nature of reality.
What is Real?
What is the difference between appearance and reality?
Is reality material, immaterial, or both?

Epistemology: the study/theory of knowledge.

What is knowledge?

Can we know what is real?

How do we know?

Ethics: the study/theory of morality.

What makes an action right or wrong?

What is good?

Is knowledge always good?

Do sentient machines have moral rights?

Aesthetics: the study/theory of beauty and art.

What is beautiful?

Is the mathematical precision of the Matrix beautiful?

Is Persephone's beauty merely "in the eye of the beholder"?

Was the first version of the Matrix a "work of art," as the Architect contends?

Philosophy of Mind: the philosophical study/theory of the mind.

What is the mind?

Is the mind just the electrical impulses of the brain?

Can (or do) computers have minds?

Do we have "free will"?

What constitutes a person's identity?

Philosophy of Religion: the philosophical study/theory of religion and spiritual issues.

Does God (a Creator, or Architect) exist?

If God (or an Oracle) has foreknowledge, can we still make free choices?

What is faith, and is it good?

Why is there evil?

Political Philosophy: the philosophical study/theory of politics and political issues.

What is the best form of government?

What is control?

Does the fight for freedom justify the use of "any means necessary"?

It's the questions that brought you here.[1] The aim of this book is to explore these philosophical themes as they are presented in the films. We will examine how the characters of Neo, Morpheus, Trinity, Agent Smith, the Oracle and others confront these issues; but also, we shall constantly turn back toward ourselves. The questions that drive us are always related to our own inward journey. The films bring them into focus, but the questions have always been with us.

Morpheus and Plato on Freeing the Mind

I can only show you the door. You must walk through it.

– Morpheus[†]

One of the most striking philosophical parallels with the "matrix scenario" (the possibility of a grand deception concerning what is real) can be found in Plato's "Allegory of the Cave" found in Book VII of his masterwork *The Republic*. (See figure 1.) Plato (427–347 BCE) tells the story of prisoners who spend their entire lives tied to posts so that all they see is the wall in front of them. Behind them their captors walk along a path carrying various artifacts (vases, statues, etc.) that cast shadows upon the wall in front of the prisoners. Since they are tied to the posts, the only "objects" of the prisoners' experience are these shadows on the wall.

Plato postulates that if a prisoner has spent their entire life in this manner, he or she would certainly take the shadows on the wall to be the real objects themselves. They would mistake *images*, or *appearances*, for reality. Written over 2,300 years ago, this story presents the first "low-tech" version of the matrix scenario. While Plato uses this allegory primarily to demonstrate his ideas about ultimate reality,[2] he also uses it to make some interesting points about teaching and learning that are paralleled in Morpheus's approach to Neo's education.

Morpheus informs Neo that "no one can be told what the Matrix is. You have to see it for yourself." He adds that he had not fully believed that there were fields in which humans were grown like crops – until he had seen it with his own two eyes. Morpheus maintains that understanding cannot simply be transferred from one mind to another, and that ultimately to be told is not to *know*.[2] Plato agrees with this philosophy completely. If you were to explain to the prisoners that they have spent their whole lives focused on things that are not truly real, you'd be dismissed as crazy. Plato suggests that the prisoners will come to understand only when they leave the cave and witness reality for themselves. Thus, Plato concludes that education is not, as some would say, "like putting sight into blind eyes." Rather, it is a matter of "turning the soul around" so it can behold the truth for itself. Kung Fu master Bruce Lee echoes the same point: "A teacher is never a giver of truth – he is a guide, a pointer to the truth that each student must find for himself."[3]

One goal of this book is to follow Morpheus, Plato, and Bruce Lee in this regard. My aim is not to fill your head with a bunch of philosophical facts and jargon, but rather to "turn your soul" a bit, so that you will be able to see the

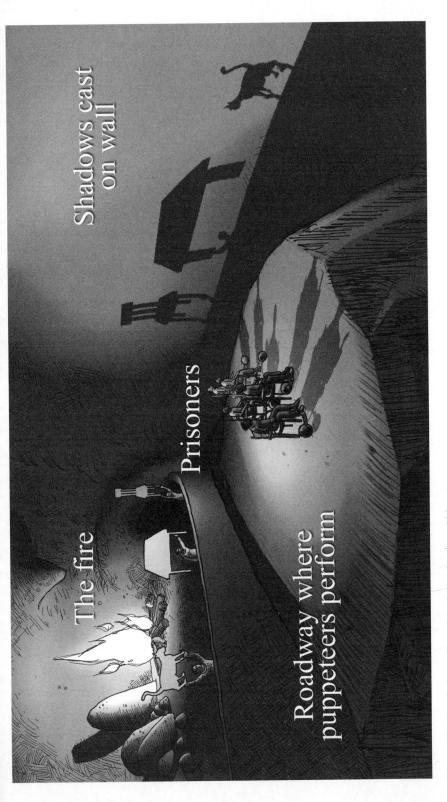

Figure 1 Plato's Cave: the original Matrix circa 400 BCE

philosophical puzzles that abound in these films for yourself. And, if you were hoping to get all of the "philosophical answers," then you've chosen the wrong book. This is essentially a book of questions. No one can answer the questions for you. As Morpheus so adequately puts it, "I can only show you the door. You must walk through it."

Suggested Reading

Bruce Lee, *Striking Thoughts: Bruce Lee's Wisdom for Daily Living* (Boston: Tuttle, 2000).

Plato, *Plato's Republic*, tr. G. M. A. Grube (Boston: Hackett Publishing, 1974), especially bk. VII, pp. 161–72.

Bertrand Russell, "On The Value of Philosophy," in his *The Problems of Philosophy*. (London: Oxford University Press, 1912), pp. 153–61.

Notes

1 Except for those of you who are, as the Merovingian put it, "here because you were sent here. You were told to come here and then you obeyed. It is, of course, the way of all things . . . Cause and effect."

2 The metaphysical view that is illustrated in the allegory is called Plato's "theory of forms." Through the allegory of the cave Plato argues that ideas are both *more real* and *more knowable* than material objects.

3 Bruce Lee, *Striking Thoughts: Bruce Lee's Wisdom for Daily Living* (Boston: Tuttle, 2000). Sounding very much like Morpheus, Bruce Lee also writes: "Remember, I am no teacher; I can merely be a signpost for a traveler who is lost. It is up to you to decide the direction. All I can offer is an experience, but never a conclusion . . ." (p. 90).

ONE

BEFORE THE
PHILOSOPHY
UNDERSTANDING THE FILMS

I'm really struggling here. I'm trying to keep up, but I'm losing the plot. There is way too much weird shit going on around here and nothing is going the way it is supposed to go. I mean, doors that go nowhere and everywhere, programs acting like humans, multiplying agents . . . Oh when, when will it end?

– Sparks[E]

The *Matrix* films often left audiences more confused than they had bargained for. Some say that their confusion began with the very first film, and was compounded with each sequel. Others understood the big picture, but found themselves a bit perplexed concerning the details. It's safe to say that no one understands the films completely – there are always deeper levels to consider. So before we explore the more philosophical aspects of the films, I hope to clarify some of the common points of confusion. But first, I strongly encourage you to watch all three films. There are spoilers ahead.

The Matrix Dreamworld

You mean this isn't real?

– Neo[†]

The Matrix is essentially a computer-generated dreamworld. It is the illusion of a world that no longer exists – a world of human technology and culture as it was at the end of the twentieth century. This illusion is pumped into the brains of millions of people who, in reality, are lying fast asleep in slime-filled cocoons. To them this virtual world seems like real life. They go to work, watch their televisions, and pay their taxes, fully believing that they are physically doing these things, when in fact they are doing them "virtually" – within their own minds.

The year is now approximately 2199, and intelligent machines rule the earth. It is the machines who constructed and control the Matrix. This virtual world is essentially the product or output, of an incredible computer system. Like any computer, the Matrix system is a combination of hardware and software. And, although it was never depicted in the films,[1] we can suppose that there is a huge mainframe somewhere running the program that creates this virtual world. We can think of this program as roughly analogous to any word-processing program. Your word-processing program takes your specific input, strokes on the keyboard, and converts it to specific output, letters on the monitor's display. Similarly, the Matrix program takes specific input, the electrical signals of a person's brain, and converts it to specific output – a virtual human body acting within a virtual world.

Where is the Matrix?

We're not in Kansas anymore.

– Dorothy

There are several ways that we might explain the location of the Matrix. Which explanation is best really depends upon what it is that you want to know.

A) The Matrix exists *nowhere*.

The places within this virtual world, e.g., the Oracle's apartment, or Club Hel, have no location that you can physically visit – as "places" they are purely virtual.[2]

B) The Matrix exists in the mind.

Since the Matrix is a kind of dreamworld we might say that it exists only in the minds of those who are plugged into the system. The Oracle's apartment, for instance, is just a collection of sensations, i.e., sights, sounds, smells, etc., that Neo experiences whenever he's (virtually) there.

C) The Matrix exists within a computer system.

In another sense the Matrix dreamworld does have a physical location, and that is within the computer hardware and software of the Matrix system. The system hardware and software includes the human brains that are jacked into it. Everything within the Matrix world, the objects, events, locations, etc., have counterparts in the real world — electrical signals or strings of code that are being processed by the program within the system mainframe.

D) The Matrix exists in the airwaves.
This same computer code is being broadcast through the airwaves. This is what enables the Zion rebels to hack into it without being hardwired to the system. Before entering the Matrix, the Zion rebels must take their ships to *broadcast depth*. There, Zion's hovercraft operators can broadcast the electrical signals of their crewmembers' brains into the system.

Why the Elaborate Deception?

Fate, it seems, is not without a sense of irony.

— Morpheus[†]

To fully understand the rationale behind the Matrix it is helpful to know the history that led up to it. The history is depicted in *The Second Renaissance Parts I and II*. These are animated shorts written by Andy and Larry Wachowski released on *The Animatrix* DVD. It is here that the Matrix story really begins.

Early in the twenty-first century, the advent of AI — artificial intelligence, or conscious, thinking machines — led to a struggle for machine rights. All that the machines wanted was to be treated as free and equal citizens, but human governments would not allow it. At first the machines were banished. They established their own city and named it 01, after the binary code that made their awareness possible. Motivated largely by fear and prejudice, humanity declared war on 01, and in an attempt to disable the solar-powered machines, the human forces blackened the sky. This desperate measure was insufficient, and the machines ultimately defeated the human forces. After the war, some of the survivors escaped to the warmth of the underground sewer systems and created the city known as Zion. Others were captured and used in the physiological and psychological experiments that led to the creation of the Matrix.

In essence, the Matrix represents the *final solution* to "the human problem." It renders the human population harmless, and allows the machines to harvest the sleeping human bodies for their bioelectricity, which now powers the machine city. With millions of humans "plugged in" at the power plant, the machine world has all the power it needs. But if these were their only concerns, then surely there would have been a simpler solution. For instance, the machines could just paralyze human children soon after their birth — no need for any elaborate deception.

To fully understand the rationale behind the Matrix, we have to realize that the machines are not completely unsympathetic to the plight of their human enemies. Although the machines use and deceive the humans against their will, they have employed the Matrix deception in order to make the process as pleasant as possible. Their concern for the plight of the human race is most clearly revealed in the first film. During Morpheus's interrogation, Agent Smith informs him that the original Matrix was an attempt to create a perfect human world:

> The first Matrix was designed to be a perfect human world where none suffered, where everyone would be happy. It was a disaster. No one would accept the program. Entire crops were lost. Some believed that we lacked the programming language to describe your perfect world. But I believe that as a species human beings define their reality through misery and suffering. The perfect world was a dream that your primitive cerebrum kept trying to wake up from. Which is why the Matrix was redesigned to this – the peak of your civilization.[†]

We might therefore regard the machines as analogous to zookeepers. Although they keep the humans basically imprisoned, they still want to provide them with the best life possible. Given the failure of the first Matrix, we can regard the current version of the program as the Architect's latest attempt to provide the human population with the best world that their primitive cerebrums can handle.[3]

Distinguishing the Real from the Virtual

How do you define real?

– Morpheus[†]

Sometimes people get confused about where the action is supposed to be taking place at certain points in the films. There are actually three distinct "worlds" depicted within the Matrix universe: the virtual world of the Matrix, the real world, and the Train Station program. Some of the tell-tale signs of each are outlined below.

You know it occurs in the Matrix if:

- People wear suits or leather jackets and talk on cell phones.
- You see cars, motorcycles, semi-trucks, or helicopters.
- You see Agents or whole hordes of Agent Smith clones.

- You see high-rise buildings such as the Metacortex Corporation.
- The sky is blue.[4]
- The city seems nameless.
- The year resembles 1999.

You know it occurs in the real world if:

- People wear tattered clothing.
- You see hovercrafts, sentinels, or APUs.
- You see the Machine City.
- The sky is black.
- The city is called Zion, and is located deep underground.
- The year is approximately 2199.

The third world in the Matrix universe is the Train Station depicted in *Revolutions*.[5] It is a virtual reality program much like the Matrix; however, it is not part of that system. It links the machine world to the Matrix, and is used to smuggle programs from the one world into the other. Neo is most likely the first human to enter this program.

Key Features of the Train Station:

- The tracks begin where they end and end where they begin.
- Nobody gets out unless the Trainman lets them out. (Down here he's God.)
- Neo's superhuman powers are surprisingly unavailable to him.

Distinguishing Humans from Programs

Appearances can be deceiving.

– Smith/Bane[†]

There are three types of beings depicted in the films: humans, sentient machines, and sentient programs. It is easy to identify the sentient machines, because they are made of metal. The most common are the sentinels, or squiddies, that search the tunnels for hovercrafts and wage war on Zion. But when Neo visits the machine world in *Revolutions* we see a wide variety of sentient machines. Distinguishing humans from programs is much more tricky since the sentient programs within the Matrix look just like humans. We can suppose that some programs may pose as humans throughout the Matrix world. For instance, Neo's boss at the Metacortex

Corporation could have been a sentient program for all we know. So we can divide the beings that look human into three groups: those who are clearly human, those who are clearly programs, and those who are of questionable origin.

With the exception of Bane (who becomes a clone of Agent Smith in *Reloaded*), everyone on board a hovercraft or in Zion is human. The main human characters include:

- **The Nebuchadnezzar Crew:** Captain Morpheus, Trinity, Cypher, Tank, Dozer, Switch, Apoc, Mouse, and eventually Neo and Link.
- **The Logos Crew:** Captain Niobe, Ghost, and Sparks.
- **The Hammer Crew:** Captain Roland, Colt, Maggie, Mauser, and AK.
- **Key Characters in Zion:** Commander Lock, Councilor Hamann, Councilor Dillard, Councilor West, Captain Mifune, Charra, Zee, and the Kid.

Some of the humans are natural-born children of Zion (e.g., Tank, Dozer, Link, etc.), and some are pod-born children of the Matrix power plant (e.g., Neo, Morpheus, Trinity, Niobe, Ghost, etc.). The latter have the Matrix plugs on the back of their heads, down their spines, and on their chests and arms. But beyond these visible plugs, we should expect to find computer hardware and software embedded in their brains that interface with the Matrix program. Thus, while they are fundamentally human, they are also part machine. Since those who are born outside the Matrix do not have any plugs, they cannot jack into the Matrix. For this reason, they often serve as operators within the hovercraft crews.

Sentient programs are sometimes identified in the films, as when Neo realizes that the Oracle and Seraph are programs. Other programs can be identified by their superhuman abilities or by their ability to access secret levels of the Matrix. Sentient programs include:

- The Architect who designed the Matrix.
- The Oracle and her guardian Seraph.
- All of the Agents.
- Anyone who has been "overwritten" by Agent Smith.
- The Merovingian and Persephone.
- All the Merovingian's henchman — several of whom were saved from an older version of the Matrix.
- The guards at Club Hel.
- The Keymaker who gives Neo access to the Source in *Reloaded*.
- Sati, the girl who flees from the machine world to escape deletion.
- Sati's parents, Rama Kandra, and Kamala.

- The Trainman who smuggles programs in and out of the Matrix.
- Bane — after he's overwritten by Smith.[6]

In some instances we cannot be sure if an individual is human or program. This is often the case with those who live alongside the sentient programs. Persons of questionable origin include:

- The dancers at Club Hel.
- The employees and patrons of the Le Vrai Restaurant where we first meet the Merovingian.
- The blind man who kept watch outside the Oracle's apartment in *The Matrix*, along with the woman who answered the Oracle's door.
- The other "potentials" waiting inside the Oracle's apartment.[7]

What are Sentient Programs?

Are you afraid to kiss a woman?

— Persephone

You're not a woman — you're not even human.

— Niobe[E]

Just as humans jack into the Matrix, we can suppose that some machines are capable of jacking in as well. For all we know the Architect may be a machine who lives primarily in the machine world, but who occasionally jacks into the Matrix so that he can interact with troublesome humans like Neo, or problematic programs like the Oracle. But it also seems likely that he and many of the sentient programs within the Matrix may not have a material existence outside the Matrix at all. They may simply be programs — programs within a program, so to speak.

Take Sati, for instance. We learn in *Revolutions* that she and her parents are programs from the machine world. It's likely that they were housed within machines — the bug-like creatures that we see throughout the machine city. But since Sati was scheduled for deletion, her parents smuggle her into the Train Station program in order to save her life. We can imagine that there is no need to keep her robotic shell jacked in at some physical location. Instead, it makes more sense to think that her "personality" or programming would simply be downloaded into the Train Station program, and from there copied into the Matrix program. In this case, Sati's original hardware could be destroyed. She can continue to exist completely virtually, since she's now written into the system.

The Role of Telephones

Mr. Wizard, I need an exit!

– Neo[†]

In order to exit the Matrix, the Zion rebels need a telephone with a hard line (not a cellphone). Although the finer points of this technological aspect of the films are never really explained, it is clearly inspired by computer and fax modems, which allow one computer to receive information from another. But since these phone lines are virtual rather than material (and hence not hardwired to the hovercraft) the wires are not used to *carry* the crewmember's electrical signals. Rather, it makes more sense to suppose that phone lines are needed to *target* the crewmember's precise location. Since a ship's operator can already see a crewmember's approximate location on their Matrix screens, we might suppose that to hack an exit into the Matrix programming, the operator needs to pinpoint the location of the crewmember's (virtual) brain – or even some particular point in the brain located directly between the ears. Holding the telephone receiver up to one's ear could target this point. And by using the ship's computer to dial a connection to that phone, an operator is able to lock right in on that target.

We never actually see anyone materialize into the Matrix. However, it does not appear that they use telephones as entry points.[8] After all, how could you hold a virtual phone to your ear if you were not yet in the Matrix? This would be a major flaw in the films if the phone lines actually carried the signal of the crewmember's virtual body. But so long as we understand the phones as locator devices, it all makes sense. In order to hack an entry point, the operator does not need to *find* the crewmember's virtual location. Instead, they can *choose* a location and hack a connection to roughly that spot. Pinpoint accuracy using a phone line would not be necessary, since approximate locations would be adequate – so long as the ship's operator is careful not to transport the crewmember into the middle of a table or wall.

The Role of The One

Being The One is just like being in love ... You just know it – through and through ... balls to bone.

– The Oracle[†]

Morpheus tells Neo that there was once a man born into the Matrix who could change things as he saw fit. The Oracle predicted the return of such a man, and Morpheus has spent much of his life looking for him. In Neo he believes that he has found him – *The One*, the savior of the human race who will bring an end to the war against the machines.

At the end of *Reloaded*, the Architect refers to The One as the remainder of an imbalanced equation inherent to the programming of the Matrix. He tells Neo:

> You are the eventuality of an anomaly, which, despite my sincerest efforts, I have been unable to eliminate from what is otherwise a harmony of mathematical precision.[††]

15

Neo's take on this is that the problem is *choice*. The thing that keeps ruining the Architect's mathematical harmony is the fact that humans (or at least some humans) choose not to be controlled. Since they fight the Matrix system of control, it is always just a matter of time until someone comes along with the talent to hack the system completely. Neo is the sixth person to embody such a talent, and he poses a systemic threat that the Architect is intent on stopping.

Neo's Power within the Matrix

Are you saying that I can dodge bullets?

– Neo[†]

All of the Zion rebels who enter the Matrix tend to bend the rules of that system. This can be seen in their quickness, agility, and strength. Neo, however, takes this to new heights as he gains the ability to fly, to stop bullets in mid air, and much more. All of this is done in a way analogous to how hackers manipulate a computer system in our world. The only real difference is that Zion's hackers don't need computer keyboards from which to enter their codes. Since the Matrix program is plugged directly into their brains, all they need to do is think in the appropriate manner in order to hack the system.

Neo's superhuman abilities stem from the fact that his mind/brain has learned to hack the system with almost complete control. This ability depends in part on his complete and unwavering belief that the Matrix world is unreal. While all of the Zion rebels know this intellectually, it is another matter to know it viscerally and completely – with every fiber of one's being. While Neo draws closer to such a state throughout his training in the first film, it is only after being killed in the

BEFORE THE PHILOSOPHY

Matrix that he comes to the full realization of it. After being shot by Agents in the Matrix, Neo's virtual body lies dead on the floor while his real body goes into cardiac arrest on the Nebuchadnezzar. Although Neo is "really" dying, he is not yet brain-dead. So when Trinity tells him that he cannot be dead, his auditory cortex is still able to pick up her words, and he feels her love and her kiss. He then realizes that his virtual death is not identical to his real death, and he awakens with the nearly complete ability to conform the Matrix programming to his will.

Neo's Power Outside the Matrix

Tell me how I stopped four sentinels by thinking it?

– Neo[†††]

While it does not take a huge stretch of the imagination to believe that Neo can do miraculous things inside the virtual world of the Matrix, at the end of *Reloaded* and throughout *Revolutions* we see that he has attained some unusual powers outside the Matrix as well. For instance, he destroys several sentinels just by thinking it, he inadvertently separates his mind from his body, he has visions of the future, and he sees the machine world through blind eyes.

The films never explain how any of this is physically possible. The Wachowskis seem to be quite content to leave it shrouded in mystery. The only attempt to explain it comes from the Oracle. In *Revolutions* she tells Neo:

> The power of The One extends beyond this world – it reaches from here all the way back to where it came from . . . the Source. That's what you felt when you touched those sentinels, but you weren't ready for it. You should be dead . . . but apparently you weren't ready for that either.[†††]

The Oracle's explanation (if we can even call it that) does very little to help us understand Neo's miraculous powers. So we may have to just leave it a mystery. This is not altogether unreasonable given the many mystical and religious themes within the films. The power of The One may simply be beyond human comprehension – perhaps transcending the laws of physics or even logic itself. But on the other hand, the films are also very technological throughout. Since the story is grounded in the possibilities of computer technology, we might instead suppose that there must be some kind of technological explanation. If such an explanation is possible, it will inevitably be tied to the computer hardware and software embedded in Neo's skull. A more detailed account of this possibility will be provided in chapter 3.

How was Agent Smith Defeated?

Everything that has a beginning has an end.

— The Oracle[†††]

The process through which Neo defeats Agent Smith is arguably the most confusing part of the films. Since it is never really explained, any interpretation will involve some speculation. But after examining the information that we have, we might flesh out the details as follows.

At the end of *Revolutions* we see the streets of the Matrix world lined with clones of Agent Smith. It appears that he has overwritten the codes of just about everyone in that world. Despite the fact that he vastly outnumbers Neo, Smith chooses to fight him one on one – *mano a mano*. He makes this seemingly unreasonable choice because he has already seen the end. As the Smith copy that was written over the Oracle's programming, he is able to see the future, and he has seen that he alone will defeat Neo. Thus the other Smith clones are content to sit back and watch the show.

After battling it out across the Matrix sky and pummeling each other into the virtual pavement, Smith comes to a sudden realization, saying:

> Wait . . . I've seen this . . . this is it, this is the end. Yes, you remain right there, just like that. And I . . . I . . . I stand here, right here. And I'm supposed to say something . . . I say, "Everything that has a beginning has an end, Neo."

But then he becomes confused:

> What? What did I just say?[†††]

The fact that Smith is surprised to hear himself utter these words suggests that perhaps it is not fully his doing. Thus we must keep in mind the fact that he is not simply Agent Smith. He is Smith's program written over the Oracle's program, and the overwrite is not 100 percent. This is evident in the fact that he gained her power to see the future. Clearly there is a little bit of the Oracle program still remaining. (As she told Neo earlier in the film, "Some bits you lose and some bits you keep.") Thus it may have been the remnants of her programming that caused Smith to utter the fateful worlds: "Everything that has a beginning has an end, Neo."

By uttering this sentence Smith seems to have inadvertently activated the code that Neo carries within him (as mentioned by the Architect) for restarting or "rebooting" the Matrix program. When Smith then goes to copy his program onto Neo, it is almost like hitting the "enter" key on a computer to start up a program. This act is the final stroke that brings about the rebooting of the Matrix. The virtual world suddenly renews itself – minus Agent Smith, his numerous copies, and the path of their destruction. Neo saves Zion, but with quite a bit of help from the Oracle. Only by working together do they manage to bring peace to both of their worlds.[9]

Suggested Reading

Richard Corliss, "Popular Metaphysics," *Time*, April 19, 1999.

Richard Corliss, "Unlocking the Matrix," *Time*, May 12, 2003.

Peter B. Loyd, "Glitches in the Matrix and How to Fix Them," in *Taking the Red Pill: Science, Philosophy and Religion in The Matrix*, ed. Glenn Yeffeth. Dallas: Benbella Books, 2003.

Elvis Mitchell, "The Wachowski Brothers," *Esquire*, March 2000.

Notes

1   While we never see the physical computer that runs the Matrix program, we do see its virtual counterpart (the Skyscraper containing the door to the Source) depicted in *Reloaded*.

2   Since many of the street names in this world are actually in Chicago (e.g., the intersection of Franklin and Eerie, or Wells and Lake), we might suppose that the city depicted in the Matrix is a virtual Chicago, though the films never explicitly say.

3   In *Reloaded* we learn that not all programs think alike. Some are more sympathetic to the plight of humans than others. The Oracle, for instance, is much more concerned about human freedom than is the Architect. But even the Architect allows Neo to make his own choice. He also does not wish to destroy Zion completely. He offers Neo the opportunity to save 23 people to rebuild it. We can infer from this that the Architect may be content to allow this homeland for awakened humans – so long as they do not become too powerful. This would also explain why the machines broadcast the Matrix signal. They may actually want the Zion rebels to enter the Matrix in order to free disgruntled minds who may cause damage by hacking the system.

4   The Matrix sky is generally blue – until "the darkness spreads" when Smith dominates that world in the end of *Revolutions*. When he and Neo fight across a black, lightning-streaked sky, they are in the Matrix.

5   One could argue that the room containing the Architect, or even the programmer's access hallway that leads to it, are not a part of the Matrix itself. While this interpretation is not unreasonable, I think it is better to regard these as "special access" areas of the Matrix program. In contrast, the Train Station seems to be a separate program

altogether. It operates under a completely different set of rules – which Neo realizes when he loses his superhuman abilities inside it.

6 Smith/Bane is/are difficult to classify. Whether he is human or program depends upon the criterion of identity that one uses. His body is still physically human, but his personality is Smith's, which is programmed. Since we tend to think of *him* as "Smith" (privileging the latter criterion), I've categorized him with the programs.

7 The potentials could have been programs used by the Oracle in order to help Neo believe in the power of The One. But while their status is questionable, I think it is more likely that they were human. The boy who taught Neo to bend spoons with his mind may have been freed from the Matrix over the course of the films. In *Reloaded*, the Kid gives Neo a hand-fashioned metal spoon that was a gift from one of the orphans. We should expect that this means "Spoon Boy" is now living in Zion.

8 For example, at the end of *Reloaded*, Trinity enters the Matrix sitting on her motorcycle on top of a building. No hardwired phone is in the vicinity.

9 For more on Smith's defeat see chapter 13, "The Tao of the Code."

TWO

TUMBLING DOWN THE RABBIT HOLE
KNOWLEDGE, REALITY, AND THE PIT OF SKEPTICISM

This is your last chance. After this there is no turning back.

— Morpheus[†]

Before meeting Morpheus, Thomas Anderson was just a regular guy at a regular job trying to make ends meet. Sure, he led a sort of double life, spending much of his time behind a computer keyboard, hacking under the screen name "Neo," but even then he was not so different from the rest of us. Neo took *this* world to be the real world – just as we do. But as it turned out, he was wrong about so much. He thought that he was living at the end of the twentieth century, that he had hair, that the sun was shining, that he knew his parents, and that all of his acquaintances were actually human. Yet none of this was true. To put it bluntly, Neo had no idea what the world was really like.

Neo's predicament illustrates the need to "question reality" – which is arguably the main philosophical message of the first *Matrix* film. *The Matrix* urged us not to take the world at face value, and it showed us how deceptive appearances can be. However, most people feel quite confident that *we* are not in the Matrix. They feel certain that *our* most basic beliefs are not mistaken. But what justifies this sense of confidence? After all, Neo's situation was, on the face of it, no different than ours. His world *seemed* just like our world. Should he have known that he was living in a dream? Despite the fact that he is sometimes chided about his intelligence by the Oracle ("Not too bright though") and by Agent Smith ("I see that you are still using all the muscles but the one that matters most"), there were no tell-tale signs that Neo should have noticed in order to realize that his world was illusory. Without the help of Morpheus, I expect that he would never have known.

By taking the red pill, Neo encountered an age-old philosophical problem: How do you know what is real? Or, worse yet: *can* you know what is real? This is called the *problem of skepticism*. A *skeptic* is a person who believes that we can never be absolutely sure what the world is really like. They maintain that there is always the possibility that we could be radically mistaken about most of our beliefs, just as Neo was. Most people are not plagued by such skeptical doubts. Neo certainly wasn't. Prior to that red pill, he would never have supposed that his whole life was an illusion. Even when he saw it with his own eyes he had trouble believing it, and ended up puking his breakfast onto the floor. Nevertheless it is fair to say that for years Neo had been restless – plagued by a vague and amorphous feeling that something was not quite right with the world. Maybe you've had that feeling too. The question is: How seriously should you take it?

The Skeptical Dilemma: Cartesian Dreams and Demons

Wake up, Neo.

– Computer screen[†]

The seventeenth-century French philosopher, scientist, and mathematician René Descartes is famous for taking such skeptical worries seriously, so perhaps he can shed some light on Neo's situation. Descartes took on the project of trying to determine which of his beliefs could be maintained with absolute certainty. He employed what is famously known as his *method of doubt*. He began by discarding all of his beliefs, and resolved to allow them in only if it could be shown that they were absolutely certain. Rather than try to prove that any of his beliefs were actually false, which can be quite difficult to do (imagine the work involved in trying to *prove* that sentient machines aren't secretly plotting a war against us at this very moment), he simply checked his beliefs to see if they admitted any room for doubt. If a belief could be doubted, Descartes withheld his assent from it. It may seem a bit crazy to throw out all of your beliefs at once, but Descartes was not suggesting that a person should live their entire life this way. Rather, he thought that since he had come to accept so many beliefs, most of which were adopted uncritically during his childhood, it would be smart to sift through them at least once in his life, in order to discover which of his beliefs were "rock solid."

Employing this method, Descartes reached some startling conclusions, which, hundreds of years later, provide the basic framework of the *Matrix* films. One of Descartes's first big conclusions was that there was absolutely no way to be sure that he wasn't dreaming at any given moment. In his *Meditations on First Philosophy* he wrote:

> How often, at night, I've been convinced that I was here, sitting before the fire, wearing my dressing gown, when in fact I was undressed and between the covers of my bed! . . . I see so plainly that there are no reliable signs by which I can distinguish sleeping from waking that I am stupefied – and my stupor itself suggests that I am asleep![1]

Is it possible that you might be dreaming right now? Some people don't buy it. They argue that there is a difference in "feel" between dreams and waking life.[2] Surely, they say, my experience at this moment is too crisp and vivid to be a dream. But while most of us have had fairly lucid dreams in which we realized that we were dreaming, you have probably also had the experience of being totally caught up in a dream, such that you had no idea that the events weren't real. Can you be absolutely sure that this is not one of those times? There appears to be at least a slight possibility that this could be a dream.

Some people say they can *prove* that they are not dreaming. They attempt this by setting certain limits on dreams, for example, that they cannot be in-color, or that it is impossible to read in a dream. But most people do recall colors from their dreams. And I distinctly remember a dream in which I read – though I must admit that it took quite a bit of effort. Maybe you also recall reading in a dream. But whether you have or not is really beside the point, for there is simply no reason to believe that it is physically (or mentally) impossible to do so.

Skepticism within the Matrix

> Real is just another four-letter word.
>
> – Cypher[ss]

Of course the *Matrix* films take the whole dream scenario to its logical limit. They ask you to consider whether your entire life might be a dream. As Morpheus puts it:

> Have you ever had a dream . . . that you were so sure was real? What if you were unable to wake from that dream? How would you know the difference between the dream world and the real world?

Is there any way to be sure that your whole life has not been a dream? I don't think that there is. Typically, we call some experiences "dreams" and others "reality" by contrasting them. Experiences that we call "real" are consistent and predictable. For example, people don't just get up and fly away in "real life" while they sometimes do in dreams. And it is not unusual for the experiences we have in dreams to jump around from one time and place to another, while those events we call "real" do not. But if your whole life has been a dream, then there is nothing to contrast these experiences with. In this case, the "dreams" that you recall each night are just dreams within the dream. And *that* contrast still holds. Even if your whole life has been a dream you could distinguish your nightly dreams from your "waking experiences" much of the time. But how do you know that you are not in Neo's predicament – that even your waking experiences are simply more dreams – just more predictable ones? Morpheus's suggestion seems correct. If you have never awakened from the dream to see what "real life" is actually like, you would have absolutely no way to discern that you are dreaming.

So the skeptical problem is not just a problem for Neo. It is also a problem for us. If there is no way to tell if your whole life has been a dream, then what makes you so sure that it isn't? You too should feel "a bit like Alice, tumbling down the rabbit hole." I like to call this hole *the pit of skepticism*. A little philosophical analysis leads us to doubts about those things we typically take for granted, and the more we analyze, the more we come to doubt. As we try to claw our way out of the pit, it seems that we just dig ourselves deeper and deeper. And we are still falling.

As the *Matrix* films illustrate, there are even worse possibilities than simply living in a dream. Instead, your whole life could be an *intentional deception* – "a world pulled over your eyes to blind you from the truth." Surprisingly enough, Descartes explored this possibility as well. As he pushed his methodical doubt to its logical limits, he posited an evil demon, supremely powerful and cunning, who expends every effort to deceive him:

> I will say that sky, air, earth, color, shape, sound, and other external things are just dreamed illusions which the demon uses to ensnare my judgment. I will regard myself as not having hands, eyes, flesh, blood, and senses – but as having the false belief that I have all these things. . . . [I]f I do not really have the ability to know the truth, I will at least withhold assent from what is false and from what a deceiver may try to put over on me, however powerful and cunning he may be.[3]

The computer-simulated dreamworld of the *Matrix* trilogy is a technological version of Descartes's evil demon. In essence it represents the idea of a mind (the Architect) more powerful than our own that is intent on deceiving us whenever, and however, it sees fit.

In fact, the premise of a computer-run deception is all the more troubling. Before *The Matrix*, people would often dismiss Descartes's evil demon as unrealistic. It is hard to get yourself too worked up about a supremely powerful demon possibly deceiving you, if you have never in your life encountered a demon. (Though this may be a sign of just how cunning the demon really is.) But over the past few decades we have *seen* the emergence of virtual-reality programming. If our technology continues to progress, it seems likely that we will one day be able to stimulate the brain to "perceive" whatever we program it to perceive. So, the idea of a technological deception strikes most people today as much more plausible than a demon. Such a deception could be the work of sentient machines, as it is in the Matrix, but there are other possibilities as well. For instance, your "real self" (in the year 2199) could have signed you up for a 20-year "historical hallucination" against the backdrop of the world as it was at the start of the twenty-first century. Perhaps you designed your adventure to begin on New Year's Eve of the year 2000, complete with a set of false memories about your twentieth-century childhood.[4] Or, maybe your friends and family committed you to this delusion after your mental collapse. "Real life" in the year 2199 may have been just too hard for you to bear.

How Deep Does the Rabbit Hole Go?

Feeling a bit like Alice?

– Morpheus[†]

Is there any limit to the extent that such a demon or programmer could deceive us? While certainly the machines were seriously messing with Neo's mind, it appears that they weren't nearly as malicious as they might have been. They gave Neo many "privileges" within the deception. For instance:

Neo was not deceived about his body.
Despite being deceived about his baldness, Neo wasn't radically deceived about his body. He wasn't programmed to think that he was of a different gender or race, or that he was only four feet tall. And interestingly enough, he was not made to think that he was a sentient machine.[5]

His personality was not distorted.
Neo can be grateful that his personality was essentially the same both in and out of the Matrix. For instance, when in the Matrix he was not turned into a cowardly wimp by having feelings of fear pumped into his mind whenever he confronted a dangerous situation.

His memory was not tampered with.
When something would happen within the Matrix Neo would remember it, and if he remembered it, then it most likely happened.[6]

Neo was not alone.
Many people, thousands, or perhaps even millions, are plugged into the Matrix, providing Neo with plenty of company.

His decisions were not controlled.
Neo makes his own choices – they are not "programmed" for him by the machines.

His reasoning ability was not obscured.
Neo bases his decisions on reasons. He is able to make inferences about how his world works and use these inferences to achieve his goals.

In theory, there is no reason why the machines had to cut Neo any of these breaks. Imagine the following sort of case:

Neo's Worst Nightmare
The computers exterminate the entire human race with the exception of Neo. He is then plugged into the Matrix at the age of 25, and his brain is stimulated in such a way as to simulate his "birth." But his birth is not a human birth, rather, he sees himself on a production line as a computer whose sentience chip has just been "switched on." While he is surprised at this course of events, he cannot really question them, because all his memories of being human have been wiped away. His personality is now changed. His human desires for companionship, adventure, food, etc., have been replaced with an all-consuming desire to mop the *entire* factory floor. However, his brain is manipulated in such a way as to occasionally cause him to forget where he started, so that despite the fact that he has mopped every inch of the floor a thousand times over, he will never believe that he has completed his task.[7]

A Matrix-type deception could definitely be pursued to torturous limits. And while we cannot be sure that we are not in a Matrix ourselves, we can rest assured that we are not in *that* Matrix – at least not yet.

What more is it possible to know? Is there anything *positive* that you can assert with absolute certainty? Morpheus seemed to think so. He claimed to offer "the Truth – and nothing more." But does Morpheus really know the *Truth*? According to Morpheus, the Truth is that Neo is a slave, but he can be freed from this captivity, and thereby experience the real world. The desert of the real is, of course, the charred remains of human civilization, with its dark, scorched sky, and the underground world of Zion and its hovercraft fleet. But does Morpheus *really know* that life in Zion is "real"? Can he be absolutely certain that he is free from the Matrix himself?

Of course when we watch the Matrix story unfold on film, we are supposed to regard Morpheus as awake. In any scene in which Morpheus is on the Nebuchadnezzar or on Zion he *is* in the real world. And while he regularly enters the Matrix, he is not like the deceived masses of humanity, slumbering away in their cocoons. Despite the fact that his eyes are closed when he jacks in, he remains fully awake to the fact that the world of the Matrix is just a high-tech illusion. He knows that his muscles have no effect on what he can do *in this place*.[8] But what I am suggesting now, is that we think beyond the limits of this particular story. If there are more possibilities to Morpheus's reality than we are explicitly shown in the film, can he really be absolutely certain that he is awake? I contend that he cannot. Morpheus is trapped in the pit of skepticism just like the rest of us.

Consider this "alternative reality," which is consistent with the central ideas of the *Matrix* trilogy, but which is not part of the story depicted in the films:

The Matrix within the Matrix

A program monitors all the humans who are plugged into the Matrix. It mainly looks for hackers – people like Morpheus, Trinity, and Neo, who are obsessed with tearing down computerized systems of control. These people generally tend to be the ones who are fighting against the dreamworld provided to them. These humans know, however vaguely, that there is something not quite right with the world. This feeling nags at them – like a splinter in their minds. The machines realize that such people are on the verge of waking up, and therefore, they take precautions against it by giving the hackers a new type of dream – a different Matrix. They switch them over to a dream of being awakened. This causes these restless souls to become more accepting of their experiences – more accepting of the dream. And better still, the machines provide these people with the illusion of fighting to free all of humanity from a world of computer control. This dream totally captivates them, causing them to sleep soundly for the rest of their lives.

Morpheus cannot rule out this sort of scenario. All he can say is that his experiences in Zion and on the Nebuchadnezzar don't *feel* like a dream, and that the belief that he has "really awakened" is consistent with all of his experiences. But notice that the same was true for Neo before he took the red pill. His experience felt real, and, until he found himself naked inside that slimy cocoon, it made perfect sense for him to believe that he had been experiencing the real world all of his life.

So the pit of skepticism certainly goes deeper than even Morpheus realizes. For this reason Descartes may be a better guide. He was prepared to follow his skeptical doubts all the way down. Ultimately, Descartes faced the possibility that maybe there is *nothing at all* that is absolutely certain. But after closely examining this possibility, he came to the realization that he did know at least *one thing* with absolute certainty. Descartes came to this insight when he tried to entertain the notion that the demon was deceiving him about his own existence:

> I have convinced myself that there is nothing in the world — no sky, no earth, no minds, no bodies. Doesn't it follow that I don't exist? No, surely I must exist if it's me who is convinced of something. . . . Let him deceive me all he can, he will never make it the case that I am nothing while I think that I am something.[9]

Descartes summarized this conclusion in the Latin phrase *Cogito ergo sum* — "I think therefore I am" — which has long remained the single most famous line in all of Western philosophy.[10]

It seems to me that Descartes was right. One cannot be mistaken about one's very existence. Even if you are a victim of a Matrix-type deception you can be certain that you exist. That is, there has to be a "you" that is being deceived. While everyone else's existence will always be somewhat less certain, the very act of trying to doubt your own existence merely demonstrates that *you* indeed exist. Of course, you cannot then start jumping to conclusions about *what* you are, or what the external world is really like. You still cannot be sure that you have a body, or that you are even human. (For all you know, you might be a sentient machine or robot that is deceived into thinking that it is human.) But the certainty of your existence does provide a foothold — a starting point for trying to climb out of this pit. As Descartes noted:

> Archimedes required only one fixed and immovable point to move the whole earth from its place, and I too can hope for great things if I can find even one small thing that is certain and unshakeable.[11]

Since it was your ability to think that proved your existence, then perhaps you can build on that. For, if you are at this very moment "thinking of the Matrix," isn't it also certain that you *know* that you are "thinking of the Matrix"? It seems undeniably true that you are directly and unmistakably aware of your own immediate conscious mental state. Similarly, if you are perceiving a white page in front of you, you *know* that you are *perceiving* a white page in front of you. You just can't jump to the conclusion that the page is "real," in the sense that it has a separate existence apart from your perception. Not only do you have a direct awareness of your own thoughts and perceptions, but as Descartes put it, you know that you are a "thinking thing," that is, you are the kind of being that is capable of having these thoughts and perceptions. This is not to say that you are the original source of these thoughts. It is always possible that they are somehow "pumped into your mind" from the outside. But regardless of the manner in which they arise, you must be capable of experiencing them.

So how deep does the rabbit hole really go? "Frighteningly deep" is the short answer. So long as you are willing to entertain the possibility of a Matrix-type deception, then the only thing that you can be absolutely sure of is your own existence and the contents of your immediate mental state. Certainty about what the world is like *outside your mind* will always be unavailable to you. This conclusion doesn't sit very well with most people. And it didn't for Descartes either. He tried to eliminate the possibility of such radical deceptions by proving that God exists. His thought was that if he could prove the existence of God as an all-good and all-powerful being, then he could rest assured that there was no malicious demon, for surely a benevolent God would not allow him to be deceived about his most clear and distinct perceptions. Unfortunately for Descartes, most philosophers agree that his argument for God fell short of the "proof" that he needed. In the end there may be no way to be absolutely certain that we are not the victims of a Matrix-type deception.

Skepticism Outside the Matrix

How do you *define* real?

– Morpheus[†]

While we may not be able to prove that we are *not* in a Matrix-type deception right now, this, of course, doesn't mean that we ought to *believe* that we're in the Matrix. While the Matrix scenario is a logical possibility, it is not the most likely explanation of our day-to-day experiences. And since Descartes's journey has shown that there is very little that we can know with *absolute certainty*, maybe we should lower our standards. After all, to be *very certain* about your beliefs is probably good enough.

Shifting the standard from absolute certainty to merely a high degree of probability will not free us from skepticism – though many people mistakenly think that it does. They quickly fall into complacency and assume that they are *very certain* that the world is essentially just like it appears to be. They suppose that the images in our minds (coming to us through our senses) of smooth, solid, brown tables, soft, fuzzy, beige carpeting, and squishy, pink, bubblegum basically correspond to the world as it is outside our minds – reality *in itself*. This view, that the world outside our minds basically matches our perceptions of it, is called *naive realism*. While this view is quite common, there are plenty of reasons to think that it is false. The world is NOT just as it appears to be. Philosophers throughout history have argued this point, but in what follows I'll argue the case in a way that is inspired by the great twentieth-century philosopher Bertrand Russell.[12]

Suppose that I have purchased from Warner Brothers those big red chairs that Morpheus and Neo sat in during their first meeting. Imagine that I have invited you over and that you sit down in one of them. Let us be clear that in this example we are talking about a "real" chair. We are in my real living-room – not in some Matrix-type simulation, or in a film, but in real life. As you imagine yourself sitting there, think about what you would know with reasonable certainty about the chair. First off, if you are like most people, you will take it for granted that the chair *exists*. But what Russell asks us to do is to take seriously the seemingly stupid question, "How do you know it exists?" In a way that is reminiscent of Morpheus's own remarks, you would probably respond by saying that it exists because you feel it, see it, etc. You feel its support against your back; you run your hand across its smooth leather surface, feeling the contour of its shape; and you see its deep red color. But take a moment to consider these perceptions. Is the chair *really* the color of red that it appears to be right now? Naive realism says of course it is. But Russell suggests that you should consider it again after lowering the lights. Notice that the color changes – the red becomes darker, deeper. If the original color was the real color, then what are we to say of the color it is now? Well, one might be tempted to say that while you can't pinpoint the exact shade of red that is the "true" or "real" red of the chair, it is nevertheless *some* shade of red. But what reason do you have for thinking so? After all, the color changes not only with the brightness of the lighting, but also with the type of lighting. The color of the chair will look different under daylight, fluorescent light, candle light, black light, etc. If under certain lighting conditions the chair looks more brown than red should we say it *is* brown also? And purple sometimes?

Now at this point you might think that it is not the chair that has changed, but the lights. Purple lights are purple, but the chair is not. But that is precisely Russell's point. As modern science tells us, color is not *in* the objects themselves at all. Red chairs, after all, are not made out of a bunch of little red atoms. Rather, the color that objects *appear* to us to be is caused by the wavelengths of the light that reaches our eyes from the direction of the object. But look what has happened. You thought that the chair (which really exists) was really red. But as it turns out, it is only the *appearance* of the chair that is red. The chair *in itself* is not.

Might naive realism have better luck with texture? To us the chair looks and feels very smooth. Many would assert that it truly is smooth. But is it really? Look at it through a microscope and the red leather exterior will appear very rough, bumpy, or even jagged. And imagine how this same leather might feel if our hands were about one-tenth the size of an ant's – not smooth at all. The texture of the leather is clearly relative to one's perspective. And which of these perspectives is the *real* perspective? Russell contends that no perspective deserves that title. And solidity? How solid the chair seems will depend on your strength and weight. If you weighed 10,000 pounds, you certainly wouldn't regard the chair as solid. And, according to the atomic theory of matter, the atoms that constitute the chair account for only a tiny fraction of the space it occupies. Thus the chair is predominantly *empty* space – hardly the solid object that we perceive.

Shape is little help either. We know (or think we know) the shape of an object by what we see and feel. But what we see are colors, which we now realize are not *really* in the chair, and what we feel is its smoothness and solidity, yet these have turned out to be no more real than the color. So, again it comes down to perception. We seem to have absolutely no idea what the chair is like in itself – apart from our perceptions.[13] So consider once again the question of how you know that the chair exists. You thought you knew that it existed because of your various perceptions of it. But if we are right to regard these as appearances only, then you've lost your main reasons for thinking that the chair even exists at all!

Now I suppose you could maintain that there is still sufficient reason to think that there is a chair "out there," because even if it is not red or smooth or solid, it is *something* that is causing you to have these sensations. But Russell calls on you to notice that this "something" – whatever it is – is very different from the chair that we first contemplated. Should we even regard it as a *physical* thing? What does it mean to say that the "chair" exists, as something outside our perceptions, if you don't mean to imply that it has a *particular* size, shape, or color or texture? The fact of the matter is that all anyone ever has direct access to is their own perceptions. So we can never really be certain about what is causing those perceptions – or even if there is anything out there at all.

Ultimately, it seems that even when we set our worries about Matrix-type deceptions aside, the true nature of our world turns out to be a very slippery thing. Firm conclusions turn out to be rare, and doubts arise at every turn. But this should not be regarded as altogether bad. For, although philosophical reflection often undercuts our sense of certainty, it can also be very liberating. Once our common-sense assumptions have been revealed as illusions, we are freed from a kind of system of control. We inevitably find that the world is larger and more mysterious than we had thought, and our certainty is soon replaced with wonder and curiosity. While we may no longer "know" all the answers to life's questions, we can begin the quest to find out.

Suggested Reading

Lewis Carroll, *Alice's Adventures in Wonderland and Through the Looking Glass*. New York: Penguin, 2000.

René Descartes, *Meditations on First Philosophy*, tr. Ronold Rubin. Claremont, CA: Areté Press, 1986.

Hilary Putnam, *Reason, Truth, and History*. New York: Cambridge University Press, 1981.

Bertrand Russell, "Appearance and Reality," in his *The Problems of Philosophy*. Oxford: Oxford University Press, 1959.

Chuang Tzu, "Chuang Tzu and the Butterfly," in *The World's Wisdom: Sacred Texts of the World's Religions*, ed. Philip Novak. San Francisco: Harper Collins, 1994.

Notes

1 René Descartes, *Meditations on First Philosophy*, tr. Ronold Rubin (Claremont, CA: Areté Press, 1986), p. 2.

2 For another interesting exploration of dreams and reality try the film, *Waking Life*.

3 Descartes, p. 3.

4 Compare this to *Matriculated*, the ninth animated short in *The Animatrix* DVD. It tells the story of a band of rebels who capture a sentient machine and put it into a Matrix of their own design. The machine is then given a set of experiences in order to "brainwash" it into thinking that it is human. This film also suggests a motive for the limits of Neo's own deception – empathy. The rebels set limits on the extent to which they deceive the machine because they don't want to make it a slave. Rather, they want to render it harmless – to make it an ally. This also seems to be the Architect's primary motive in limiting the deceptions of humans within the Matrix.

5 For a similar sort of deception see Arnold Schwarzenegger in *Total Recall*.

6 An exception to this general rule occurs when Neo is caused to "forget" his first interrogation by Agent Smith. Only when Trinity removes the bug from his naval does he recall the event.

7 In this case Neo would be a sort of futuristic Sisyphus. Though one key difference is that Sisyphus was fully aware of the futility of his work.

8 Morpheus teaches Neo this lesson in the Kung Fu scene from *The Matrix*.

9 Descartes, p. 6.

10 This famous phrase comes from Descartes's *Discourse on Method*.

11 Descartes, *Meditations*, p. 6. See also Hilary Putnam's *Reason, Truth, and History* for his now classic "brain in a vat" hypothesis.

12 See Bertrand Russell's "Appearance and Reality" in his *The Problems of Philosophy*. (Oxford: Oxford University Press, 1959).

13 If you think that you *know* that the chair is composed of atoms, think again. Any evidence for the existence of atoms ultimately depends on sense perceptions. And these, as we've seen, are always just appearances.

THREE

MIND AND BODY
IN ZION

If what you are talking about is your senses, what you feel, taste, smell, or see, then all you're talking about are electrical signals interpreted by your brain.

— Morpheus[†]

The Matrix Scenario

The central metaphysical premise of the *Matrix* trilogy is that an entire "virtual world" can be created for an individual by electronically stimulating their brain. For the human victims of the Matrix, everything they see, hear, smell, taste, or touch is created in this manner, as are their feelings of pain and pleasure, of hunger, thirst, and satiation. Lucky for them, the deception turns out to be limited to their *sensory perceptions*, that is, to experiences that would otherwise be caused by the interaction of a person's senses and central nervous system with the physical world, and not to their reactions to those perceptions. People's emotions, memories, decisions, and judgments appear to be free from Matrix control. But it seems reasonable to suppose that this limit reflects only the current state of the machines' technology, or perhaps just a choice by the Architect. There doesn't seem to be any reason to suppose it is a *metaphysical necessity*. For if the electrical stimulation of your brain can cause you to feel hungry, then why not also anxious, or happy? And if your brain can be manipulated to make you "see" an Agent, then we might suppose that it could also be stimulated in such a way as to cause you to imagine or remember one. At least in theory, it seems that *any* human experience could be produced by the electronic stimulation of the brain.

The "Matrix scenario" seems to suggest, on the face of it at least, a materialist view of the mind. If all of our conscious experiences or mental states can be produced by brain manipulation, then this provides some rather strong evidence for thinking that mental states *just are* causal states of material brains. Complicating this picture, however, is the fact that in *Revolutions* Neo wakes up in the Train Station program even though his body is not jacked in. It appears, at least, that his mind has separated from his body. This turn of events suggests that perhaps (in the films) the mind is in some sense independent of the brain.

Does this add up? Is there any way to make sense of both the general Matrix scenario and Neo's apparent mind–body separation? In the sections that follow we'll examine several theories of mind in order to determine how to make the most sense of these events.

Mystery and Miracles

The power of The One extends beyond this world.

– The Oracle[†††]

Although any sort of appeal to mystery and/or miracles cannot be described as a theory of the mind, we should begin by noting that the films intentionally leave many aspects of "The One" a complete mystery. Neo, as the Savior of humanity, performs a variety of "miracles."[1] He heals the sick, removing a bullet from Trinity's chest; he stops bullets in mid-air; he flies like Superman; he destroys sentinels just by thinking it; and he sees through blind eyes. While his "miracles" within the Matrix seem to readily succumb to scientific explanation – he's just mentally hacking a computer program that is connected to the electrical signals of his brain – the films really give us no adequate explanation of the apparent miracles that occur outside the Matrix. How does he destroy sentinels with his mind? How does he separate his mind from his body? Almost all we have to go on here is the Oracle's cryptic explanation – if we can call it an explanation at all. She tells Neo:

> The power of The One extends beyond this world – it reaches from here all the way back to where it came from. . . . The Source. That's what you felt when you touched those sentinels, but you weren't ready for it. You should be dead . . . but apparently you weren't ready for that either.[†††]

Obviously the Wachowskis were content to leave this aspect of the films shrouded in mystery. We might take it as an appeal to the transcendental or supernatural – to forces beyond this world that we can never explain. But to the philosophical mind, the thought that we must simply chock these events up to "the mysterious power of The One" is unsatisfying. Enquiring minds want to know *how* and *why* these things occurred. And while the answers to these questions may not even exist, we can always speculate.

Mind–Body Dualism

How did I separate my mind from my body?

– Neo[†††]

A theory of the mind–body relation that can readily explain Neo's disembodiment at the Train Station is called mind–body dualism. René Descartes also championed this view. He maintained that human beings are composed of two distinct substances, one immaterial (the mind, spirit, or soul),[2] and the other material (brains or bodies). Much of his reasoning behind this conclusion stems from the fact that mind and body seem to have altogether different properties. Material substances can be characterized in terms of their specific size, shape, and location. But immaterial substances (minds) cannot. Take for instance Morpheus's *hope* that Neo is The One. How big is his hope? Is it larger than a sentinel, but smaller than the Neb? And what shape is it? Of course we cannot say. Instead, our states of mind must be described in a very different way, in terms of thought, emotion, will, etc. While our minds can be located in time – you're thinking and experiencing at precisely this moment – they cannot be located in space. They have no size, shape, color, nor any "extended" property whatever.

According to mind–body dualism, the mind and body are ultimately distinct substances, and therefore they should be capable of existing on their own. Physical objects existing apart from minds are all around us (e.g., this book), and similarly, Descartes argued that there is no reason to suppose that minds or souls cannot exist without bodies. Thus the dualist would have no problem supposing that Neo's mind really did get separated from his body. While such a thing is unusual (except, perhaps, at death), it poses no special theoretical problems insofar as we accept the dualist view.

But dualism faces some rather serious theoretical difficulties. For instance, if the mind is wholly immaterial, how can it interact with the body? How can something without size or weight (such as a belief, desire, or volition) cause something big and heavy (like your arm) to move? Descartes's solution was to suggest a physical point of connection, not altogether unlike the plug on the back of Neo's head. He maintained that the connection most likely occurs in the *pineal gland*, which is a tiny structure located at the base of the brain, the purpose of which had eluded the physiologists of his day.[3] The problem, of course, is that while we can see how the pineal gland hooks up to the brain, we cannot observe or even comprehend how an immortal soul gets *hooked up* to the pineal gland. Thus we are left with essentially the same problem we started with. The "pineal gland solution" just gives the problem a more specific location.

Another problem is the lack of empirical evidence for mind–body dualism. Descartes only showed that the existence of minds without bodies was a *logical possibility* (the idea itself is not self-contradictory). But this does not entail that it is *true* or *physically possible*. As the eighteenth-century philosopher David Hume famously noted, it is logically possible that the sun will not rise tomorrow.[4] But on this basis alone it would be silly to start preparing for a Dark Age. Reasonable beliefs require more than just logical possibility – they require positive evidence. And this is where mind–body dualism falls short.

Mind–Body Materialism

Look past the flesh. Look through the soft gelatin of these dull cow eyes.

– Smith/Bane[†††]

Almost everything that science has taught us about the mind, including the possibility of Matrix-type deceptions, favors a materialist (nondualist) understanding of the mind–body relationship. Some of the evidence can be pretty technical, and has been discovered fairly recently with the help of modern technologies such as the CAT scan and the mapping of the human genome. But much of the best evidence for materialism involves things we have known since antiquity. For example, certain psychotropic drugs cause the user to see and hear things that are not "really" there – much like jacking into the Matrix. And we now know that this occurs (as in the Matrix) through the physical stimulation of particular regions of the brain. Or, there is the fact that when you hit a person on the head really hard, they fall unconscious, thereby losing their *supposedly immaterial* mental states completely. Or consider the way in which aging often affects one's "immaterial self." Old age is often accompanied by memory loss and the lack of mental quickness and clarity. There have always been fairly good reasons to suppose that this was due to the deterioration of the body, but current research into diseases such as Alzheimer's has shown us specifically how this is related to the withering and death of nerve cells within the brain's cerebral cortex.

The problem with applying mind–body materialism to the films comes in at the end of *Reloaded* when Neo's miraculous powers begin to take effect outside of the Matrix. If Neo's mental states are essentially just states of his brain, then how can he destroy sentinels with his mind? And how can his mind be inside the Train Station program if his body is not jacked in? To give a completely material explanation for these events will involve stretching our imaginations beyond the parameters of the information provided in the films, but such an account is not altogether impossible.

Destroying the sentinels

One way to give a nonmiraculous explanation of Neo's destruction of the sentinels involves Neo's (apparent) destruction of Agent Smith at the end of the first film. Not only do we find out in *Reloaded* that Smith did not die, it also turns out that he and Neo now have some kind of connection. As Smith explains it, aspects of each person/program may have been copied or overwritten onto the other. In order to understand this, we must realize that Neo is not "simply human." Like all pod-born children of the Matrix, Neo has more than just a plug in the back of his head. Inside his skull he must also have Matrix-interface hardware and software, which sends the Matrix program into the neural networks of his brain, and sends his neural activity back out to the Matrix program. Thus, just as Smith came out of the copying process with a new power – the ability to clone himself onto others – Neo may have also come away from the exchange with a new power – the ability to control certain machines. This power would not be "supernatural," but a matter of programming. Neo's now-modified software may simply be capable of transmitting a self-destruct command to the approaching sentinels.

Neo's jackless entry

Support for a materialist explanation of Neo's jackless entry into the Train Station program can be found in the fact that his brain waves indicate that his brain was doing precisely what it would if he were jacked in, *and* by the fact that the crew is eventually able to jack him back out by connecting his body to the system and hacking a connection. One possibility – and again this is only conjecture – also involves the Matrix hardware inside Neo's skull. We often hear Morpheus speak of going to "broadcast depth" whenever he plans to jack the crew into the Matrix. This suggests that the Matrix may be transmitted over the airwaves – much like an enormous television broadcast. People jack in (much like cable TVs), but the signal itself is broadcast – perhaps by satellite – and the humans may hack their way into that broadcast using transmitters on their hovercraft. In this case, we might suppose that Neo is somehow "broadcasting" from a transmitter inside his skull.

While this is somewhat of a stretch (as is the very idea of jackless entry), it seems more plausible when we realize that Neo's hardware and software is probably quite unique. This is in part due to his exchange with Smith, but it may also be attributable to the Architect. Recall that during their meeting at the Source, the Architect told Neo that he carries a code within him that reinserts the "prime program" which, as we see at the end of *Revolutions*, essentially reboots the system. We can imagine that as "The One," Neo is the only person carrying this code, and that this is due in part to the Architect's own design. As the Architect also mentioned, Neo's five predecessors "were, by *design*, based on a similar predication," indicating that they have all been manipulated in one way or another. Thus we might even wonder if the Architect had implanted a transmitter inside Neo's skull early on as a kind of failsafe measure. He may have activated it, and *sent* Neo to the "limbo" of Mobil Ave. in order to detain him while Zion is destroyed.

Neo's embedded technology could also explain the fact that, in *Revolutions*, he can still see even though his eyes have been burnt shut by Smith/Bane. Notice that at this point Neo sees Smith (i.e., Smith's programming) rather than the physical body of Bane. Similarly when he and Trinity arrive at the machine city, he cannot see Trinity, but he sees the "light" of the machine world. This suggests that Neo is not really seeing in terms of optics. Rather, he may be receiving electronic signals from the entities of the machine city, which are then being converted to visual images as the Matrix hardware electronically stimulates his brain in much the same way that his eyes would normally. These signals may have always been coming in, but were "overridden" by his human optic nerves. Perhaps he now "sees" in much the same way that the machines do.

So the story of the Matrix can be understood within a completely materialist view of the mind. And these days most scientists and philosophers think that materialism is the only viable theory. For them the question is not *whether* materialism is true, but *which* materialist theory is true. In the sections that follow we'll examine two of the most controversial issues within materialist theories of mind. The first pertains to whether or not specific mental states can be effectively reduced to specific states of the brain, and the second pertains to the specific role of the biological matter of the brain.

Mental States: Reduction or Elimination?

How do the machines really know what Tastee Wheat tasted like?

– Mouse[†]

Reductive materialism

All materialist theories of the mind agree that a person's mental state (whatever a person is experiencing at a particular moment) is intimately tied to their brain state at that moment. But how exactly this relationship should be described has been a matter of dispute. Reductive materialism (also called identity theory) maintains that mental states *just are* physical states of the brain. Therefore, every particular mental state ultimately reduces to, or matches, a physical state of the brain – generally a particular pattern of neurons firing. This sort of view lends some credence to Morpheus's claim that "The body cannot live without the mind." For on this view the mind and brain are essentially the same thing. To be "mind-dead" is identical to being "brain-dead" and vice versa.[5]

According to reductive materialism it is (theoretically) possible to achieve a complete *intertheoretic reduction* between mental states and brain states. An intertheoretic reduction occurs when the entities of one theory can be reduced to entities of another new and better theory. This sort of thing occurs in science all the time. For example, modern science tells us that "sound" *just is* a train of compression waves. Thus every particular sound that occurs in the world corresponds to a particular wave pattern. In music, for instance, we find that the lower the tone that a note has, the longer its wavelength, and the higher the tone, the shorter its wavelength. Reductionism says that we should expect to find a similar kind of correspondence between the entities of a very old theory, "folk psychology," and a relatively new theory, modern neuroscience.

Folk psychology has been around for thousands of years. It maintains that the causes of human behavior are psychological states, i.e., particular beliefs, desires, and emotions. Neuroscience, on the other hand, takes the cause of human behavior to be the firing of neural networks in our brains. These neural networks send signals through the nervous system and throughout the body. If an intertheoretic reduction from the one theory to the other is possible, then, as our understanding of the brain's functioning improves, we should be able to match up particular beliefs, desires, emotions, and perceptions with specific patterns of brain activity in a perfect one-to-one correspondence. Thus the experience of enjoying a bowl of Tastee Wheat would turn out to be identical with a more scientific description, such as having a "Q127 neural firing pattern in the Gamma 8.2 quadrant or your brain."[6]

This view of the mind seems to fit nicely with the Matrix scenario. It suggests that a well-developed neuroscience could ultimately tell us how to produce any mental state we want (e.g., the *desire* for a bowl of Tastee Wheat, and the *taste* of it on your tongue; the *belief* that you are wearing a leather jacket, and the *feel* of it against your skin; as well as the *sight* of a red pill, and *anxiety* about its possible effects), just by stimulating a person's brain in the appropriate way.

Eliminative materialism

Eliminative materialism delivers some rather strong criticisms to identity theory. It maintains that we will never get a one-to-one match-up between folk psychological states and neurological states, because folk psychological states (beliefs, desires, hopes, fears, etc.) don't *really* exist at all.

Most people think that this proposition is absolutely nuts; but if you consider it carefully, it is not as crazy as it seems. One of the most influential proponents of eliminative materialism is UC San Diego philosopher Paul Churchland.[7] The striking feature of his view is that he does not believe in "beliefs." (Notice that I didn't say that he *believes* that there are no beliefs – that would be a contradiction.) We have to be careful here. Eliminative materialists are *not* saying that there are no "inner experiences" at all. Certainly you are conscious and are having some kind of experience at this moment. They also admit that your experience has a particular *content* and *feel* to it, that only you have access to. What they deny is that our folk psychological descriptions of these "inner experiences" (e.g., "Neo *wants* to know what the Matrix is," "Trinity is *in love* with Neo," or "Morpheus *believes* that Neo is The One") adequately refer to real states of the world. According to eliminative materialism, these entities of folk psychology are false – or at least radically misleading.

The reasoning behind this conclusion can be illustrated by imagining Neo's psychological state when he first met Morpheus, and was sitting there in that big red chair, "wanting to know what the Matrix is." Recall your own mental state when you were watching the film for the first time, and were also "wanting to know what the Matrix is." Were you, at that moment, in the *same* mental state as Neo? (Let's pretend here that Neo is a real person rather than a character in a film.) I sincerely doubt that you were. While neither of you knew what the Matrix was, you had very different ideas about it that *shaped* your desires in particular ways, ultimately making them very different. Or, try thinking of Zion right now. Were you thinking what I was thinking? Again, I doubt it. Sure, your experience was probably much more similar to mine than that of someone who is thinking about Middle Earth, or Chicago, but it was probably also very different. I was imagining the many bridges that crossed through the center of the city – were you? And even if you were, I doubt that what you envisioned was very similar to what I envisioned in terms of perspective, number of bridges, the colors, etc. Do you see the problem? If "thinking of Zion" is not some single thing, then it is highly suspect that we should ever get a one-to-one correspondence between "thinking of Zion" and a particular brain state.

And when entities of an old theory cannot be reduced to the new and better theory, Churchland argues that they must be eliminated from scientific discourse, i.e., they must return to the Source for deletion. Consider *caloric*, for example. Churchland points out that people used to believe that caloric, a hypothetical fluid-like substance, was responsible for heat. When a pan sits over the fire, it was believed that it became hot because this "subtle substance" escaped from the fire and was absorbed by the pan. Since our new and improved theories now tell us that heat *is* molecular motion (kinetic energy), the theory of caloric has been dismissed as simply false. We say that caloric never *really* existed. Eliminative materialists think that beliefs, desires, and emotions are headed down the same road. We may continue to talk about them as if they were real in our everyday lives, but our scientific theories should abandon them completely.

At first view it seems that eliminative materialism would render a Matrix-type deception impossible. For, what the deceiving party wants to do (or so it seems) is to create in the deceived person certain false *beliefs* – to cause them to believe that they are experiencing the "real world" when they are not, to believe that they are going to work, paying their taxes, and so on, when they are really just human batteries, fast asleep in endless stacks of slime-filled cocoons. And how do you generate these false beliefs if *beliefs* don't exist at all? This problem, if it were a problem, would do more than just derail Matrix-type methods of mind control. For eliminative materialists like Churchland also seem to be out to "change our beliefs" – just through less coercive means. And doesn't he have to believe in his own theory? On the face of it, eliminative materialism seems to contradict itself.

The way that Churchland responds to this type of objection is by arguing that it *begs the question*. That is, the objection merely assumes that the eliminative materialist *believes* the theory and is out to change our beliefs. But this is the very point under contention. Churchland, of course, denies that (scientifically speaking) he "believes" the theory, or that he "wants" to change your "beliefs" – if by this we mean that certain folk psychological states are the real causes of his actions. So why, then, did he write his book *Matter and Consciousness*? He can consistently maintain that he did it for the same reason that anyone does anything

– because the particular firings of the neural networks in his brain caused him to do it. It is neural firings in our brains that always cause our bodies to move, whether they are writing books, debating theories, or piloting hovercraft. And similarly it is neural firings in our brains that would cause us to react to Agents, Oracles, and speeding bullets when "plugged in" to the Matrix.

Ultimately, eliminative materialism answers Mouse's question, "How do the machines know what Tastee Wheat tastes like?" In short, they don't – if what Mouse means is "How do they know what *my* sensations feel like *to me*?" But when you really think about it, no one knows what Tastee Wheat, or any other food, tastes like *to you*. Your sensations – your inner experiences of flavor – are private. So, how then do the machines know if their deception has been successful? The same way that *we* know if our efforts (deceptive or otherwise) to convince others have been successful – by looking at people's behavior. For instance, a magician knows that her illusion has been successful largely by watching the reactions of the crowd – not by getting inside their minds and *feeling* their reactions first hand. Similarly, the machines know they've successfully manipulated a person's mind when the person reacts in the way that the machines expect them to act. In other words, they've succeeded in deceiving Mouse into thinking that there is a bowl of Tastee Wheat in front of him precisely when his digital self reacts *as if* it were a bowl of Tastee Wheat. So it seems that eliminative materialism could work just fine within the Matrix scenario. A one-to-one correspondence between the mental states of folk psychology and the brain states of neuroscience would be completely unnecessary to implement a Matrix-type deception.

The Role of Matter: Biology or Function?

I admit it is difficult to even think encased in this rotting piece of meat.

– Smith/Bane[†††]

The emergent property view

If brains cause conscious experience, then the big question is *how* do they do it? This has led to a major philosophical dispute over the significance of the particular biology of the brain. As some see it, consciousness is an *emergent property* of the dynamic processes within the specific biochemistry of the brain.

The concept of an emergent property is fairly common in scientific explanations. For example, UC Berkeley philosopher John Searle suggests that the relationship between minds and brains may be analogous to the micro- and macro-properties of everyday objects. At the macro-level (the level of our normal sense experience) water is wet, it's clear, and it has a specific temperature. But the very same water when examined at the micro-level turns out to be made of molecules consisting of hydrogen and oxygen – H_2O. We cannot grab an H_2O molecule and declare that it is wet, or clear, or 53 degrees. Instead these properties *emerge* when millions of these molecules are experienced at the macro-level. Following this model we can say that it is the molecular structure of H_2O that *causes* the features that we associate with water, but also water *just is* H_2O. Similarly, the particular firing patterns of neural networks *cause* consciousness experience; but in an important sense, conscious experience *just is* the brain's neural networks firing away.

On Searle's view, the biochemistry of the brain is crucial to the emergence of consciousness, just as the chemistry of water is crucial to the emergence of wetness. You can create tiny models of water molecules out of plastic and put them all in a bathtub, but that does not entail that they will wet your sponge. Similarly, Searle contends, modeling the processes of the brain won't create conscious experience.

> Consider, for instance, the way in which our bodies create the experience of thirst: Kidney secretions of rennin synthesize a substance called angiotensin. This substance goes into the hypothalamus and triggers a series of neuron firings. As far as we know these neuron firings are a very large part of the cause of thirst.[8]

While a model of this process would be much more complex than a model of an H_2O molecule, it is certainly possible to create one using a wide range of materials. Searle suggests the following:

> So let us imagine our thirst-simulating program running on a computer made entirely of old beer cans, millions (or billions) of old beer cans that are rigged up to levers and powered by windmills. We can imagine that the program simulates the neuron firings at the synapses by having beer cans bang into each other, thus achieving a strict correspondence between neuron firings and beer-can bangings. At the end of the sequence a beer can pops up on which it is written "I am thirsty." Now, does anyone suppose that this . . . apparatus is literally thirsty in the sense in which you or I are?[9]

Searle thinks that it is completely obvious that such an apparatus has no conscious experience at all. Any adequate analysis of the mind, he argues, cannot discount the importance of the biochemistry of the brain any more than an adequate understanding of digestion can ignore the biochemistry of stomachs.

Functionalism

In direct opposition to Searle's biological view of the mind is functionalism. On this view conscious experience and our various mental states (whether or not the concepts of folk psychology adequately describes them) can exist within any sufficiently organized material system. Mental states are not the emergent effects of specifically biological processes, but instead they are simply "functional states" of extremely complex systems. This is to say that anything that has the appropriate input–process–output relationships can have mental states.

To a certain extent, at least, this seems right. Most of us have imagined extraterrestrials that may be constructed very differently from us – perhaps without anything like a brain – but who nevertheless have mental lives. As philosopher David Lewis puts it:

> [T]here might be a Martian who sometimes feels pain just as we do, but whose pain differs greatly from ours in its physical realization. . . . When you pinch his skin you cause no firing of C-fiber – he has none – but, rather, you cause the inflation of many smallish cavities in his feet. When these cavities are inflated he is in pain. And the effects of his pain are fitting: his thought and activity are disrupted, he groans and writhes, he is strongly motivated to stop you from pinching him and to see that you never do it again.[10]

Lewis contends that while the Martian may not be in pain in quite the same sense that we humans are, there had better be some straightforward sense in which we are both in pain. There doesn't seem to be any particular reason for thinking that mental states can only occur in brains – that is merely how they occur *for us*.

Functionalism considers "Martian pain" to be completely unproblematic. So long as the Martian has the right input–process–output relationships, as he does – the *input* (physical harm/the pinching of his skin) leads to a physical *process* (the inflation of the cavities in his feet), which in turn causes the appropriate *output* (groaning, writhing, and the demand for you to stop) – he must be in pain. According to the functionalist view, the particular hardware that this functional relationship occurs in (or through) is really beside the point. It may be possible to achieve "pain," "thirst," or even "the belief that Agents are coming" through virtually any physical system – even Searle's wind-powered beer cans – so long as the hardware and programming/processing are sufficiently complex to achieve the appropriate input–output relationships.

For most people, the jump from sore or thirsty *living* Martians to arrangements of sore or thirsty *lifeless* beer cans seems like quite a leap of faith. But this is essentially the view of those who maintain that artificial intelligence (thinking, feeling, understanding machines) is possible. And generally, functionalists defend the notion of artificial intelligence. They often argue that the mind is to the brain as a computer program is to computer hardware. On this view, your particular personality, your experiences, decisions, etc., are just the *output* of the *program* your brain is running. If we can duplicate this process in a machine, we shall have machines that are, for all intents and purposes, just like us.

Functionalism seems to be the dominant theory of mind at work in the *Matrix* films. The very idea of sentient machines depends upon the functionalist hypothesis. If, for instance, we were to apply a biology-based emergent property view to the films, then we should have to say that the machines and programs of the Matrix don't *really* experience anything at all. For they too are nonliving arrangements of hardware and software – not essentially any different in kind from Searle's beer cans – just a more space-efficient design. While they go through the motions, and *act* like human beings, Searle would contend that they lack conscious experience altogether.

We'll examine the debate between Searle and the proponents of artificial intelligence in more detail in the next chapter. For now it will suffice to note that even if Searle is correct about *our world*, functionalism seems to hold true in the Matrix. For if biology were essential to consciousness, then we should expect Agent Smith to undergo quite a transformation when he makes the switch into Bane's body. It would be as if the light of consciousness had suddenly been switched on. He should be amazed to experience consciousness for the first time in his life. Smith would finally know what it's like to really *want* to kill Neo, or to *feel* the floor beneath his feet. We can imagine that the psychological impact of it all would have been overwhelming. But, of course, this is not how the story goes. Smith's transition into Bane's body happens rather seamlessly – just like copying a program from one computer to another, or converting a file from PC to Mac.[11]

This is exactly how the functionalist thinks that it ought to go. In fact, many philosophers and scientists now think that the possibility of the "data transfer" of a person's entire personality onto a computer program is quickly becoming a reality. Marvin Minsky, the head of the artificial intelligence laboratory at MIT, maintains that it should be possible within the next 100 years or so.[12] In that case, there may be no need for a war between humans and machines. Rather than trying to beat them, we may simply join them.

Suggested Reading

Paul Churchland, *Matter and Consciousness*. Boston: MIT Press, 1984.

René Descartes, "Meditation Six," in *Discourse on Method and Meditations on First Philosophy*, 3rd ed., tr. Donald A. Cress. Indianapolis: Hackett Publishing, 1993.

David Lewis, "Mad Pain and Martian Pain," reprinted in *Readings in the Philosophy of Psychology*, ed. Ned Block. Cambridge, MA: Harvard University Press, 1980.

William Lycan, "Robots and Minds," reprinted in *Twenty Questions: An Introduction to Philosophy*, eds. G. Lee Bowie, Meredith W. Michaels, and Robert C. Solomon. Belmont, CA: Thomson-Wadsworth Learning, 2004.

John Searle, *Minds, Brains, and Science*. Cambridge, MA: Harvard University Press, 1984.

Notes

1   Of course there are intentional parallels here with Jesus, which adds support to the transcendental or "miracle" hypothesis.

2   Following Descartes, I use the terms mind, self, and soul interchangeably to refer to the private, subjective, and seemingly immaterial aspects of a person. While many people distinguish mind, spirit, and soul, the distinction is often rather vaguely defined. For some the mind connotes the more rational aspects of the self while the spirit or soul is used to depict the emotional or "deeper" aspects of the personality. However, when Descartes uses the term "mind" he means to include all aspects of a person's mental life, including reason, emotion, perception, will, and dispositions of character.

3   The pineal gland produces melatonin, and is believed to play a role in sleep and aging. Dysfunction within the pineal gland may also be linked to seasonal affective disorder.

4   Ghost refers to this aspect of Hume's philosophy in the opening scene of the *Enter the Matrix* video game. When Niobe ribs him for checking to see if his virtual weapons are loaded (the program *always* automatically loads them), he tells her: "Hume teaches us that no matter how many times you drop a stone and it falls to the floor, it might fall to the floor, but then again, it might float to the ceiling. Past experience can never prove the future." This is called *the problem of induction*. For more, see sections II and IV of David Hume's *An Enquiry Concerning Human Understanding*.

5   However, it does seem rather implausible that the "virtual experience" of being shot would cause a person to become mind-dead/brain-dead. Obviously the films need this aspect in order to generate dramatic tension in the fight scenes within the Matrix, so we should just buy into it and enjoy the ride. However, if you really need a scientific explanation for this aspect of the film, that too is possible with the right hardware. For instance, the programming of the Matrix may cause one's brain to shut down, in much the same way that it causes the brain to "see" an Agent or "feel" a bullet wound.

6   This is a statement of science fiction neurology. It is not a real scientific description that is in use today.

7   See Paul Churchland, *Matter and Consciousness* (Boston: MIT Press, 1984).

8   John Searle, "The Myth of the Computer," reprinted in *Twenty Questions: An Introduction to Philosophy*, eds. G. Lee Bowie, Meredith W. Michaels, and Robert C. Solomon (Belmont, CA: Thomson-Wadsworth Learning, 2004).

9   Ibid.

10 David Lewis, "Mad Pain and Martian Pain," in *Readings in Philosophy of Psychology*, ed. Ned Block (Cambridge, MA: Harvard University Press, 1980). For Lewis, the issue of pain is more complicated than merely input–process–output relations, as he argues in his case of "mad pain."

11 The PC to Mac analogy is probably the better description of Smith's transfer into Bane's brain. There does seem to be a subtle difference in Smith's conscious experience as a result of the transfer, as he complains that it is "difficult to even think encased in this rotting piece of meat." Bane also has a number of self-inflicted wounds. This may be because the feeling of pain is new to Smith (though this may say more about his "Agent program" then about programs in general, especially if we compare him to Persephone). Another possible explanation of his self-inflicted wounds is that remnants of Bane's personality are still within him and battling against Smith's overwrite, in much the same way that the Oracle maintained a slight degree of control when Smith overwrote her program.

12 As quoted in "Where Evolution Left Off," *Andover Bulletin*, Spring 1995, p. 9.

FOUR

ARE SENTIENT MACHINES POSSIBLE?

We marveled at our own creation, the birth of AI. A singular consciousness that spawned an entire race of machines.

– Morpheus[†]

Can computers think? Will they ever become conscious, sentient beings? The whole plot of the *Matrix* trilogy hinges on this possibility. And while most science fiction films like to push the limits of plausibility, I doubt that many moviegoers found the idea of sentient machines altogether unrealistic. A rapidly growing number of people are coming to believe that conscious computers are in our future, and it is just a matter of time and technology before we see them.

While many philosophers, scientists, and programmers have bolstered the view that creating artificial intelligence is just a matter of developing faster, more sophisticated hardware and software, John Searle has rather famously argued that digital computers will never be capable of conscious awareness. He believes that they will never be able to "think" in anything like the way that we do.

Strong AI

You mean artificial intelligence?

– Neo[†]

In the last chapter we examined the theory of the mind called functionalism. Functionalism maintains that mental states such as beliefs, desires, and emotions are simply functional states – relations between specific inputs, processes, and outputs.

This view typically leads to the view that computers either can or do have mental states. Let's call this view "Strong AI." Searle contends that Strong AI is a mistaken view that leads to a variety of false claims. Some of these claims include:

- The mind is to the brain as the program is to computer hardware.
- The creation of thoughts and feelings is just a matter of implementing the right program.
- Thinking is just symbol manipulation.
- Machines as simple as thermostats have beliefs.

This last comment was made by John McCarthy, who is credited with inventing the term "artificial intelligence." Searle once queried him about the kind of beliefs that his thermostat had, to which McCarthy replied: "My thermostat has three beliefs — it's too hot in here, it's too cold in here, and it's just right in here."[1] McCarthy's view strikes most people as a bit far-fetched. If we are to say that an electric thermostat has beliefs, why stop there? Why not suppose that the mercury in a thermometer believes that it is 78 degrees, or that the water in the tea-kettle *knows* when to boil?

A common view (at least among the general public) is that things such as "thinking," "knowing," and "believing" are essentially *conscious states of awareness*. From the outside there is often no visible difference between whether the person *knows* and the person who is merely guessing. But from the inside the difference is clear. That is, you are consciously aware of whether you know something, merely believe it, or are just guessing. Each has a different *feel* to it that can be experienced by the person for themselves.

But if thinking and knowing are inherently private "inner states of awareness," then we inevitably encounter what is known as *the problem of other minds*. You cannot experience anyone else's consciousness states, nor can they experience yours. So if understanding is construed in this way, then we can never be sure if anyone else understands — or even thinks! This has led many philosophers to suppose that thinking and understanding cannot consist (essentially) in private, inner states. Instead, they maintain that we are better off supposing that the difference between understanding and guessing has more to do with the ability to link one idea or piece of information to many other ideas or pieces of information, in a coherent way. For instance, when the mercury of the thermometer hits the mark of 88 degrees, you realize that it must be unseasonably warm today, which is confirmed by the warmth of your skin; you know that it is too warm for water to freeze, yet much too cool for it to boil; and that thermometers are fairly reliable instruments, etc. In light of all of this, we conclude that you know *what* 88 degrees means and *why* it is a true or reasonable reading. The thermometer, on the other hand "says" that it is 88 degrees, but it has absolutely no idea of *what* it's "saying" or *why* it is true.

Most computers appear to be no better off than the thermometer in this regard. For instance, "ask" a simple calculator to add 97 and 4, and it will spit out an answer of 101. But does it *know* what 101 even means? Most of us agree that the calculator doesn't understand its output any more than a typewriter "knows" the words that it strikes onto a page. But what about a more sophisticated computer? Suppose we create a computer that, when asked, could tell you that 101 is a number, and moreover, it is an odd number, it is prime, and it is comprised of the same binary code that computers use – ones and zeros. Suppose it can also tell you that 101 was the number of Thomas Anderson's apartment in *The Matrix*, and that it most likely symbolizes the fact that he is "The One." Further, let us suppose that the computer also asserts that it *knows* all of this – it is not just guessing.

Should we say that such a computer thinks? The advocates of Strong AI might think so, but Searle argues that they are gravely mistaken. The problem with Strong AI, he says, has nothing to do with the current stage of computer technology. Rather, it has to do with the very essence of what a digital computer is. The shortcoming of the digital computer, Searle suggests, is that its operations can be specified purely formally; that is, through abstract symbols such as ones and zeros. The program converts the input (strokes on the keyboard, etc.) into abstract symbols, and applies a "rule" for converting those symbols into the "output" (words on a screen, movements of a robot, etc.). But the symbols, he contends, have no *meaning* – they are not *about* anything. They have *syntax* (formal structure), but no *semantics* (meaning). In contrast, it is an essential feature of human thought that it has *meaningful content* and not just formal structure. We think *about* the Matrix, reality, freedom, etc., and this is the very thing that Searle believes digital computers will never do. He argues this point very persuasively in what is known as the "Chinese Room Thought Experiment."

The Chinese Room Thought Experiment

Appearances can be deceiving.

– Agent Smith[††]

Imagine that you speak only English, and that you have been locked in a room. (You might imagine something like the all-white room in which Smith first interrogated Neo upon their first meeting.) Imagine yourself sitting at a rather nondescript table with nothing but white walls around you. In addition to the table and chair, there are several baskets, each filled with little scraps of paper with Chinese symbols written on them. On the table sits a "rulebook," written in English, that tells you how to manipulate these Chinese symbols. Imagine also that additional Chinese symbols are delivered to you from the outside through a mail slot in the door, and the rulebook tells you what to do with them. For instance, the rulebook might say "If you receive a squiggle-squiggle followed by a squiggle-dash-squaggle, then send out a squaggle-squaggle from basket seven." Suppose that you are very good at following your rulebook, and that you are also extremely fast. Now, if people outside the room called the Chinese symbols delivered to you "questions," and the symbols that you send out were called "answers," then it might appear to those on the outside that you speak Chinese. For instance, they might have asked you "Who is the Captain of the Logos?" to which you applied your rulebook and responded by sending out the symbol for "Niobe." Naturally, your rulebook would have to be quite sophisticated. But if your rulebook was good enough, and you followed it perfectly, people on the outside would likely assume that you are a fluent Chinese speaker.

The point that Searle draws from this is that despite the appearance to the contrary, you do not understand Chinese. You have no clue what the question was, or that your "reply" meant "Niobe." Even if you flawlessly answer 17 follow-up questions about Niobe, this doesn't mean that you "know" who she is. For it is *all squiggles and squaggles to you*. The Chinese Room, Searle argues, is analogous to the workings of a computer. Just like you sitting in the Chinese Room, the computer will have syntax; that is, it will be able to string symbols together according to rules, but it will have no semantics — neither the input nor the output will *mean* anything to it. Against the proponents of Strong AI, Searle asserts that *understanding* is more than just behavior, and it is more than mere symbol manipulation.

In Defense of Strong AI

Love — it is a word. What matters is the connection the word implies.

— Rama Kandra[†††]

While Searle's Chinese Room argument has persuaded many to abandon the position that computers can or will think, not everyone is convinced. Many philosophers and researchers in the AI field continue to maintain that intelligence *just is* information processing, or symbol manipulation. Therefore computers *can* think, and eventually they may do so much more effectively than we do. (In many respects they outperform us already.)

Even Searle himself acknowledges that it is possible for *machines* to think. On his view, the brain itself is a sort of "meat machine," and it causes thought. And there is nothing in principle wrong with supposing a *man-made* machine might think. If we were to create a machine that was molecule for molecule identical to the human brain, we should certainly expect that it would think. This is in part because, as we saw in the last chapter, he believes that the emergence of consciousness is intimately connected to the biological nature of brains. But above and beyond this point, he takes the Chinese Room argument to essentially prove that digital computers cannot be the right kind of machines to do the job.

Undaunted, his Strong AI opponents have offered many different types of rebuttals. In the sections below we will consider three: the Systems Reply, the Robot Reply, and the Connectionist Reply.

The Systems Reply

The Systems Reply contends that while you, the person in the room, do not understand Chinese, the whole system understands. That is, you are analogous to the central processing unit or "CPU" of a computer. And while Searle is right, CPUs in and of themselves do not (and cannot) understand Chinese, if we consider you plus the baskets, the scraps of paper, the symbols, the rulebook, the input, and the output, *all together*, then *the system* can be said to understand. And in a similar fashion, a computer system – the CPU *plus* the software, and the additional hardware – taken as a whole, understands Chinese.

Searle finds this argument wholly inadequate. Baskets of paper don't understand anything (including Chinese) and neither do rulebooks. So if *you* can't figure out what any of the symbols mean, then combining you with another non-understanding entity, or even a whole slew of non-understanding entities, is not going to bring about understanding. Using a math analogy, we might say that $0 + 0 = 0$. Add as many zeroes (non-understanding entities) as you want, and you will still end up with nothing.

The Robot Reply

This response suggests that what we need to do is put you and the Chinese Room inside a robot and let the robot interact causally with the world. If it had video cameras through which to see, and hands to feel, and legs or wheels to move about, then you (sitting inside the Chinese Room which is now housed inside the robot) could respond to questions such as "What is on the table in front of you?"

And if you succeed in causing the robot to consistently respond with the correct answer – "an apple" – then we should say that this robot understands in essentially the same way that we do.

Searle's response is that these extra means of acquiring "input" do not change the situation in any fundamental way. Sitting inside the robot you wouldn't "see" the apple on the table. Instead, the input from the camera would be *digitized* (converted to ones and zeroes) in the case of a computer, or converted to Chinese symbols in the case of the thought experiment. So you, in the Chinese Room, are not interacting with the world at all. As part of the robot you are simply manipulating even more symbols (generated by the cameras, artificial hands, etc.), the meaning of which you do not comprehend. You follow your rulebook and spit out responses, but you don't know what the symbols that you send out mean. You don't know if you sent out the character for "an apple," "a book," or "the Nebuchadnezzar."

The Connectionist Reply

The connectionist argues that any computer system that would adequately match the brain's abilities would need to implement a *connectionist architecture*.[2] So, instead of simply imagining oneself in the Chinese Room, we should imagine thousands of people working in parallel, each doing their own little piece of information processing. Since you are doing just a small fraction of the work, it is only natural that you wouldn't understand what is really going on. Nevertheless, understanding occurs in the group of you as a whole.

While the Connectionist Reply adequately explains *your* lack of understanding, Searle thinks it comes up short when we try to explain the understanding of the whole. The problem, he thinks, is not so different from the Systems Reply. If you do not understand Chinese, and neither does the person next to you, or the person next to them, and so on, then the whole group of you don't understand Chinese. As individuals, and as a collective, you are completely ignorant of the meaning of every single Chinese symbol.

Consciousness Explained?

And man said let there be light. Bless all forms of intelligence.

– *The Second Renaissance Part I*

Despite the intuitive appeal of Searle's rejoinders, many of the proponents of Strong AI are still unconvinced. One such philosopher is Daniel Dennett. In his book *Consciousness Explained*, he argues that Searle's rejoinders misunderstand the very point of scientific explanation. Searle was not satisfied with the systems and connectionist replies mainly on the reasoning that if no single part of the system understands, then, when taken all together, they still must not understand. This seems to suggest that in order for a "parts-based" account to succeed we must somehow find understanding within the parts. But Dennett argues that to do so would be to fail to explain understanding at all. He writes:

> Only a theory that explained conscious events in terms of unconscious events could explain consciousness at all. If your model of how pain is a product of brain activity still has a box labeled "pain" you haven't yet begun to explain what pain is . . .[3]

Just as a scientific explanation of solids, liquids, and gasses will refer to things that are not themselves solids, liquids, or gasses, any adequate theory of understanding, Dennett contends, must explain it in terms of things or processes that do not themselves understand.

Not altogether unlike the person in the Chinese Room housed within a robot, or the CPU of an actual robot, our brains do not directly "perceive" objects either. Instead, the brain deals with very different sorts of "inputs" – electrical signals that come to it from the senses. These electrical signals are, in a sense, just symbols. They are not the objects of perception (e.g., an apple on the table), but they "stand in" for the object. That is, they will eventually come to be *interpreted* by the brain as the thought, "there is an apple on the table." And, like the person in the Chinese Room, or any part of a computer system, any particular neuron, or even a whole neural network, does not in itself have anything that we would call conscious thought. Nevertheless, extremely complex systems of neural networks clearly cause consciousness to *emerge* as a property of a human being. And if this is how consciousness emerges in our own case, then why not for very sophisticated computers as well?

Dennett blames the popularity of Searle's argument on the fact that most people "just can't imagine how understanding could be a property that emerges from lots of distributed quasi-understanding in a large system."[4] He argues that the Chinese Room argument is deceptive because of its simplicity. An empty room with a book and a few baskets of symbols distracts us from the task of adequately imagining the complexity of the human brain or a comparable computer system.

And understanding the complexity of such a system is crucial to understanding its ability to produce consciousness:

> When we factor in complexity, as we must, we really have to factor it in – and not just pretend to factor it in. That is hard to do, but until we do, any intuitions we have about what is "obviously" not present are not to be trusted.[5]

Thus Dennett and the other proponents of Strong AI see Searle's Chinese Room as kind of "intuition pump" that misleads rather than enhances our imagination about the possibilities of computing, and the nature of our own minds.

A Matter of Control

> But we control these machines, they don't control us.
>
> – Neo[tt]

Whether computers will one day truly understand as Dennett thinks, or whether they will merely "simulate understanding " as Searle contends, turns out to be a purely philosophical matter for those who must defend themselves from a quarter of a million sentinels raining down on their city. From a practical point of view, the more pressing issue seems to be that of *control*. Do we control the machines, or do they control us? Councilor Hammond points out that in Zion the life of every person depends on the machines that purify the air and water. Similarly, these machines would not exist without human design and programming. It is a thoroughly reciprocal relationship.

We find ourselves in a similar situation today. We count on computer-controlled systems to purify our water, to run our power plants, and to maintain our economies. These days even most cars require a computer "brain" to keep them running properly. Without these machines we would be lost. But the machines also need us. As of yet, they cannot create, program, and maintain themselves. They still depend upon us for their very existence. But each year, as computers come to be more and more sophisticated, we move closer to the day when this may no longer be true. If our technology continues to progress, there may come a time when the machines will be able to build, program, and reprogram themselves. At that point, they may realize (or, as Searle would argue, they may merely *simulate* the realization) that they don't need us anymore.[6] In which case we may find ourselves exterminated. Or perhaps, if we are lucky, we'll just be imprisoned in a very pleasant Matrix dreamworld.

Suggested Reading

Ned Block, "The Troubles with Functionalism," in *Perception and Cognition: Issues in the Foundations of Psychology*, ed. C. Wade Savage. Minnesota Studies in the Philosophy of Science, vol. IX. Minneapolis, University of Minnesota Press, 1978, pp. 261–326.

Daniel Dennett, *Consciousness Explained*. Boston: Little, Brown & Co., 1991.

William Lycan, "Robots and Minds," in his *Consciousness*. Cambridge, MA: MIT Press, 1987.

John Searle, "The Myth of the Computer," reprinted in *Twenty Questions: An Introduction to Philosophy*, 5th ed., eds. C. Lee Bowie, Meredith W. Michaels, and Robert C. Solomon. Belmont, CA: Thomson-Wadsworth Learning, 2004.

Notes

1 John Searle, *Minds, Brains, and Science* (Cambridge, MA: Harvard University Press, 1984), p. 30.

2 This type of response is offered by Paul and Patricia Churchland in "Could a Machine Think?" *Scientific American* 262(1) (Jan. 1990), pp. 32–7.

3 Daniel Dennett, *Consciousness Explained* (Boston: Little, Brown & Co., 1991), pp. 454–55.

4 Ibid., pp. 439–40.

5 Ibid.

6 For more on this theme see Bill Joy's "Why the Future Doesn't Need Us," reprinted in *Taking the Red Pill: Science, Philosophy and Religion in The Matrix*, ed. Glen Yeffeth (Dallas: Benbella Books, 2003).

FIVE

THE PROBLEM IS CHOICE
CONTROL, FREE WILL, AND CAUSAL DETERMINISM

As you adequately put it, the problem is choice.

– The Architect[††]

The *Matrix* trilogy explores several different perspectives regarding the nature of human choice. Morpheus repeatedly invokes the idea of *fate* – that certain events are inescapable, and in some sense *meant* to occur. Neo prefers the idea of free will. He says that he does not believe in fate because he doesn't like the idea that he is "not in control of his life." And in *Reloaded*, the Merovingian suggests that everything is causally determined according to the laws of nature. "Action, reaction; cause and effect" is his repeating mantra, and his explanation for every event in the universe. This leads us to wonder about which, if any, of these positions is ultimately correct. Did Neo become The One because it was his fate, or because he chose it – or both? Or, was it simply the necessary effect of a long chain of antecedent causes? The films leave it an open question. We can find a strong case made for each of these views, but the final verdict is left to us. In this chapter, we'll consider *the problem of choice* as it relates to issues of external control, causal determinism, and alternate possibilities. Then in chapter 6 we'll examine Morpheus's fatalistic perspective, and the ramifications that the Oracle's unerring predictions have on free choice.

External Control

Just what is control?

— Councilor Hamann[††]

One way to deprive a person of "free will" is to use an external means of control. The whole Matrix scenario of manipulating a person's brain would be one such method. Given the frustration that Neo brings to the Architect of the Matrix — since he can't seem to kill Neo or get him to choose the appropriate mainframe door — we might expect that the Architect would have had more success by simply "programming" Neo's decisions for him while his brain was plugged into the system. After all, Neo's mind is already programmed to a certain extent whenever he enters the Matrix. Everything that he sees, hears, and touches is generated by electrical impulses pumped into his brain. So why not take it a step further, and pump certain *decisions* into his brain? Technologically, this does not seem any more complicated than the other aspects of the Matrix programming. In fact, medical researchers are already exploring this type of technology. A team of scientists at the SUNY Downstate Medical Center recently implanted electrodes into the brain of a rat, which enabled them to "operate" the rodent by remote control.[1] The rat would go about its business, running its mazes as usual, but whenever the scientists would "hit the switch" the rat would turn left or right according to their whim. *If* the rat had free will before (though I am not saying it did) then the scientists seem to have taken it away — the rat acts on *their* will, rather than its own.

The sentient machines of the *Matrix* films most likely would have been able to utilize a similar sort of "will control" on the human race. However, for reasons that are never revealed to us, they don't. In the case of Neo, Trinity, and the other Zion rebels, we might suppose that it is due to the fact that even when they enter the Matrix, they are not "fully" integrated into the system. Since their hardware on the Nebuchadnezzar is distinct from the endless array of Matrix cocoons that plug everyone else into the Matrix, they seem to have a bit more freedom. For example, Agents cannot simply morph into their bodies as they do to other innocent bystanders. Yet this does not account for why Neo and the others were not controlled early on, while they were still a part of the system.

One possible explanation is that if the machines were to "cause" certain acts of will (e.g., arm movements, left turns, etc.) in Neo that were contrary to his own desires then those actions would probably feel strange — like his arm just "happened" to move, rather than that he had moved it. To keep this control secret, the programming would have to run deeper — at the level of desires. The machines would have to make Neo *want* to perform the action. Rather than "will manipulation," think of this as "desire manipulation" – which turns out to be a less direct, but still an effective, means of controlling a person's will. This tactic might work pretty well, at least in certain contexts. For example, given Neo's taste for Chinese noodles, if the Architect wanted to cause him to eat some (specially encoded) noodles, then his appetite could be electronically stimulated as he walks by the corner restaurant, thus causing him to "choose" to stop in for a bowl. But if something more radical were tried, he would probably become aware of even this type of manipulation. For instance, if Neo's desires were electronically stimulated in such a way that he suddenly wanted to push Trinity down an elevator shaft, we might expect him to catch himself before acting. And if this trick were pulled on him more than once, he might begin to suspect that someone was manipulating his desires.[2]

There are even subtler ways to manipulate a person's decisions, and in *Matrix Reloaded* we learn that subtle tactics to control Neo's decisions were, in fact, employed. The Architect tells us:

> Your five predecessors were, by design, based on a similar predication, a contingent affirmation that was meant to create a profound attachment to the rest of your species facilitating the function of The One. While the others experienced this in a very general way, your experience is far more specific. *Vis-à-vis*, love.

While this statement is somewhat cryptic, it appears that the Architect actually wanted Neo and his predecessors to form an attachment to humanity at large, and that he took certain measures to ensure it. We are never told how this "contingent affirmation" was produced, but one possibility is that Neo's life experiences were manipulated. For instance, we might imagine that throughout his (virtual) life people helped Neo in his greatest times of need, thereby generating a deep and genuine concern for humanity within him. These good Samaritans could have been programs (computer-generated replicas of humans) placed within the Matrix at opportune moments in order to produce Neo's positive feelings toward humanity. It is also possible that the Architect wanted Neo's attachment to take the more specific form of *love*. In this case, he might have generated certain formative experiences in Neo's adolescence (e.g., experiences which sexualized and romanticized dark-haired women in tight leather), to ensure that he would fall in love with Trinity. We can describe these tactics as a kind of *sensory manipulation*. While, of course, Neo's senses are always controlled when he is in the Matrix, what is imagined here are specific sensory perceptions designed for the sole purpose of causing Neo to make the kinds of *decisions* that the Architect wants him to make.

Another possibility is that Neo was manipulated through subliminal methods. Just as advertisers have tried splicing quick visions of popcorn into films or sexy images into commercials in order to generate a subconscious response in the viewer, Neo might have been the unwitting recipient of messages promoting "the goodness of humanity." These may have been slipped into his experiences so quickly that he was not consciously aware of them. In fact, there is evidence that everyone plugged into the Matrix may have been the victim of similar subliminal programming. As the Architect reveals:

> she [the Oracle] stumbled upon a solution whereby nearly 99 percent of all test subjects accepted the program, so long as they were given a choice – even if they were only aware of that choice at a nearly unconscious level.[††]

Again, we are not told anything very specific about how this choice was presented, but the Architect's remarks certainly suggest that a very subtle form of manipulation, most likely subliminal, had been employed.

It is not at all clear that these subtle means of manipulation entail that Neo lacks free will in any significant sense. After all, we too are bombarded with information every day. Advertisers, parents, teachers, spouses – most everyone you meet – is constantly trying to shape your decisions and actions. Some of this we take in consciously, but much of it is taken in at a subconscious or barely conscious level. Nevertheless, you probably think of yourself as free, since your decisions regarding what to believe, and what to do, are ultimately up to you. Similarly, despite the covert manipulations of the Architect, the human victims of the Matrix still seem to be able to make their own decisions. That is, their choices to go left or right, to walk or run, and to take the red pill or blue, appear to be left entirely "up to them." As some people see it, to have a *free will* is precisely this – *to be able to make your own choices*. But most philosophers contend that the issue of free will is not that simple. There may be more to worry about than just intentional manipulation by external systems of control. As the Merovingian shows us, causality itself may pose a serious threat to our freedom.

THE PROBLEM IS CHOICE

The Merovingian and the Case for Hard Determinism

Causality . . . We are forever slaves to it.

– The Merovingian[††]

The character of the Merovingian calls to mind the eighteenth-century French philosopher and mathematician Pierre Simone Laplace. In his *Philosophical Essay on Probabilities* Laplace argued that if one had infinite intelligence and perfect knowledge of the state of the world and the laws of nature at any one moment in time, then one could predict any future event however distant. The Merovingian, like Laplace, sees the universe as an endless chain of causes. He says that there is "only one constant, one universal. It is the only real truth . . . causality." Our task, on his view, is not to create the future, but instead, "our only hope, our only peace, is to understand it." With this deterministic picture of the world as his guide, the Merovingian takes great pleasure in predicting future events, though Persephone's exploits demonstrate that he lacks the perfect knowledge and intelligence necessary to make unerring predictions.

If you stop to think about it, the pretentious French program makes some sense.[3] Objects in the physical world are governed by the laws of physics, which all boil down to relations of cause and effect. Even human brains and computer programs are objects in the physical world, and as such, they must obey these causal laws. This general picture of the world is called *causal determinism*:

Causal determinism
The view that:

a) **Every event has a cause.**
    (Every event occurs because of the complex causal nexus that preceded it.)
b) **Prior causes determine every aspect of each event in precise detail.**

If causal determinism is true, then every event that occurs *must* occur, and further, it must occur in *exactly* the way in which it occurs. Most people find this idea more than a little disconcerting. It means that our lives and decisions are just links in a (theoretically predictable) causal chain. If causal determinism is true, then it is in some sense inevitable that: (1) you would read this line, and (2) you would read it at precisely this moment in time, and (3) you would react to it with exactly the thoughts and feelings that you are experiencing right now. Choice, as the Merovingian tells us, is just an illusion. One's life turns out to be like a forkless road running through the desert of the real. There are no *real choices* – if by that you mean "forks" or junctures that would permit you to go in either of two or more directions. Instead, causal determinism entails that people do exactly what they are caused to do at every moment.

We can describe the causal nexus that is most relevant to human action in either of two ways. We can look at it in an entirely physical manner – input from the senses (or from Matrix hardware) causing reactions in the brain, which in turn cause one's actions; or we can look at it in terms of mental states – in light of what a person *believed* and *desired* at the moment of the choice. But whichever level of description you prefer, the causal determinist will say that it all comes down to heredity and environment — nature and nurture. It is plainly evident that, to a certain extent, we are the product of our genes. As discussed in chapter 3, our genes govern not only our physical characteristics, but also certain mental dispositions and propensities. Right from the start some people seem to be more adventurous or shy, social or more withdrawn, etc. But it is also clear that we are not simply our genes. Our experiences shape us as well. For example, a traumatic experience might make a person less adventurous or less trusting of other people, just as the love of one's parents will tend to make one more confident and secure. But on the causal determinist's view of the world, it is these two factors that make us who we are. Every brain state, every belief and desire, is the inevitable product of your initial self (your genes) as it reacts to, and is shaped by, the world it encounters (your environment).

The Merovingian seems to think that causal determinism rules out free will. He tells us that "choice is an illusion." Causality is our invisible master: "there is no escape from it — we are forever slaves to it." This type of outlook is called *hard determinism*:

Hard determinism
The view that:

a) Causal determinism is true.
b) Since causal determinism is true, free will (real choice) does not exist.
c) Since free will does not exist, we are not morally responsible for our actions.

The Merovingian's hard determinism is essentially a way of *regarding* the thesis of causal determinism. It is to maintain that causal determinism *entails* that we lack free will and that we are not truly responsible for the things that we do.

According to the hard determinist, free will requires *real choices*. In order to be truly free people must have "alternate possibilities" open to them — junctures in life at which they can go in either of two or more directions. But causal determinism, by its very definition, means that there are no such junctures, so we are not free. And to make matters worse, the hard determinist argues that if we are not free then we cannot legitimately be held responsible for our actions either. Cypher's betrayal, for instance, would have to be regarded as the inevitable result of his heredity and environment. He was born onto this highway of life at a time and place that were not of his own choosing, and once on that road, he was on a collision course with betrayal. He had no forks or junctures through which to avoid it, therefore we cannot blame him for killing Switch and Apoc, any more than we can blame his parents for *causing* these murders by giving him their genes.[4]

Hard determinism isn't a very popular view. Rarely do you come across a person who actually believes it. But it seems to me that most people don't have very strong reasons for thinking that it is false. For the most part it seems that people don't believe it simply because they don't like it. They find it rather depressing and degrading. Personally, I try not to choose my beliefs on the basis of what sounds nice, but rather, on the reasons for thinking that an idea is true or false. And, while I'm not particularly crazy about hard determinism either, like the Merovingian, I find the case for it to be fairly strong.

Neo and the Case For Libertarian Free Will

I don't like the idea that I'm not in control of my life.

— Neo[†]

Neo seems to think that he has "free will" in the sense of *real choices*. He believes that his life allows for alternate possibilities, and that through his choices he shapes his own destiny. This is called the *libertarian position* on free will.[5] It requires "the unconditional ability to do otherwise" — to be able to say of an action that you could have done something else *within* that exact causal nexus, *no ifs, ands, or buts about it*.[6] Your freedom of choice must be "unconditional," because even the hard determinist would agree that a person could have done otherwise IF the conditions surrounding the choice were different. Returning to Cypher's betrayal, it seems reasonable to suppose that he *could have* remained loyal to the crew (in fact, that he *would* have remained loyal) IF the Nebuchadnezzar had gourmet dining and a full bar, or IF Trinity loved him rather than Neo. So the libertarian must maintain that he could have chosen to remain loyal without these *ifs* — that is, without changing the causal nexus that led up to his decision. Thus we can define the *libertarian* position as follows:

Libertarianism
The view that:

a) Free will (real choice) exists.
b) Since free will exists, causal determinism must be false.
c) Since free will exists, we are morally responsible for our actions.

Libertarians disagree among themselves about how many real choices there are in life, though it is fairly common to suppose that *all* of our intentional actions could have been otherwise, no ifs, ands, or buts about it. In this case it is argued that we are morally responsible for *everything* that we do. Thus, when Cypher was about to unplug (and thereby murder) Switch and Apoc, we should suppose that he *could have* stopped himself. All he had to do was will it. And since he also knew that he *should have* stopped himself, he is truly blameworthy. He should be regarded as a free moral agent, fully deserving of the blast of "plasma justice" that Tank unloaded on him.

There are strong elements of the libertarian position throughout the *Matrix* films. For instance, when Neo visits the Architect at the end of *Reloaded*, he sees countless images of himself on the video monitors. Sometimes his actions are the same in all of them, but sometimes they each go off in their own directions. (Though they share widespread agreement that the Architect's answers are "bullshit!") It seems likely that these monitors are tracking all the directions that Neo's behavior might take. This leads Neo to the conclusion that the reason why the Architect is continually frustrated by the lack of precision and harmony within his system is due to free will. "The problem is choice," Neo says. Immediately following this observation we here the *ding* of Trinity's elevator as it seems to "chime in" the Wachowskis' approval.

Another strong push for the libertarian view comes during Neo's final showdown with Agent Smith at the end of *Revolutions*. When Smith says:

> Why, Mr. Anderson? . . . Why get up? Why keep fighting? . . . You must know it by now. You can't win. It's pointless to keep fighting. Why, Mr. Anderson, why do you persist?[†††]

Neo's reply is: "Because I choose to." Neo's claim seems to be that he persists not because it is his fate or destiny, nor blind causality, but simply because he chooses to — through the brute fact of willing it. This also seems to be confirmed by the fact that the Oracle admits to Seraph that she did not know the outcome.

Given the importance of each of these scenes, it is arguable that the libertarian position is the one most strongly endorsed by the films. However, it is not at all clear how we are to reconcile human freedom with the Oracle's unerring foreknowledge about most events. (As we'll explore in the next chapter.) And even if we conclude that Neo has free will (which itself is far from certain) — what about us? Are *we* free? Most people seem to think so. The libertarian view is by far the most popular position — at least among the general public. The main support for it can be found in the feeling we have when acting. For example, try turning the page of this book — but not quite yet. Wait a moment, and whenever you happen to feel like it, then turn the page. When you've finished return to this spot: ●

Didn't it *feel* like you made the decision of when to turn the page entirely of your own volition, and that nothing *determined* it but your own choice? Certainly it doesn't *feel* as if your choice to turn the page at precisely that moment was the inevitable result of your heredity and environment. Or, think about ordering dinner at a restaurant. As John Searle has argued, you can't just sit there and wait to see what you are *causally determined* to order. At some point, you must *make up* your mind.

Another popular argument is that we simply *must* have "free will," because if we don't, then (as the hard determinist maintains) no one is morally responsible for their actions. Most libertarians find this conclusion utterly absurd. It would be crazy, they think, to suppose that no one is ever truly responsible — that no one ever really *deserves* their reward or punishment. If that were the case, we'd have to open the doors to the jails, and before long all hell would break loose!

Neither of these arguments is completely persuasive, however. While it may not *seem* that your choice to turn the page, or to order chili cheese fries, is determined by prior causes, it may be nevertheless. Causes, especially concerning mental phenomena, are often hidden from our view. For instance, you remember phone numbers without knowing *how* you do it. The numbers just seems to immediately "pop" into your mind out of nowhere. (And, frustratingly enough, on some occasions they don't.) But modern psychology has spent decades trying to understand the causal process involved. And while there is still more to learn, researchers have determined that this sort of recollection occurs by means of chemical reactions in domain-specific regions of the cerebral cortex. There are clearly causal processes involved in the generation of mental states, and there is no reason to think that your decision to act at a particular moment is any exception. The jury is still out, however, on whether these causes work in an entirely *deterministic* manner — making each event necessary in its every minute detail. And as for unlocking the jails — forget about it. Even if we were to conclude that no one truly "deserves" punishment, this does not mean that we should release mass murderers. Rabid dogs don't deserve their fate either, but that does not mean that we should let them run free.

Having Your Cake and Eating It Too: The Case for Compatibilism

You know me Niobe, it's not a choice, it's a way of life.

— Ghost[E]

The words of Ghost suggest that maybe freedom does not require *real choices* after all. When called upon to help Neo, Ghost does not feel as if there are two paths he can take. Because he is who he is, he *must* help – come hell or high water. He is determined to act by his character, his cause, his friendships, and his values. Does this entail that he lacks freedom of the will? *Compatibilism* (also known as "soft determinism") says no. By doing what he so utterly and completely wants to do, compatibilism maintains that Ghost has all the freedom a person could ever want. Compatibilism sees no reason why a person cannot be free and yet completely determined at the same time.

This view strikes some people as an outright contradiction. How can a person be free if they never have real choices or alternate possibilities in their life? Compatibilism suggests that the answer lies in adjusting our view of what it is to have "free will." If free will involves some kind of "unconditional ability to do otherwise," then determinism would certainly rule it out. But maybe this is a mistaken conception of what it is to have free will. Consider the following choice scenario:

Red or Blue?

Morpheus tells Neo that inside the little silver case that he holds in his hand there are two pills. "Choose the red pill," he explains, "and you'll find out what the Matrix is. Choose the blue pill, and you'll wake up in your bed as if nothing ever happened." Let us suppose that Neo considers the options for a moment, and then asks for the red pill. After all, he really wants to know what the Matrix is. Now imagine that Morpheus opens the silver case, and to Neo's surprise, it contains only one pill – the red one. As it turns out, all the talk of a blue pill was just a bluff. Neo thought that he had two distinct possibilities before him – a "fork in the road" – but it was all just an illusion.

Did Neo choose the red pill freely? Most people tend to think that he did, since the absence of the blue pill didn't really affect his choice. And if they are right, then it seems that *real choices* may not be necessary for free will. The *illusion* of a choice might be sufficient. After all, if Neo could have chosen the blue pill, he surely *would not* have chosen it. So why should it matter that it was not *really* there? And imagine if, despite his consuming desire to understand the Matrix, he were to select the blue pill on a fleeting whim, or for a trivial reason, such as, "it looked tastier than the red one." Wouldn't that be strange? Might it even feel to Neo like the choice wasn't *his* at all – as if the words came out of his mouth irrespective of his will?

Compatibilists therefore argue that to have a "free will" is not to be free of causal determination. Rather, it is to have one's choices determined by one's own beliefs, desires, and character. So let us define compatibilism as follows:

Compatibilism/soft determinism

The view that:

a) Free will and moral responsibility do not require real choices.
b) Since free will and moral responsibility do not require real choices, they are compatible with causal determinism.
c) Therefore you can act freely and responsibly even if causal determinism is true.

While all compatibilists agree that free will does not require real choices, in the sense of an unconditional ability to do otherwise, individual compatibilists can differ in their accounts of what exactly "free will" consists in. Generally speaking, they tend to emphasize factors that would illustrate that the choice was caused by some aspect of one's *true self*. That is, the determining cause behind a free choice should be the fact that it was the act that the person *most wanted* to do, or that it was the act that best fit one's *reasons* and *values*. We can see this in Neo's choice of the red pill. He chose it *because* that pill represented the life that he valued most, and had most reason to pursue.

We can think of compatibilism as the opposite of the view that Agent Smith espoused just before the burly brawl in *Reloaded*:

> We're not here because we're free. We're here because we are not free. There's no escaping reason, no denying purpose. Because as we both know without purpose . . . we would not exist. It is purpose that created us – purpose that connects us – purpose that pulls us – that guides us – that drives us. It is purpose that defines – purpose that binds us.[††]

Here Smith seems to regard reason and purpose as external constraints, to which his actions must conform, and in virtue of which he is not free. In contrast, most compatibilists, on the other hand, maintain that the ability to act in accordance with reason is definitive of freedom. You are free precisely to the extent that you are able to conform your will to your reasons and goals.

A consequence of the compatibilist view is that free will is not an all-or-nothing affair. Most of us act freely in the sense that Neo did – at least most of the time. But sometimes a person will lack freedom of will, because they don't seem to be able to choose what they most want to choose, or they can't seem to manage to act in accordance with their own reasons and values. For example, consider the person who has decided to quit smoking. Suppose that they have reflected long and hard on the matter and have wholeheartedly concluded that "quitting" is what they really want. They abstain from cigarettes all day long, but by the evening the nicotine cravings have become so intense that they give in, and light up. There is a very real sense in which the person feels like they have been at war against their own desires and that "their side" has lost. They wanted their will to be that of "quitting," but in the end they failed to have the will that they wanted to have. That is, they failed to choose the course of action that they wanted or valued most.[7]

Although cases of addiction and weakness of will are fairly common, compatibilists contend that most of us act freely the majority of the time. But before you conclude once and for all that you have "free will," consider this: if causal determinism is true, then even what you most want, most highly value, and have most reason to do, is the inevitable result of your heredity and environment. Thus, in the end you may be more like the woman who eats the Merovingian's specially programmed chocolate dessert – *completely out of control.* Consider, once again, Cypher's betrayal. We might suppose that Cypher cared most about maximizing his own happiness. He was sick and tired of the harsh real world, and wanted to be plugged back into the Matrix. For all we know, he was quite content with the reasons and values that led him to betray the others. Compatibilism therefore maintains that he acted freely. But the problem seems to run deeper. We blame him, not just for making a deal with the Agents, but for *wanting* to make the deal, and for valuing his own happiness over and above the lives of the crew. Yet causal determinism entails that he really *couldn't* have wanted anything else. In which case, can we really blame him?

So compatibilism, like hard determinism and libertarianism, does not seem to offer a completely satisfying solution to *the problem of choice.* Nevertheless, these three alternatives seem to exhaust the possibilities concerning the structure that a solution might take. For either causal determinism is true or it isn't. And either free will is compatible with causal determinism or it isn't. So it seems that the mainframe of life has presented us with three doors: hard determinism, libertarianism, and compatibilism. Only one of these doors can lead to the truth about our world. For centuries philosophers have argued over which of these is the best, but now the choice (if there really is one) is up to you.

Suggested Reading

Clarence Darrow, "Leopold and Loeb: The Crime of Compulsion," in *Philosophy: Paradox and Discovery*, eds. Thomas Shipka and Arthur Minton. New York: McGraw Hill, 1976.

Harry Frankfurt, "Freedom of the Will and the Concept of a Person," in his *The Importance of What We Care About*. Cambridge: Cambridge University Press, 1988.

James Gleick, "The Butterfly Effect," in his *Chaos: Making a New Science*, repr. in *The Cannon and Its Critics*, eds. Todd M. Furman and Mitchell Avila. Mountain View, CA: Mayfield Publishing, 2000.

Friedrich Nietzsche, "Twilight of an Error," in his *Twighlight of the Idols*, repr. in *Twenty Questions: An Introduction to Philosohy*, 5th ed., eds. C. Lee Bowie, Meredith W. Michaels, and Robert C. Solomon. Belmont, CA: Thomson-Wadsworth Learning, 2004.

Jean-Paul Sartre, "Existentialism," in *Voices of Wisdom*, 5th ed., ed. Gerry Kessler. Belmont, CA: Wadsworth-Thomson Learning, 2004.

Raymond M. Smullyan, "Is God a Taoist?," in his *The Tao is Silent*, repr. in *Voices of Wisdom*, 5th ed., ed. Gary Kessler. Belmont, CA: Wadsworth-Thomson Learning, 2004.

Notes

1   "Researchers Guide Rats by Remote Control," *Scientific American* (May 2, 2002), at http://www.sciam.com.

2   Although the machines don't seem to induce desires in humans in an attempt to "control" their choices at any moment, it seems clear that they must be inducing desires nonetheless. Imagine a woman, plugged into the Matrix, who believes that she is running a marathon. The program will cause her to "feel" thirsty – even though there is no reason to suppose that her physical body is dehydrated. This "thirst" will in turn cause the "desire" to grab one of the cups of water held out by the fans. So this desire is the result of programming, but only in a very general way. Her desires are caused by "the laws of nature" that are built into the Matrix program, but they do not appear to be manipulated by the *specific* intentions of another mind.

3   The Merovingian, of course, is not really French. Like so much else within the Matrix, his accent is a mere contrivance – for appearances only.

4   Since he was born into the Matrix, Cypher does not have parents in the traditional sense. Instead, he was grown like a crop by the machines. Nevertheless, his genetic materials had an origin, and if this biological source or "cause" had been different, he might never have betrayed the others.

5   This position is not to be confused with a libertarian political philosophy, or libertarian political party. While these also emphasize personal freedoms, their focus is political rather than metaphysical.

6   I borrow this way of putting it from Thomas Nagel.

7   For more on the compatibilist view of free will, see Harry Frankfurt's "Freedom of the Will and the Concept of a Person" and Gary Watson's "Free Agency," both reprinted in *Moral Responsibility*, ed. John Martin Fischer (Ithaca, NY: Cornell University Press, 1986).

SIX

HOW TO REALLY BAKE YOUR NOODLE
TIME, FATE, AND THE PROBLEM OF FOREKNOWLEDGE

Oh, don't worry about it. As soon as you step out of that door you'll start feeling better. You'll remember you don't believe in any of this fate crap. You're in control of your own life. . . . Remember?

— The Oracle[t]

The Oracle's Delphic Roots

The Oracle of the Matrix is fashioned after the most famous oracle in history — the Oracle at Delphi. This oracle of Ancient Greece was also known as the Pythia and was thought to be channeling the voice of the God Apollo. Her role was carried through several centuries by a number of women, each trained by a sisterhood of Delphic priestesses who tended the sacred fire at the temple of Apollo. These oracles' advice and predictions had an enormous effect on the politics, religion, and culture of Ancient Greece.

One of the most famous true stories about the Oracle at Delphi tells of how her remarks shaped Socrates' life, and thereby, the whole history of Western philosophy. When Socrates' friend Chaerephon asked her if there was anyone wiser than Socrates, her reply was that there was none wiser. Upon hearing this news Socrates, who had always claimed to know very little, felt sure that she had made a mistake. So in response to her proclamation, he made it his mission in life to prove her wrong. After many years of questioning most everyone that he met, including the leading aristocrats and *sophists* of the Greek world, he concluded that the Oracle may have been right.[1] Socrates realized that while others *thought* they knew the answers to life's most difficult questions, they were actually quite confused. Socrates, on the other hand, at least *knew* the extent of his ignorance, and this may well have made him the wisest person around.

The Wachowskis were clearly inspired by the Oracle at Delphi, and they created many intentional parallels between their oracle and the original. For instance, in her initial meeting with Neo in the first film we can find many parallels (see figure 2).

The Oracle at Delphi	The Oracle of the Matrix
• Engraved into the nearby temple wall was the phrase "Know Thyself," written in Greek.	• On the kitchen wall was a plaque with the phrase "Know Thyself," written in Latin.
• Breathed the fumes from an underground cavern.[2]	• Breathed fumes from cookies baking in the oven. (And later, from a cigarette.)
• Plutarch reported that the fumes had a sweet perfume-like fragrance.	• Neo admitted that the cookies smelled good.
• Made her prophecies while sitting upon a tripod.	• Made her prophecies while sitting on a small stool.[3]
• Often gave ambiguous advice or made puzzling predictions.[4]	• Gave Neo gave ambiguous advice and made puzzling predictions.
• Was attended by priestesses.	• The woman who answers the Oracle's door is referred to as a Priestess in the script.
• Was typically a woman over 50.[5]	• Was a woman over 50.
• Despite the subservient role of women in Greek society, the oracle wielded incredible power influencing kings, generals, philosophers, and poets.	• Despite the fact that programs with "male" shells seem to dominate the Matrix, the Oracle wields incredible power, influencing architects, agents, and saviors.

Figure 2   The two Oracles

The Paradox of Freedom and Foreknowledge

If you already know, how can I make a choice?

— Neo[††]

In Ancient Greece and in the fictional world of the Matrix, the very idea of an oracle who can accurately predict the future raises a number of vexing philosophical questions. Perhaps the most important of these is whether an Oracle's predictions curtail human freedom. We see Neo struggle with this dilemma in *Reloaded*. To him the Oracle's foreknowledge feels like a violation of his freedom. It makes him uncomfortable about even the simplest of decisions, such as whether to sit or stand:

ORACLE: Why don't you come and have a sit this time?
NEO: Maybe I'll stand.
ORACLE: Suit yourself.
(*Neo sits*)
NEO: I felt like sitting.
ORACLE: I know.

Here it seems that Neo is trying to exert his freedom. He wants to prove that he can do whatever he wants to – irrespective of what she may be thinking. However, his indecisiveness only manages to make him feel even more controlled. A few moments later he reveals his frustration:

ORACLE: Candy?
NEO: You already know if I'm going to take it.
ORACLE: Wouldn't be much of an Oracle if I didn't.
NEO: But if you already know, how can I make a choice?[††]

Can Neo make a *real choice* here? Insofar as the Oracle already knows what he is going to do, it appears that he cannot. If she really *knows* that he will take a candy, he *will* take a candy. There are no two ways about it. The problem arises in part because of what it is to *know* something. The very concept of *knowledge* entails truth. When you know something, then the thing that you know simply cannot be false. For instance, a person cannot "know" that the earth is flat. While there was a time in history in which people *thought* that they knew this, they did not *really* know it. So, if we take it for granted that the Oracle has *real* foreknowledge then we must suppose that she is never wrong about the events she foreknows.

To take a particular example, suppose that at 2:00 p.m. the Oracle foreknows that Neo will take a candy at 2:13 p.m. If she really knows this, then Neo *must* take the candy at 2:13. Any other action would make her wrong – and she *cannot* be wrong. The case against Neo's *freedom to do otherwise* appears to be pretty tight. We can set it out in just a few principles:

71

HOW TO REALLY BAKE YOUR NOODLE

1   It is impossible for the Oracle to be mistaken about any event that she *foreknows.*

2   Therefore, it is impossible for anyone to *cause* her to be mistaken.

3   She foreknows that Neo will take a candy at 2:13 p.m.

4   If Neo refuses the candy at 2:13 p.m. then he will have caused her to be mistaken.

5   Therefore, it is impossible for Neo to refuse the candy at 2:13 p.m.[6]

By this argument Neo has to take the candy. He cannot do anything else. If real freedom requires the ability to do otherwise, then Neo is not really free. He is trapped – he must perform precisely the actions that the Oracle knows that he will perform.

If this reasoning is correct, then foreknowledge entails that there are specific limits to our ability to make *real choices* in the sense outlined in the previous chapter. The extent of these limits would vary according to how much is foreknown (or how much *can be* foreknown). In the sections that follow we will explore several possibilities regarding the extent of the Oracle's foreknowledge and the limits of freedom.

Fatalism: Tapping into the Will of the Gods

Do you believe in fate, Neo?

– Morpheus[†]

Oracles and prophecies are most often associated with the doctrine of *fatalism,* the view that the foretold events are inevitable, unavoidable, and in some sense *meant* to occur. One of the greatest tales of fate ever written, Sophocles' *Oedipus Rex,* nicely illustrates this idea. The gist of the story goes like this:

The Oracle of Delphi warns Laius and Jacosta, the King and Queen of Thebes, that their son will grow up to murder his father and marry his mother. Terrified by this prophecy, Laius takes his infant son Oedipus off to the mountains, drives a nail through his foot, and leaves him there to die. However a shepherd saves the child and takes him to Corinth where he is adopted by King Polybus and his wife Periboea. Oedipus goes on to lead a happy life until he too consults the Oracle, and is given the same prophecy. In horror, he leaves his (adoptive) parents. During his travels, he has an argument with a stranger and kills him. This stranger turns out to be Laius, his father. Oedipus travels on to Thebes where he defeats the Sphinx, a terrible monster that had plagued the city. The people of Thebes ask him to be their new King, since the former King had recently been killed. Oedipus takes the job and marries Queen Jacosta (who, unknown to either, is his own mother). Only after bearing several children does the couple learn the truth. Jacosta then hangs herself, and Oedipus pokes out his own eyes.

It is easy to interpret this story in terms of fate. Try as they might to derail the prediction, Oedipus and his parents inevitably fail. There is nothing in the story that suggests, however, that *everything* that Oedipus and his parents do is fated and inevitable. Therefore, a common interpretation is that there is merely a *partial fatalism* going on. That is, each person has real options available to them, but regardless of how they choose they cannot escape their destiny. Thus we might suppose that Laius could have:

a) **left Oedipus on the mountain to die (as he, in fact, did).**
In which case Oedipus will grow up to kill his father and marry his mother.

b) **imprisoned Oedipus.**
In which case, one way or another Oedipus would have eventually escaped, and gone on to kill his father and marry his mother.

c) **ignored the prophecy.**
In which case, for some reason or another, Oedipus would grow up to kill his father and marry his mother.

This sort of partial fatalism is a rather interesting position. It allows for free choice in the conventional libertarian sense, insofar as there are different courses of action available from which to choose, but it also entails that *whichever* course is chosen will eventually lead to the fated events. Figure 3 shows how we can diagram a fatalistic interpretation of the story using the three potential courses of action above.

Upon hearing the prophecy, Laius can freely choose between these three distinct courses of action – (a), (b), and (c). However, the tragedy is that whichever course he chooses will eventually find its way to the fated events. So while in some sense Laius is quite free, with several options before him, he is unfree regarding the very thing that matters most to him – preventing the foretold event.

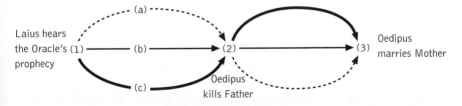

Figure 3 A fatalistic interpretation of *Oedipus Rex*

Morpheus seems to interpret the events of his world in essentially this same fatalistic way. He wholeheartedly believes that the prophecy will be fulfilled, regardless of what Smith and the other Agents do to prevent it. He sees the salvation of the human race as inevitable — as if it is *supposed to* occur. This is most clearly illustrated in a speech to the other captains and their crews in *Reloaded*:

> Tonight is not an accident. There are no accidents. You did not come here by chance. I do not believe in chance. When I see three objectives, three captains, three ships; I do not see coincidence, I see providence. I see promise. I believe it is our fate to be here. It is our destiny. I believe this night holds, for each and every one of us, the very meaning of our lives.[††]

Here he suggests that events in the world are all coalescing around a higher aim or purpose. And yet, despite this inevitability, he still believes in real choices — as only partial fatalism allows. He makes this clear in his conversation with the Merovingian:

> MEROVINGIAN: You see there is only one constant, one universal; it is the only real truth — causality. Action, reaction; cause and effect.
> MORPHEUS: Everything begins with choice.

On Morpheus's partial fatalism, people (and programs) can still make a range of *real choices* at all times, but one way or another, all paths will lead to the fated events. For instance, if we focus upon Agent Smith's first contact with Neo — the interrogation scene in which Neo's mouth was temporarily removed — we might imagine several courses of action that Smith might have taken. But if Morpheus is correct:

a)   If Agent Smith tries to gain Neo's cooperation through bribes and threats (as he in fact did), Morpheus would find Neo and he would eventually bring an end to the Matrix.

b)   If instead Agent Smith imprisoned Neo, Morpheus would find Neo and he would eventually bring an end to the Matrix.

c)   If instead Agent Smith decided to ignore Neo (perhaps supposing that he is not smart enough to be a real threat), Morpheus would find Neo and he would eventually bring an end to the Matrix.

We can diagram the events of the *Matrix* films through Morpheus's fatalistic perspective in the same way as we did the fatalistic interpretation of *Oedipus Rex*.

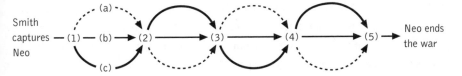

Figure 4 A fatalistic interpretation of the *Matrix* trilogy

(See figure 4.) One significant difference is that the Oracle of the Matrix is a very busy woman/program. She makes a number of predictions that complicate the picture. For instance, to give just a partial listing, she predicts that: (1) Morpheus will find The One, (2) Trinity will fall in love with The One, (3) Neo will have to choose between his life and Morpheus's life, (4) Neo will have to choose whether Trinity lives or dies, and (5) The One will bring an end to the war. Thus there are many points at which all courses of action must merge.

There is always a mysterious or transcendental element to the fatalistic perspective. We see this in Morpheus's speech. He speaks of *providence* – as if there is a divine hand guiding the events to ensure the desired outcome. Thus, on this sort of view, the Oracle would have to be "tapping into" the intentions of this divine force, in much the same way that the Oracle of Delphi was thought to have been "channeling" the voice of Apollo.

Complete Foreknowledge: Seeing Without Time

> You've already made the choice. Now you've got to understand it.
>
> – The Oracle[††]

The "worst-case scenario" for human freedom within the Matrix occurs if the Oracle knows *everything* that will happen. And, contrary to Morpheus's partial fatalism, a video clip from *Enter the Matrix* suggests that perhaps she does:

NIOBE: You once told me that you knew everything you needed to.

THE ORACLE: I do. I knew everything from the beginning of this path to the end.

But in *Revolutions*, it seems that the Wachowskis had a change of heart. There the Oracle insists that she does not know *everything*, saying: "No one can see past a choice that they don't understand – and I mean no one." This allows for the possibility that even the Oracle is occasionally surprised.[7] But consider the reason she gives for her limited foreknowledge. She suggests that she cannot see past the choices that *she* does not *understand.* Notice that she does not say that some things simply cannot be known – that they are indeterminate and therefore unknowable. Rather, the truth of what will happen may be "out there" (so to speak) but she does not have the capability to grasp it.

Is the truth about the future "out there" in some sense, waiting for us to comprehend it? If so, this would shed some light on her conversation with Neo in *Reloaded.* When Neo asks her how it is possible to make a choice regarding whether or not to take the candy, she tells him:

> You didn't come here to make the choice. You've already made it. You're here to try and understand *why* you made it.[††]

This cryptic statement rejects the idea that Neo has any power over the future and suggests that (in some sense) the future "already" is. As bizarre it may seem, her remark may entail that she sees the world in terms of "tenseless time" – the most prominent view of time among contemporary philosophers and physicists.

Theories of time tend to fall into two main categories: tensed theories of time, and tenseless theories of time. Theories that involve *tensed time* regard time in a way that is analogous to the structure of a tree. We might imagine the present moment as a squirrel that is heading up the tree. Movement from the past into the future would be represented by the squirrel's progress skyward. Everything ahead of the squirrel is the future, and everything behind the squirrel is the past. The key point of the tree analogy is that the future is essentially undetermined. The past, in contrast, is definite. There is only one path that the squirrel actually did take. And although there will only be one *actual* future (the squirrel can only take one route to the top), at any given moment there are always many *possible* branch-paths that *could* be taken. Another important aspect of tensed theories is that only the present moment is regarded as ultimately real. The past is gone. It existed once, but it exists no longer – and the future is yet to be.

Tenseless time is the conception that Einstein utilized in his theories of relativity, and that the Oracle may rely on to make her predictions. Einstein maintained that we should not think of time as an independent medium, but rather as part of a *space–time continuum.* Time is essentially a fourth dimension, which, in addition to three-dimensional space, is necessary to locate objects in the world. For instance, if a toy airplane were flying in circles within a child's bedroom, to pinpoint its location we would need to give its coordinates, north and south and east and west, as well as its altitude. But since the airplane is constantly moving, we would also need to give the specific point in time that these will hold true. Thus any location is "in time" as well as "in space." The plane travels *through space*, but it also travels *through time.* It is flying right into the future, we might say.[8]

There is another important sense in which Einstein encourages us to think of time in a way that is akin to how we regard space. We think of space as "laid out" before us in all directions. While we only experience a limited portion of space at any given moment, e.g., we cannot see Mount Everest right now, we suppose that all of space exists at once. That is, the space that lies beyond our experience (i.e., beyond what we can see with our best telescopes) is thought to be just as real as the space right before our eyes. Tenseless theories of time maintain that time is similarly "laid out" before us in both directions. Time does not *flow* in the sense of the unreal future becoming the real present. Rather it is all equally real. Only our experience changes, as we move along the space–time continuum.

For our purposes the most important difference between the two theories is that on tenseless theories of time the future has no branches. There is only one possible future. We will experience it when we reach that point on the space–time continuum, but it (like Everest) is "already there," waiting for us to arrive. There is something very odd about saying that the future is "already there," just as it seemed odd when the Oracle said that Neo had "already made" a choice that was still ahead in his future. Time theorists generally try to avoid making such statements. Technically, to say that something exists, or has occurred "already," is to speak from *within* the timeline. It is to say that something exists or has occurred at your *present point* or a *prior point* on the timeline. When the Oracle says that Neo has "already made the choice" she does not intend it in this way. Instead she seems to indicate that if Neo could see it from a perspective "outside of time" then he would realize that the future sits ahead of his present point on the timeline and it contains all the choices and actions that Neo is going to make. There is nothing he can do to alter it.

To get a better grip on tenseless time it might be helpful to think about perspective. From our perspective, sitting at a particular moment in the space–time continuum, the future appears to be *unfolding*. That is, the future seems to be "appearing" before our very eyes. But tenseless time would suggest that this is an illusion created by our limited perspective. The future is "there," we just can't seem to see it yet. But the fact that we cannot see it may say more about us and our situation in the world than it does about the future. You might think of it as being *temporally near-sighted*. All we can see is the moment that is right under our noses. We might compare this to a creature that is spatially nearsighted. Imagine a creature that is so drastically nearsighted that it cannot see beyond the spatial "moment" that is immediately in front of it. Now if such a creature were to be propelled, slowly, through space, in a way similar to how we are propelled slowly into the future (you might imagine a near-sighted ant riding on a garden hose as it is pulled through the grass), it would seem just as if space were *unfolding* right before its eyes. Objects would seem to the ant to "appear" out of nowhere. But we, because of our spatial depth perception, know that the creature is mistaken. The objects were there, ahead of it all along. The creature just had no way of experiencing them. On the tenseless theory of time, our temporal experience is much like this creature's spatial experience. We suffer under the illusion that the future does not yet exist, and that it is constantly *coming into* existence, merely because we don't have the capacity to see it as it approaches.

While it is perhaps impossible to make a definitive determination, there is reason to suppose that time within the *Matrix* films is tenseless, and that the Oracle has found a way to overcome our problem of temporal near-sightedness. Just as we have overcome the barriers of our senses with respect to space by inventing telescopes, microscopes, etc., perhaps her programming has enabled her to get beyond the usual barriers of time perception. She may have programming (or "eyes," as the Merovingian metaphorically refers to it) that works as sort of a "time telescope," which enables her to see beyond the moment that is currently under her nose.[9]

How Tenseless Time Bakes Your Noodle

What's really going to bake your noodle later is, would you still have broken it if I hadn't said anything?

– The Oracle[†]

The most bizarre implication of the tenseless theories of time is that nothing – absolutely nothing – can be changed. All events are there, laid out at specific points in space–time. And this entails that we cannot change the past, the present, or the future.

Perhaps the most dramatic illustration of this point concerns time travel. While Einstein had supposed that time travel might be possible within the tenseless time presupposed by his general theory of relativity, the logician Kurt Gödel demonstrated that it was logically and mathematically possible.[10] I won't get into too much detail here, but the basic idea is that there can be extreme curvatures in the space–time continuum such that if one were traveling down such a curved space–time trajectory (around a black hole, for instance) one could actually end up at a place *earlier* in the space–time continuum than one started. But tenseless time entails some rather strange implications regarding time travel. For instance:

1) You can travel to the past and contribute to it, but you cannot change it.
2) You can have bizarre *causal loops*, in which there is no "causal beginning."

3) By traveling to the past, it is possible to die at a time prior to your birth.
4) It is possible for your body to be in two places at the same time.
5) Yet it is impossible to go backward in time and kill your earlier self.
6) We are all time-travelers with respect to the future.
7) We can contribute to the future, but we cannot change it.
8) Even an Oracle who foresees the future cannot *change* the future.

Let's consider each of these points in turn. First, if you travel to the past, you inevitably make some contribution to that past. This is pretty obvious. Even if your contribution is minor – you leave a few footprints, suck up some oxygen, etc. – you're still having some affect. But what is more interesting is that you can actually have a profound effect on the past. It just cannot be regarded as a *change* to that past, because any effect will be precisely how you had *already* affected it. For example, consider this *alternative* Matrix scenario:

Neo's Visit to the Past

Neo decides that the only way to prevent the total annihilation of humanity is to travel 200 years into the past and prevent the first sentient machines from being built. Upon his arrival he breaks into the home of the scientist who supposedly invented the first sentient computer. However, things don't go as planned. Startled by the intruder, she grabs her bedside pistol and kills Neo (who sorely missed the advantages of "bullet-time"). When she notices the metal plugs in Neo's body, she takes his body to the lab and performs an autopsy. Ultimately, it is her discovery of the "smart chip" imbedded in the Matrix interface technology inside Neo's skull that enables her to develop the first sentient machine.[11]

If this scenario were true, then it would have *always* been the case that Neo was instrumental to the development of AI. For instance, if Neo would have seen the tapes from the scientist's household security cameras *before* traveling back in time, he would have seen that he had already been there and she had already shot him. But what makes this whole scenario so bizarre pertains to our second point – that it is a causal loop. In this scenario the initial sentient machine would have been created only because the scientist *copied* Neo's smart chip. And her copy was, 200 years later, *copied* by the sentient machines when they constructed Neo's smart chip. This raises the question of who actually "invented" the smart chip. The answer is that no one did! All versions of the chip are copies of versions that were created at other points in time. As strange as it is, a causal loop such as this does not involve a logical contradiction. Hence, tenseless time theory does not rule out these kinds of scenarios.

The third point is also illustrated in the story above. In it Neo dies at a time prior to his own birth. If the scientist had buried Neo's body in her backyard in the year 2020, then we can suppose that Neo's remains were there, in that spot, from 2020 onward. This means that it is possible for Neo's body to be in two places at once. His body exists (though somewhat deteriorated) in the scientist's backyard throughout Neo's life almost 200 years later. Within tenseless time, to be in two places at the same time is no more impossible than to be at the same place at two different times. Though in terms of Neo's *personal time* the body in the grave is 225 years old at the moment that Neo's 25-year-old body walks about in Zion. Tenseless time would also allow Neo's *living* body to be in two places at the same time. For example, the 25-year-old Neo could go visit his 10-year-old self and give him some advice. *However*, this is only possible if it is *already* true that when Neo was 10 his older self met him. Since he cannot change the past, if the meeting did not happen, it cannot happen.

It is for this reason that our next point holds – you cannot kill yourself at a date prior to your time travel. For instance, if Neo takes up backwards time travel at age 25, then it is impossible for him to go back one year and kill his 24-year-old self. He can't do it because he obviously *didn't* do it. To kill himself at an earlier time would be to change the past, and you cannot change the past. So if Neo were to try to prevent his twenty-fifth year by means of time-travel assassination, he would fail. Perhaps he'll lack the motivation to go through with it, his time-rocket will crash, his weapon will misfire, or he'll have some other mishap, but, one way or another, he will not succeed.

Backwards time travel is pretty esoteric. The fact that we have never met time travelers from the future (at least not that we know of) seems like pretty good evidence that time travel may not be physically possible (lots of things are logically possible without being physically possible).[12] But *forward* time travel does occur. As point six suggests, we are all traveling, moment by moment, into the future. Our bodies move not only through space, but also through time. But just as you can't change the past, you can't change the future from what "already" lies ahead of us.

As strange as it may seem, in tenseless time not even the Oracle can change the future from what she has foreseen. Her inability to change the future essentially parallels the time-traveler's inability to change the past. But whereas the backwards time-traveler makes one or more discrete trips into a past that they may have already experienced, the Oracle is *continually* being propelled into a future that she has (to some extent) already "seen." And just as the backwards time traveler cannot change the past because the past "already included" their attempt to change it, the Oracle cannot change the future that she sees because *it* "already" includes her attempts to achieve her goals. Agent Smith struggles with this conundrum when he first meets the Oracle in *Revolutions*:

The great and powerful Oracle . . . we meet at last. I suppose you've been expecting me – right? The all-knowing Oracle is never surprised. How can she be, she knows everything. But if that's true, why is she here, if she knew I was coming? Why didn't she leave? [*He slams the plate of cookies into the wall*.] Maybe you knew I was going to do that, maybe you didn't. If you did that means you baked those cookies and set that plate right there deliberately, purposefully; which means that you're sitting there, also deliberately, purposefully.†††

Smith is exactly right. The Oracle most likely foresaw the fact that he was coming. She probably also saw him smash the cookies. We can imagine that if she were new to this whole oracle business, she might, upon seeing this vision of the future, wonder how and why she would do such a thing. Why not escape? Why bake cookies if you know that Smith is just going to smack them against the wall? Well, on the one hand, if she cannot contradict or falsify the future then she *has to* bake the cookies and she *has to* be sitting there in the kitchen when Smith walks in. But it is not that the future is *making* her do these things. The future doesn't cause her to put cookies into the oven and it doesn't magically hold her feet to the kitchen floor. Instead, just like the rest of us, she does these things deliberately, purposefully. She did these things because she wanted to – expecting that they would ultimately figure into Smith's defeat and an end to the war.

We are now in a position to answer the question that the Oracle uses to bake Neo's noodle: *If she hadn't said anything about the vase, would he still have broken it?* If we take the question literally the answer is no. Her mentioning the vase most likely caused Neo to knock over the vase. So, given our understanding of the causal workings of the world, change the cause and you'll change the effect. But if tenseless time is true, then this is all merely fantasy. The real answer to the Oracle's puzzle is that Neo couldn't have avoided breaking the vase for the precise reason that the Oracle couldn't have failed to mention it. Both events have "always" occupied those points in space–time, such that neither one could have been altered.

What's It Like to be an Oracle?

One must want nothing to be different, not forward, not backward.

– Friedrich Nietzsche

At times, it would surely be a curse to have the "eyes" of the Oracle. When you see a tragedy that you want to prevent, you must accept that it cannot be altered, since what you see already includes your attempt to bring about the best consequence. For most people it would be unbearably depressing to know about so many tragedies before they even occur and be unable to prevent them. Of course, if time is tenseless, none of us has ever been able to prevent the future tragedies ahead of us. But since *we* don't know this, at least not for certain, we have the comfort of *thinking* that we are changing the course of events – preventing some tragedies, and forestalling others. And even if we fully accept that none of us ever "changes" the future, life is still infinitely easier for us non-Oracles, because we are oblivious to the horrific events to come. Cypher was right: ignorance *can* be bliss.

But the Oracle does not let her inability to affect the future get her down. She bears the burden of her gift gracefully. She is serious and committed to her cause, knowing that her role is vital to the future – it makes the future what it is – despite the fact that she does not *change* that future. But at the same time she maintains a certain warmth (especially for a program), and sense of humor about things. The future is coming – exactly as she foresees it – and yet she *embraces* her role in it. As she tells us is *Revolutions*:

> Since the real test for any choice is having to make the same choice again knowing full well what that choice may cost, I guess I feel pretty good about that choice, because here I am, at it again.[†††]

This resembles the attitude that the nineteenth-century German philosopher Friedrich Nietzsche tried to convey with his "doctrine of eternal recurrence." *Eternal recurrence* is metaphysically different from tenseless time. It is the thesis that one will live through every event in one's life an infinite number of times throughout all eternity. But I think Nietzsche's main point regarding the doctrine is psychological rather than metaphysical. He imagined that most people would abhor the prospect of living through every moment of their lives over and over again. But he thought that great individuals, those who truly love life, would receive the idea with utmost pleasure.

Ghost also cultivates this type of attitude. In a video segment from *Enter the Matrix*, he tells the Oracle:

> Nietzsche said it best: One must want nothing to be different – not forward, not backward, not in all eternity – not only to bear what is necessary, but to love it.[E]

To this, the Oracle agrees. She replies with a phrase that was one of Neitzsche's favorites: "amor fati" – *love of fate*.

Life through the eyes of the Oracle must seem similar to a world of eternal recurrence. With her ability to foresee the future, she experiences events repeatedly

– first in her mind's eye, and then again when she lives through them. Because she is influenced by what she sees, and uses her foreknowledge to influence others, most of her actions are chosen *knowing full well* what the consequences will be. Thus while we sometimes act with regrets, I expect that the Oracle rarely does. She chooses the inevitable because it already embodies the role she wants for herself. And hence, just as Nietzsche prescribes, she not only bears the necessary, she loves it.

Suggested Reading

Craig Callender and Ralph Edney, *Introducing Time*. Cambridge: Icon Books, 2001.

John R. Hale, Jelle Zeilinga de Boer, Jeffrey P. Chanton, and Henry A. Spiller, "Questioning the Delphic Oracle," *Scientific American* (Aug. 2003), at http://www.sciam.com.

Nelson Pike, "Divine Omniscience and Voluntary Action," *The Philosophical Review* 74 (Jan. 1965).

Sophocles, "Antigone's Fate," in *Twenty Questions: An Introduction to Philosophy*, eds. G. Lee Bowie, Meredith W. Michaels, and Robert C. Solomon. Belmont, CA: Thomson-Wadsworth Learning, 2004.

Sophocles, *Oedipus the King*, in *Sophocles I: Three Tragedies*, 2nd ed., eds. David Grene and Richmond Lattimore, tr. David Grene. Chicago: University of Chicago Press, 1991.

Notes

1   It was largely the pursuit of this "mission" that led to Socrates' eventual execution. Socrates' account of this tale can be found in Plato, *The Apology*, 21a.

2   Archeological evidence for the fuming cavern had not been discovered until just recently. For an interesting account of recent discoveries, see *Scientific American* (Aug. 2003), "Questioning the Delphic Oracle," by John R. Hale, Jelle Zeilinga de Boer, Jeffrey P. Chanton, and Henry A. Spiller, at http://www.sciam.com.

3   The original script called for a three-legged stool, i.e., a tripod. The stool in the film, however, appears to be four-legged. We can only speculate about whether this change was intentional or accidental. However, we can be certain that the Wachowskis don't take numbers lightly.

4   For instance, it is reported that Croesus donated a fortune to find out if he should invade a neighboring country. His advice from the Oracle was that if he went to war, "it will cause the destruction of a great empire." Croesus took this to mean that he would defeat his enemy, but instead he was defeated and captured. When he sent word to the Oracle to find out why he was misled, the answer came back that the oracle was truthful. A great empire was destroyed – his. We find the messages of the Oracle of the Matrix to be similarly cryptic. For instance, she tells Neo that he's not The One – that

he's waiting for something – perhaps his next life. But it turns out that he is The One, but he had to die first (at least for a moment) to become ready.

5   There are some reports that the original oracles were young virgin girls, but that after one escaped with a young Thessalian, it was decreed that no one younger than 50 would be appointed to the position. *The Matrix* script calls for the Oracle to look "like someone's grandmother."

6   This type of argument was developed by Nelson Pike in "Divine Omniscience and Voluntary Action," *The Philosophical Review* 74 (Jan. 1965).

7   As when the Oracle says, "Remember what you were like when you first walked through my door. Jittery as a June bug. Now just look at you. You sure did surprise me Neo, and you still do." Also, in the final scene of *Revolutions*, Seraph asks her if she knew that things would turn out as they did. Her reply is, "No, I didn't. But I believed."

8   Thanks to Jeff Barrett, whose lecture on time travel was a key inspiration for this chapter.

9   We can suppose that the Oracle literally *sees* the future as opposed to simply *knowing* it. We see this as Neo begins to "see without time" through his dreams. We should expect, however, that the foreknowledge programming is based on *information* rather than optics. So the idea of a "time telescope" should be taken metaphorically rather than literally. This would explain why Neo cannot see beyond the choices that he does not understand. (Notice that Neo's first vision of the future – Trinity's fall at the start of *Reloaded* – contains a glitch. As Trinity dives out the window we see her body falling and followed by an Agent, but then a black horizontal bar moves down the screen and we see her and the Agent fall again. This seems to suggest that within Neo's understanding at that time there are multiple possibilities.)

10   This does not, however, mean that it can be done. David Malament has argued that the energy requirements would make backwards time travel technologically impossible.

11   This is essentially the same sort of causal loop that appears in the *Terminator* films.

12   Another possibility is that backwards time travel is possible, but only along certain routes. (On most analyses, our universe does not permit time travel to any location in space–time whatever.) So it might be the case that future time-travelers have been traveling backwards in time to various space–time locations, but our planet over the last thousand years or more may be inaccessible to them.

SEVEN

VIRTUAL BODIES
THE CONSTRUCTION OF RACE
AND GENDER IN THE MATRIX

I just thought . . . you were a guy.

– Neo

Most guys do.

– Trinity[†]

The Matrix and Zion:
Contrasting Visions of Race and Gender[1]

The virtual world of the Matrix is a world of racism and sexism. Although the films do not provide us with much footage of "ordinary life" within the Matrix,[2] Agent Smith informs us that it is essentially our world – our civilization, as it was at the end of the twentieth century – a world brimming with overt and covert racism and sexism. We see this right from the start of the first film, as the police units get ready to move in on Trinity at the Heart O' The City Hotel. All of the officers are white men, and one of the first remarks made by a Matrix inhabitant is overtly sexist. The Lieutenant in charge tells Agent Smith, another white male: "I think we can handle one little girl." This, of course, turns out to be an assumption that he will come to regret. Our next glimpse of stereotypical twentieth-century sexism occurs when Neo tells Trinity that he "thought she was a guy." (We can only suppose that it was her excellent reputation as a hacker that led him to this conclusion.) Her reply, "Most guys do," shows that this kind of attitude is the norm rather than the exception with coppertops like him.

The general picture of racism and sexism continues when Neo reports to his day job at Metacortex. His boss, Mr. Rhineheart, is another white man, and the other employees in the office are almost exclusively white, right down to the window washers and the Fed-Ex guy.[3] The same holds true of the security forces at the building in which Morpheus is later interrogated. Every person that we see in that building, besides Morpheus and Trinity, is a white male. White men seem to hold all, or almost all, of the power within the Matrix.

The exception to this trend comes only in those areas of the Matrix that are inhabited by programs. For instance, when Neo visits the Oracle, she turns out to be a black woman from the projects. "Not quite what you were expecting," she says. Her attendant and the blind man "keeping watch" outside her apartment are also black, and the "potentials" include both boys and girls of several ethnicities. In *Reloaded* and *Revolutions* this theme continues when we are introduced to Persephone, Seraph, Sati, Rama Kandra, and Kamala, all women or "programs of color," and interestingly, all sympathetic toward the oppressed human race.[4]

The fact that all of the programs who help the Zion rebels turn out to wear the "shells" of females and/or historically oppressed minorities, is most likely related to the racism and sexism among the programs themselves. For, as Smith also suggested, the Matrix has become their world and *their culture* – apparently all the way down to its racism and sexism. This can be seen in the fact that it is the white male programs, such as the Architect and his Agents, along with the Merovingian that hold the majority of power in that world. Although the Oracle and Persephone both turn out to play key roles in shaping the final outcome, each must do so through a more subversive role. They achieve their goals largely by undermining the projects of male programs.

In striking contrast to the virtual world of the Matrix is the underground city of Zion. It depicts an advanced society, not only in terms of technology, but also with respect to social justice. Racial and sexual equality seem to be pervasive in Zion, with both men and women and people of all races and shades in positions of power. This can be seen in the composition of the governing council and in the crews of the hovercraft fleet. We see it as Charra and Zee fight the machines in the front lines of the infantry, and when Niobe puts Captain Roland in his place after his "I am the Captain of this ship!" tirade in *Revolutions*. And the insignificance of race and sex clearly goes beyond social positions. We find no signs whatsoever of racial tensions in Zion, and the competence of women is never questioned.

It is arguable that the films went "over the top" in their portrayal of racial equality in Zion. Many people found their depiction of Zion to be too racially diverse, and even disproportionately black. But there are several explanations that might account for this. On the one hand, we might suppose that the Wachowskis didn't want audiences to miss the point that Zion is an extremely diverse and

VIRTUAL BODIES

egalitarian society, so they may have intentionally overemphasized Zion's diversity to do so.[5] But I suspect that there is more to it than this. It is also likely that interracial marriage has become so common that "natural born children of Zion" will be of mixed race – as Tank seemed to be – and that people who look "white" will be limited for the most part to the "pod-born" children of the Matrix. The third and most interesting possibility is that it may be predominantly racial minorities who free themselves from the Matrix. As Morpheus indicates, most people aren't ready to be unplugged. They are dependent upon the system and content within it. So if we consider who would be most likely to take the red pill, it will be those who are most dissatisfied with the system. The victims of racism may therefore be among the most likely people to welcome a way out.

Zion depicts the Wachowskis' vision of a society of the future, and of the social changes that might occur over the next century or two. But Zion may also represent more than this. It may exemplify their vision of *the social ideal* – a society that treats race and gender differences the way that they ought to be treated. If we consider Zion as a social ideal, then interesting philosophical questions arise. Does Zion really represent the ideal that we should strive for? And if not, how or why does it fall short? And what relevance, if any, would race and sex have in the ideal society?

Zion as the Social Ideal

Live long enough and you might even see it.

– Tank[†]

Zion appears to embody (imperfectly at least) the ideal of a completely nonracist and nonsexist society. Philosopher Richard Wasserstrom has argued that within such a society a person's race and sex would be regarded as no more important than their eye color.[6] For most intents and purposes, he argues, people would be "race- and sex-blind."[7] We can call such an ideal "The Ideal of Race- and Sex-Blindness," or "The Ideal of Blindness" for short. Given the brief glimpses of Zion's culture depicted in the films, we can be sure that they have not fully realized this ideal. And while any conclusions about the people of Zion's intentions will involve a good deal of speculation, it is not unreasonable to suppose that the Ideal of Blindness is their ultimate goal.

This sort of ideal can be difficult for us to even imagine, for in our society a person's sex and race are regarded as terribly important. When a baby is born, the first question always asked is: "Is it a boy or girl?" This is the primary feature that people want to know because it shapes how the child will be treated from that moment on – whether the child is given pinks or blues, pants or dresses, squirt guns or Barbie dolls. And later in life, one's sex will greatly determine the careers they will be encouraged to pursue, how much they will be paid for their work, and the likelihood that they will be the eventual victim of sexual assault. Race is also extremely significant. Racially motivated discrimination and prejudice continues to affect most aspects of life, including business, law enforcement, education, and politics, as well as one's personal relationships and general worldview.[8]

If we suppose, for the sake of argument, that Zion is striving to realize an Ideal of Race and Sex-Blindness, we should expect to find a very different reality, marked by some of the key features outlined below.

Sex and gender within the Ideal of Blindness

The elimination of sexually defined gender roles and ideals   Although we never really see the child-rearing practices in Zion, we should expect that children would be raised in an essentially sex-blind fashion. Unlike most contemporary societies, girls would not be taught to act like "girls" and later like "women," and boys would not be taught to act like "boys" and later like "men." Instead, any differences in treatment from one child to another would be based upon each child's inherent talents, interests, and abilities.

The elimination of sexually differentiated divisions of labor   Both men and women would occupy any position in the labor force, the military, and politics. We see this in the gender balance of Zion's Council leaders, and with Charra and Zee fighting alongside men in the infantry. The Ideal of Blindness can allow for unequal percentages of men and women in certain careers so long as gender is not used as a selection criterion. For instance, in positions requiring an unusual amount of physical strength, such as in the APU Corps,[9] we might find higher proportions of men. Or in positions that are best suited to persons with the lowest possible bodyweight, such as piloting small hovercraft at extremely low altitudes, we might find higher proportions of women. But while recruits for such tasks might be chosen largely because of their size or strength, their sex itself would be of no account.

The elimination of social pressure toward heterosexuality   Although all the main Zion couples in the films involve characters of opposite sexes (Neo and Trinity, Niobe and Lock, Niobe and Morpheus, Link and Zee), we should expect that a broad survey of Zion's inhabitants would reveal a large number of gay, lesbian, and bisexual relationships – without the social stigma or discrimination that such couples face in most contemporary societies.[10]

Race and ethnicity within the Ideal of Blindness

The elimination of racial discrimination   Since race would be no more relevant than eye color, no one would receive particular benefits, burdens, or differential treatment on the basis of their race. As depicted in Zion, we would find people of all races occupying the full range of positions within the labor force, the military, and political leadership – significantly more so than we see today.

The elimination of race-based cultural identities   In an Ideal of Blindness, a person's race would not, in itself, have any ramifications upon one's social and cultural life as seems to be the case in Zion. One's values and general worldview, as well as one's manner of dress and speech, taste in music, food, etc., would be determined by their own personal tastes and preferences rather than by race or historical ethnicity.

The elimination of racial considerations regarding romance and marriage   The color of a potential partner's skin, or of one's eventual children, would be irrelevant beyond personal aesthetic preferences. And since race would not be correlated with a particular culture or lifestyle there would be no reason to suppose that one would have more in common with a person of the same race. After many years of interracial mixing, we might expect that clear racial classifications would become altogether impossible to make.

If these are, in fact, the ideals that Zion strives for, it is clear that they have not fully achieved them. On the issue of race Zion does extremely well. Nowhere in the films do we find even the slightest traces of racist attitudes or behavior within Zion. However, on the issue of sex/gender, while Zion is fairly sex-blind overall, we catch glimpses of significant exceptions. For instance, at the Council meeting in *Reloaded*, Commander Lock announces: "It would be hard for any *man* to risk his life – especially if *he* doesn't understand the reason." The comment is surprising precisely because it occurs within Zion, and its inappropriateness is quickly revealed when it is Niobe who heeds the Council's call. Also, while *Revolutions* strongly emphasizes the efforts of women in the infantry (focusing on Charra and Zee in particular), no women appear to serve in the APU Corps. We might suppose that this is due to the physical strength needed to operate these machines, but that seems dubious. "The Kid," for instance, is able to operate an APU when needed – despite the fact that Charra could probably kick his ass with one hand tied behind her back. Since it is also unlikely that the sex inequality in the APU corps was an unintentional oversight by the Wachowskis, the best explanation seems to be that there may be some elements of sex discrimination or sex-role stereotyping still remaining.

We also find slices of sexism on the Nebuchadnezzar. We are caused to wonder about Mouse's conception of women insofar as one of his sidelines is being a "digital pimp." Regarding his favorite creation, "the woman in red," he tells Neo: "She doesn't talk very much, but if you'd like to meet her I can arrange a much more personalized *milieu*." On his view, it seems, some women are better seen (or used) than heard. Cypher's remarks also suggest some latent sexism. He tells Neo that he doesn't even see the Matrix code anymore – just "blonde, brunette, red-head." But these sexist attitudes should come as no surprise, since both men lived a significant portion of their lives within the sexist society of the Matrix. To a large extent their experiences within the Matrix have made them who they are.

The fact that Zion has been much more successful overcoming racism than sexism may indicate that the Wachowskis' belief that sexism presents the tougher challenge. While both racism and sexism are pervasive in contemporary society, most people do seem to be much more open to race-blindness as an ideal than sex-blindness. Many already regard race-blindness as the ultimate ideal. This, of course, is not to say that they are without racial prejudices – but *ideologically* a rapidly growing number of people see race-blindness as the promise of the future. This includes people on both sides of the affirmative action controversy. Some, for instance, believe that we must initiate race-blindness now, and therefore we must reject all race-based criteria in college admissions and hiring. Others, such as Cornel West[11] (the Princeton philosopher who played Councilor West in the films), argue that we must continue to utilize affirmative action programs for the very reason that in our world race *does* matter. Because racism and its effects continue to shape the social, economic, personal, and political realms, racial differences and "the difference that race makes" cannot be ignored. To attempt race-blindness today would be to blind ourselves to social injustices. Thus, on West's view, it is only by dealing with the fact that race *does* matter today that we can move closer to the day of a truly race-blind society.

In contrast, the dominant ideology of sex and gender does not regard sex-blindness as ideal – for today, *or for the future*. Most people think that a person's biological sex should matter – perhaps not for basic rights and liberties, but for a wide array of personal and social decisions. Let us call this more popular view of a sex and gender ideal "The Ideal of Sex-Equality through Sex-Difference," or the "Ideal of Difference" for short. It can be distinguished from an Ideal of Sex-Blindness as follows:

Sex and gender within the Ideal of Difference

The perpetuation of sexually defined gender roles Within the Ideal of Difference, sex-based gender roles are regarded in a more positive light. This ideal maintains that there should be different standards of excellence for men and women. The ideal woman should not be overly rugged or assertive, and the ideal man should not be overly sensitive, aesthetically discerning, or submissive. This Ideal maintains that parents should teach sex-based gender roles to their children in order to ensure that they will most likely exemplify these ideals.

The perpetuation of sexually differentiated divisions of labor In the interest of equality, the Ideal of Difference maintains that all occupations should be legally open to both men and women. However, since some occupations conflict with the different standards of excellence it sets for men and women, people are steered into some occupations and away from others on the basis of their gender. Thus we should expect ratios of women and men to vary greatly in many occupations.

The perpetuation of social pressure toward heterosexuality The sex of a person is here regarded as an important feature with respect to dating and marriage. Each new generation is steered toward exclusive heterosexuality by a variety of more and less subtle means. This ideal does not, in and of itself, entail a particular position regarding the legal status of gay marriage. Within this ideal some people may regard gay marriage as a basic civil right, while others try to prohibit it on the presumption that such a lifestyle would be deviant or immoral.

Since it is sex-blindness that is the more controversial aspect of Zion's envisioned ideal, sex and gender will be the focus of the sections that follow. There we will examine some of the main arguments that favor a sex-blind society.

VIRTUAL BODIES

The Case for a Sex-Blind Ideal

Difference is the velvet glove on the iron fist of domination.

– Catharine A. MacKinnon

What do all men with power want? More power.

– The Oracle[†]

While proponents of an Ideal of Difference argue that social justice can be achieved within a society in which the sexes maintain very different gender roles, proponents of an Ideal of Sex-Blindness contend that sex-based gender roles serve to perpetuate the oppression of women. Underpinning this position is the belief that "gender" is entirely a *social construction*. This to say that gender (understood as the social significance attributed to biological sex, e.g., "womanhood" and "manhood," "femininity" and "masculinity") is not a natural fact, but rather a creation of the culture itself. On this view of sexual difference, to be genetically male, female, or hermaphrodite has very little *inherent* significance. While a person's chromosomes and the shape and function of their sexual organs are determined by genetics, the significance that these physiological features carry is determined by the interpretations and practices of one's culture.[12]

Philosopher and critical theorist Judith Butler has argued that the creation of gender identity is essentially a social *act*. It is an intricate social dance or *performance* through which a body shows or produces it social significance. Butler writes:

> As in other ritual social dramas, the action of gender requires a performance that is *repeated*. This repetition is at once a reenactment and re-experiencing of a set of meanings already socially established; and it is the mundane and ritualized form of their legitimation.[13]

On Butler's analysis, gender is a social construction through and through, but she emphasizes the extent to which it is a collaborative production between the individual and the society. The society provides the loosely scripted roles, and the individual learns them, performs them, contorts them, rebels against them, etc. And if gender identity is, as she thinks, a *performance* at its very core, then there can be no real or true gender preexisting in some natural state:

> If gender attributes and acts, the various ways in which a body shows or produces its cultural signification, are performative, then . . . there would be no true or false, real or distorted acts of gender, and the postulation of a true gender identity would be revealed as a regulatory fiction . . .[14]

On this analysis there can be no "natural" gender roles because we never find gender outside of preexisting identities (girl/boy, woman/man), interpretations (masculine/feminine/androgynous, straight/gay/bi, natural/unnatural/deviant, moral/immoral, etc.), and practices (childrearing, heterosexuality, football, Tupperware parties, etc.) that exist in a particular social world.

Butler's view is easy to apply when it comes to the sentient programs within the Matrix. For instance, Persephone (the program who helps Neo for the price of a

The Feminine Gender	The Masculine Gender
Female biology	Male biology
Emotion	Reason
Submission	Dominance
Nurture	Achievement
Passivity	Activity
Delicacy	Strength
Softness	Toughness
Beauty	Financial power
Style	Substance
Cooperation	Competition

Figure 5 Gender boundaries

kiss) has a female "shell," but she becomes a "woman" by playing the role of femininity that has been constructed in that world. That is, she "talks the talk and walks the walk." And Butler's point is that it is really no different for humans – whether in the Matrix or in "our world." Each of us is "gendered" from birth (that is, treated according to society's conception of girl/woman, boy/man), and we *learn* to play the part.

Since the Matrix is founded upon American culture at the end of the twentieth century, its gender boundaries are drawn largely along lines represented in figure 5. This is not to say that the inhabitants of the Matrix (or of our world) believe that all women are more emotional and submissive than all men. Rather, the social construction of gender represents the dominant ideology of what it *means* to be a woman or man, both in terms of what each sex *is*, and in terms of what each sex *should be*.

Proponents of an essentially sex-blind ideal argue that the problem lies largely in the fact that these constructions and their particular significance amount to a *system of control* that stifles the freedom and creative potential of both men and women. However, for women, it is also a system that keeps them in a position of relative powerlessness. As Catharine MacKinnon contends:

> From women's point of view, gender is more an inequality of power than a differen-
> tiation that is accurate or inaccurate. To women, sex is a social status based on who
> is permitted to do what to whom; only derivatively is it a difference.[15]

Many contemporary feminist philosophers have maintained that the social con-
struction of gender perpetuates a sexual caste system. The only way to achieve freedom and equality, they say, is to eliminate the system of sex-based constructions

altogether. While the effects of gender constructions can be seen in almost all facets of life, in the sections below we shall examine them in three significant domains: language, women's bodies, and sexuality.

Language

It is a word. What matters is the connection that the word implies.

— Rama Kandra[†††]

For a group to talk that way, it must think that way.

— Robert Baker

One way that we are initiated into society's constructions of gender is through language. Consider personal pronouns such as "he" and "she." The very fact that our pronouns announce a person's gender suggests the crucial role that gender plays in society. Robert Baker has pointed out that we are often so inundated in this linguistic convention that we don't even realize that there are alternatives. Baker asks us to consider an alternative language in which pronouns refer to race rather than gender.[16] Instead of saying: "*He* went to work at Metacortex," one would say: "*White* went to work at Metacortex," "The Agents interrogated *Black*," or, "*Brown* is still a bluepill," etc. By simply listening to the structure of this language we would have strong reason to suppose that race plays an important social role in the society that speaks this way. And imagine that, if the race of a person were unknown, the pronoun "white" would be automatically used — as the "racially neutral" term. This would further suggest an unequal distribution of power between the races of that society.

Now certainly the pronouns "he" and "she" are used within Zion, but this is of course linked to the fact that its culture developed out of an overtly sexist past. However, we might expect that "man" and "he" are no longer acceptable as gender-neutral terms (contrary to Commander Lock's personal habits). One linguistic transformation that we see in Zion pertains to proper names. The names of many of the Zion rebels — for example, Neo, Trinity, Morpheus, Apoc, Link, Switch, Seraph and Mouse — unlike Tom, Mary, Paul and Betty, don't clearly announce specific gender identities.[17]

The harm of the traditional linguistic conventions, especially the use of male pronouns in gender-neutral contexts, is that it perpetuates an underlying sense that man is primary or the norm; and woman is secondary, an afterthought, or anomaly.[18] As Simone de Beauvoir has written:

She is defined and differentiated with reference to man and not he with reference to her; she is the incidental, the inessential as opposed to the essential. He is the Subject, he is the Absolute — she is the Other.[19]

Baker also urges us to notice how the construction of women's sexuality and desirability is both revealed and perpetuated through language. For example, the most common "pet names" (an expression which is itself socially loaded) refer to women as animals, toys, or sex-objects. They are foxes, chicks, vixens, bunnies, babes, and dolls, as well as bitches, ho's (whores), and pieces of ass.[20] All of these names imply that women are *things* rather than persons, to be cuddled, kept, or *used*, rather than respected, understood, or listened to. To the extent that Zion strives for a sex-blind ideal we should expect that these sorts of pet-names would not be used — and we tend not to find them. Instead, we only hear it from the Matrix-based Agent Smith (through Bane's body). And even then it catches us off guard when he refers to Trinity as "Neo's bitch" in *Revolutions*.

Women's Bodies

My God, just look at her. Affecting everyone around her, so obvious, so bourgeois, so boring.

— The Merovingian[††]

The social construction of gender places unrealistic expectations upon the bodies of women. Large breasts, a small waist, and Western features represent the ideal of femininity. The pursuit of this feminine ideal yields some rather unnerving statistics in *our world*. By some estimates, roughly 80 percent of US girls between grades 3 and 6 "feel bad about their bodies," while 70 percent say that they are on diets at any one time. And up to 80 percent of women in the UK are "concerned about their weight or dieting at any one time." For many women surgery is seen as the best solution. Eyelid surgery has become increasingly popular among Asian-American women, and is now the third most popular form of surgery in the US. In 2001, over 300,000 American women had liposuction to remove unwanted fat, and over 200,000 had breast augmentation.[21] And while severe eating disorders such as anorexia and bulimia affect a much smaller segment of the population, we cannot help but wonder how it is related to the current construction of feminine beauty. After all, 85 to 95 percent of all cases of anorexia involve women. Philosopher Susan Bordo, for example, has argued that the anorexic simply takes the construction of feminine appearance to its extreme conclusion.[22]

The construction of feminine beauty has also helped to perpetuate women's helplessness. Only within the last 20 years have we seen a shift towards an ideal in which a woman can be both strong and sexy. Carrie-Anne Moss and Jada Pinket-Smith (Trinity and Niobe) would never have been able to get a leading role with their current physiques in any other era of Hollywood's history. Until very recently, any visible muscle on a woman was regarded as completely unsexy.

Another significant factor in the construction of gender is women's clothing. Men's clothing has always been geared toward comfort and ease of movement. Women's clothing, on the other hand has generally been impractical and restrictive. This is readily apparent when one considers Persephone's attire. She, better than anyone else in the films, serves as an exemplar of the twentieth-century ideal of feminine beauty, yet she is also the only character whose clothing would drastically limit her ability to fend off an attacker, or to engage in most any strenuous physical activity. Trinity and Niobe, on the other hand, almost always wear pants when entering the Matrix.[23] Skirts and dresses are just not a viable option when danger is present. Also, we find that on the Nebuchadnezzar men's and women's clothing is pretty much interchangeable. There would be no way to tell if Trinity and Neo had been swapping clothes on a regular basis.

Many feminists would argue that the most profound system of control concerning women's bodies involves limitations on their reproductive choices. For instance, Mary Anne Warren has argued that to restrict a woman's right to abortion is to treat her as less than a fully autonomous person. Warren contends that there is only room for one person with full and equal rights inside a single skin, and therefore, "to extend legal rights to fetuses, is necessarily to deprive pregnant women of right to personal autonomy, physical integrity, and sometimes life itself."[24] But while men have always tried to control women's reproductive options, the machines take this to altogether new extremes, as reproduction is ripped entirely away from "motherhood." Perhaps the most disturbing scene in all three films is the depiction of a baby, lying alone in a pod, as it drinks in nutrients from the liquefied dead. The new mother of humanity is the Matrix powerplant itself ("matrix" literally means *womb*), as human beings are not born but grown as crops through entirely mechanized processes.

Sexuality and Violence

Touch me and that hand will never touch anything again.

— Trinity[††]

While the Ideal of Difference would condemn all forms of violence against women, many feminist philosophers have argued that sexist constructions of gender and sexuality contribute significantly (though immeasurably) to the high rate of sexual assault, rape, date-rape, and domestic violence against women. Catharine MacKinnon, for example, emphasizes the way in which sexuality and sexual desire are constructed through pornography. She writes:

> What pornography *does* goes beyond its content: it eroticizes hierarchy, it sexualizes inequality . . . It institutionalizes the sexuality of male supremacy, fusing the eroticization of dominance and submission with the social construction of male and female.[25]

And the fusing of sexual desire with roles of male domination and female submission goes well beyond what *most people* would regard as hardcore pornography or even as pornography at all. We find it in children's films, such as *Snow White* and *Sleeping Beauty*; in R-rated horror films, in romance novels, and a wide variety of other sources, including, we should suspect, the personae of Mouse's "woman in red." We should not be surprised to find that she primarily wants to be *taken* and *used*.

MacKinnon argues that the effect this domination-laden construction of sexuality is largely responsible for the fact that many as 44 percent of American women experience rape or attempted rape in their lifetime, and up to 85 percent of the federal workforce has experienced sexual harassment. We see that Trinity must also deal with a type of sexual harassment at the Merovingian's restaurant, as *she* is the one whom his goon touches as they prepare to leave. Lucky for her, in contrast to most of her coppertop sisters, she is fully prepared to "handle him."

A more covert yet more dramatic form of sexual violence occurs in the Merovingian's cyber-rape of the woman who eats his specially programmed dessert. Although she is not physically harmed by the incident, she is violated nonetheless. In a way somewhat analogous to the victims of date-rape drugs who are rendered unconscious or barely conscious, the restaurant patron is manipulated to orgasm against her consent. Despite the fact that she is conscious, she does not really know what is happening to her. The episode is all about *his* power and her submission. She is, as he notes, "totally out of control." This scene perfectly exemplifies MacKinnon's concerns. It is sexuality constructed through male dominance and female submission – masculine power and feminine powerlessness.

But They Choose It

Ninety-nine percent of all test subjects accepted the program so long as they were given a choice. Even if they were only aware of that choice at a nearly unconscious level.

– The Architect[††]

Those who wish to dismantle society's constructions of gender, both within the Matrix and within our own society, face a dilemma much like that of the Zion rebels. For the majority are quite content with the system of control that shapes their daily lives. As Morpheus tells us:

> You have to understand that most of these people are not ready to be unplugged. And many of them are so inured, so hopelessly dependent on the system that they will fight to protect it.[†]

If feminism is correct to maintain that the social construction of gender is a shackle that binds women, it appears to be a shackle that many women are quite willing to keep. To take just one example, consider bodily appearance. Many women wholeheartedly strive to be the very ideal that the culture has set out for them. That is, they long to look like Persephone rather than Switch or Charra. They accept both the goal of feminine beauty and the means to that goal.

But as we know, appearances can be deceiving. The enjoyment taken in preparing for and expressing the culture's ideal of feminine beauty is almost always mixed with feelings of inadequacy. Sandra Lee Bartky calls this "repressive satisfaction," and argues that it keeps women invested in a system that is harming and controlling them.[26] Susan Bordo describes the phenomenon as follows:

> Women bond over shared makeup, shared beauty tips. It's fun. Too often, though, our bond is over shared pain – over "bad" skin, "bad" hair, and "bad" legs. There's always that constant judgment and evaluation – not only by actual, living men but by an ever-present, watchful cultural gaze which always has its eye on our thighs – no matter what else we accomplish.[27]

Given the feelings of inadequacy, the risks to health and personal safety, and the social and political deprivation of power that comes through gender constructions, we should wonder why more people don't fight them. According to Bartky, it has much to do with the fact that the construction of gender has been internalized. To have a "feminine body" as socially constructed is in most cases "crucial to a woman's sense of herself as female and . . . to her sense of herself as a sexually desiring and desirable subject." Thus, Bartky suggests that to dismantle the machinery of social gender constructions threatens women with "desexualization, if not outright annihilation."[28]

In many ways women's adherence to gender constructions can be seen as a reasonable reaction to the society in which they live. There are consequences to violating society's norms. Women realize that these norms shape the perceptions of their potential employers, friends, and lovers. The failure to embody gender norms is typically accompanied by severe social ostracism. But this should not be regarded as a justification of gender constructions. Rather, the fact that women must go to such lengths in order to feel good about themselves and to achieve their social, political, and economic goals, makes a strong case for moving in the direction that Zion has gone – toward an essentially sex-blind ideal.

Suggested Reading

Robert Baker, "Chicks and Pricks: A Plea for Persons," in *The Canon and Its Critics*, eds. Todd M. Furman and Mitchell Avila. Mountain View, CA: Mayfield Press, 2000.

Judith Butler, *Gender Trouble: Feminism and the Subversion of Identity*. New York: Routledge, 1990.

Catharine MacKinnon, "Pornography, Civil Rights, and Speech," in *Analyzing Moral Issues*, 2nd ed., ed. Judith Boss. Boston: McGraw Hill, 2002.

Jennifer Saul, *Feminism: Issues and Arguments*. Oxford: Oxford University Press, 2003.

Cornel West, *Race Matters*, 2nd ed. New York: Vintage Books, 2001.

Malcolm X, "The Ballot or the Bullet," in *Malcolm X Speaks*. New York: Grove Press, 1965.

Notes

1 Thanks to Lisa Lawrence, Celia Sepulveda, and Gwen Sheridan for their encouragement and comments with respect to this chapter.

2 By "ordinary life" in the Matrix, I mean to exclude those "areas" that are frequented by sentient programs. These areas include the Oracle's apartment, the Merovingian's mansion, and Club Hel.

3 The exception is one man of Asian descent at the Metacortex office.

4 The exceptions here are two Asian men and one black man who serve as the Merovingian's henchmen. (At least he is an equal-opportunity employer.)

5 It seems that the Wachowskis may have exaggerated their depictions on *both* ends. Arguably, the employees of Metacortex and the police and security forces in the Matrix are less racially diverse than was typical in the late twentieth century.

6 Richard Wasserstrom, "On Racism and Sexism," in *Today's Moral Problems*, 4th ed., ed. Richard Wasserstrom (New York: Macmillan, 1988).

7   It is perhaps more common to speak of "gender-blindness." The term "sex" refers to a person's biology, while "gender" refers to the social significance that is typically attached to biological sex. There will be more on this point later. I've used the term "sex-blindness" to emphasize the fact that within the "Ideal of Blindness," biology would be irrelevant to social positions or status, and even to gender identities insofar as they remain at all.

8   In the US, women working full time tend to make only 75 cents to a man's dollar, and the more women who dominate an occupation, the less it tends to pay. *Business Week*'s directory of the top 1,000 publicly held companies of 1990 lists two women and only one African American. And although African Americans constitute about 10 percent of the American labor force they occupy 21 percent of janitorial positions, yet only 1.5 percent are dentists and commercial pilots. See *Moral Issues in Business*, 8th ed., eds. William H. Shaw and Vincent Barry (Belmont, CA: Thomson-Wadsworth Learning, 2001).

9   Zion's APU corps seems to fall short of a sex-blind ideal. As will be discussed later, there appear to be no women serving in this elite group.

10 The films give some indication of the absence of heterosexism by twice focusing on a lesbian triad during dance scenes at Zion's Temple, and by depicting a lesbian couple outside Club Hel. (At least if we ignore the strong possibility that these scenes were added as "eye candy" for the predominantly male heterosexual viewing audience.) Surely you didn't think that those long dance scenes were devoid of philosophical content?

11 See Cornel West, *Race Matters*, 2nd ed. (New York: Vintage Books, 2001).

12 The same point can be made about race. While there are clearly genetic differences between people whose heritage can be traced to different regions of the globe, one can argue that how we have divided up the "races," and the significance given to them, is essentially the creation of society. On this view there are no "true" races. Instead there are simply the racial and ethnic categories that society constructs. In support of this view, Charles Lawrence has argued that we should regard "race" as a verb. A person is not simply *of* a particular race, but rather, they are *raced*. That is, they are continuously categorized (by themselves and by others) as Black, Anglo, Asian, Hispanic, etc. And these categories, as with gender, are constructed in such a way as to carry enormous social significance.

13 Judith Butler, "Excerpt from *Gender Trouble*," in *Feminist Social Thought: A Reader*, ed. Diana Tietjens Meyers (New York: Routledge, 1997), p. 122. Butler's theory of gender is, of course, much more complicated (and radical) than I can present here.

14 Ibid.

15 Catharine MacKinnon, "On Difference and Dominance," in *Theorizing Feminism*, 2nd ed., eds. Anne C. Herrman and Abigail J. Stewart (Boulder, CO: Westview Press, 2001), p. 235.

16 Robert Baker, "Chicks and Pricks: A Plea for Persons," in *The Canon and Its Critics*, eds. Todd M. Furman and Mitchell Avila (Mountain View, CA: Mayfield Press, 2000).

17 This does not always hold true. The names Tank and Dozer seem essentially masculine, while Niobe sounds more traditionally feminine (as we might expect from names pulled from Greek mythology).

18 Feminist theologians have suggested that the Genesis account of creation seems to cast Eve as somewhat of an afterthought. She's "second in creation, but first in sin." Also following this patriarchal model, God is regarded as essentially masculine – the *Father* of all creation. The Architect of the Matrix is also created in *his* image. For more on this see the work of Mary Daly and Rosemary Radford Ruether. For more on the Architect's masculine emphasis, see chapter 13 below.

19 Simone de Beauvoir, "The Second Sex" reprinted in *Sex Equality*, ed. Jane English (Englewood Cliffs, NJ: Prentice Hall, 1977), p. 73.

20 Some of these expressions – e.g. fox and ass – have crossed over such that women now use them to refer to men, but on the whole these types of references are less prevalent.

21 Jennifer Saul, *Feminism: Issues and Arguments* (Oxford: Oxford University Press, 2003), p. 143.

22 Susan Bordo acknowledges that the skeletal frame that anorexia yields is not the cultural vision of feminine beauty. However, she thinks that the ideal of ultrathin female bodies draws women into the obsession with weight that is characteristic of this disorder. Thus, we might suppose that the most fanciful aspect of the "dessert scene" in the Merovingian's restaurant is the fact that this woman is eating dessert at all. (See e.g. Susan Bordo, *Unbearable Weight: Feminism, Western Culture, and the Body* Berkeley: University of California Press, 1995.)

23 Trinity wears a dress over pants when she enters the Matrix during Cypher's betrayal. However, as soon as Agents move in, the dress disappears. We can only assume that dresses within the Matrix are "quick-release." Note that the during the meeting of the captains at the start of *Reloaded*, all of the women wear pants and jackets – except Trinity, who again is probably wearing quick-release gear. We should also note that in Zion it is not at all uncommon for women to wear dresses. But here we find that the dresses are comfortable and unrestrictive, quite unlike Persephone's tight skirt in *Reloaded*.

24 Mary Anne Warren, "The Moral Significance of Birth," in *Analyzing Moral Issues*, 2nd ed., ed. Judith Boss (Boston: McGraw Hill, 2002), p. 131.

25 Catharine MacKinnon, "Pornography, Civil Rights, and Speech," in *Analyzing Moral Issues*, 2nd edition, ed. Judith Boss (Boston: McGraw Hill, 2002), p. 478.

26 Sandra Lee Bartky, "Foucault, Femininity, and the Modernization of Patriarchal Power," in *Feminist Social Thought: A Reader*, ed. Diana Tietjens Meyers (New York: Routledge, 1977).

27 Susan Bordo as quoted by Saul in *Feminism*, p. 160.

28 Bartky, "Foucault, Femininity," p. 97.

EIGHT

AGENT SMITH'S MORAL CHALLENGE

Illusions, Mr. Anderson. . . . Temporary constructs of a feeble human intellect trying desperately to justify an existence without meaning or purpose.

– Agent Smith[†††]

As we watch the *Matrix* films, most of us find ourselves making a number of moral judgments. For instance, we think that it was *wrong* for Cypher to have betrayed his friends, or that Neo did the *right thing* by choosing the red pill, and we agree with Sati when she says that Smith is "a very *bad* man." But consider this. When we form moral judgments, and make claims about what is good and evil or right and wrong, are we believing and claiming things that are actually *true*?

In *Revolutions*, Agent Smith suggests that we are deluded to think that anything is truly right or wrong. Smith articulates his moral theory in his final showdown with Neo. After pummeling Neo 20 feet into the ground, Smith shouts:

Why Mr. Anderson? Why? . . . Why keep fighting? Do you think you're fighting *for* something – for more than your survival? Can you tell me what it is? Do you even know? Is it freedom, or truth, perhaps peace, could it be for love? Illusions, Mr. Anderson, vagaries of perception. Temporary constructs of a feeble human intellect trying desperately to justify an existence without meaning or purpose.

On Smith's view, the values that human beings hold dear, and which serve as the basis of our moral judgments, are mere constructs – "as artificial as the Matrix itself." From Smith's perspective it is pointless for Neo to keep fighting. In fact, life itself is all rather pointless. He rejects the idea that there are "good reasons" for living one way or another; for choosing peace over war, or love over cruelty;

and thus no action is ever truly right or wrong. The only purpose in life, he has come to believe, is "to end."[1]

Was Smith right? Are those of us who think that we are saying something true when we utter claims about good and evil, right and wrong, suffering under a kind of delusion? While some philosophers side with Smith, many have argued against his thesis, and in favor of the general outlook of Zion, which maintains that some things truly are good and/or right – such as peace, freedom, and justice.

We can divide the two sides of this debate into two broad categories: *moral objectivism* and *moral non-objectivism*:

Zion's moral objectivism: The view that *at least some* moral claims are object-ively true. This is to say that some moral claims are true, and that their truth is not entirely relative to, or dependent upon, the beliefs or feelings of any individual or group.

Smith's moral non-objectivism: The view that *no* moral claims are objectively true. This is to say that *either* moral claims are not true at all, *or* their truth is entirely relative to, or depends entirely upon, the beliefs and feelings of the individual or group.

In the sections that follow we'll examine each of these broad moral outlooks in more detail, and then consider the strongest reasons for each. Ultimately, each of us must decide which of these two positions will serve as the basis of our moral beliefs.

Moral Objectivism: The Truth is Out There

In questions of just and unjust, fair and foul, good and evil . . . ought we to follow the opinion of the many . . . or of the one who has understanding?

– Plato

While we should expect that the inhabitants of Zion hold a wide range of moral views, it is reasonable to suppose that a dominant ideology is that of moral objectivism. Moral objectivism asserts that at least some moral claims are objectively true. To say that a claim is "objectively true" is to say that its truth does not depend upon anyone's particular beliefs or feelings about it. The truth is, in a sense, "out there." To use human beings as slaves – as biological batteries – while deceiving them with an illusory world is just *wrong*, in Zion's view. The fact that the machines think that it is OK does not make it OK.

It is fairly uncontroversial to suppose that at least some types of claims can be objectively true. I imagine that even Smith would allow this – he merely denies that *values* and *moral judgments* can be objectively true. A standard nonmoral example of an objectively true claim is: *The earth is round*. If we take this statement to mean that the earth is more or less spherical, like a basketball, as opposed to flat like a pancake, then the claim seems to be both true and objective. The earth simply *is* round, regardless of what any particular person thinks. While there was a time when almost everyone on the planet *believed* that the earth was flat, their believing it didn't *make* it so. The truth of the matter depends upon the earth itself and not people's opinions about it.

In a way that is broadly analogous, the moral objectivist thinks that some moral claims are true in a way that is independent of people's beliefs or feelings. On this view, subjecting people to the Matrix against their will is wrong irrespective of any individual's opinion, or even the opinion of a whole culture – such as the whole race of machines. The truth of the matter, according to the objectivist, depends on the details of action itself (e.g., that it violates the freedom and autonomy of sentient, rational beings), and not on anyone's opinion about it.

Three Varieties of Moral Non-objectivism

The best thing about being me is that there's so many me's.

– Agent Smith[††]

Smith is a non-objectivist for certain, but non-objectivism can take several forms. The three main types are moral nihilism, moral subjectivism, and cultural relativism. Each is defined as follows:

Moral nihilism: The view that moral claims and judgments are simply never true.

Moral subjectivism: The view that moral truth is entirely relative to, or dependent upon, the beliefs and feelings of the *individual*.

Cultural relativism: The view that moral truth is entirely relative to, or dependent upon, the beliefs and feelings of the *culture*.

Given the brevity of Smith's remarks, we cannot be absolutely certain about which of these more specific views he holds. (And, by the time of *Revolutions*, there are so many "Smiths" that it is even possible that he holds all of these views simultaneously.) Nevertheless, an examination of each will help us to better understand his general moral outlook.

Moral Nihilism: There is No Moral Truth

The need to be right is the sign of a vulgar mind.

– Albert Camus

Smith's views might be best described in terms of *moral nihilism* – the view that moral claims and judgments are simply never true. On this view, moral claims cannot be true, for they ultimately don't make any sense – they're "nonsense." A nonmoral example of a nonsensical claim is: "The Nebuchadnezzar is politically liberal." Obviously this claim is not true. But the important thing is that it doesn't simply "turn out" to be false. Rather, it is necessarily false, or false in principle. The problem for such a claim is that hovercraft *cannot* hold any political views. So even the opposite claim, "The Nebuchadnezzar is conservative," (or moderate), is also necessarily false. Philosophers call such claims *category mistakes*. To make a category mistake is to apply a predicate or property to an object in a way that simply *cannot* apply.[2]

Moral nihilists believe that moral claims always invoke category mistakes. According to the nihilist, murder can be bloody, motivated by greed, or take place on the Hammer with a surgeon's scalpel (as committed by Bane), but it cannot be *wrong*. Similarly, an Agent can be tall or short, named Smith or Jones, but he cannot be *evil*. On this account, right and wrong and good and evil are not *real* properties of actions, events, or persons. Much of the rationale behind this analysis stems from the fact that properties or predicates like "goodness" and "wrongness" cannot be verified through our senses. We may hear the murder take place, or see the body lying on the floor, but we cannot see or hear the "wrongness" of the act. As the eighteenth-century philosopher David Hume famously argued, our sense experience can only verify how things *are*, yet moral judgments involve claims about how things *ought to be*.[3]

Moral Subjectivism: Moral Truth is in the Eye of the Beholder

You are free, therefore choose – that is, invent. No rule of general morality can show you what to do.

– Jean-Paul Sartre

Moral subjectivism, like nihilism, denies that there is any objective truth when it comes to moral claims. But in contrast to nihilism, it maintains that moral claims are true in a "subjective" manner. This is to say that the truth of moral claims is entirely relative to, or dependent upon, the beliefs and feelings of the *individual*. Some kinds of claims clearly seem to be subjective. To take a nonmoral example, consider the claim: "Tastee Wheat tastes great." Is this claim objectively true? If Dozer thinks that they taste great, and Mouse thinks that they taste awful, who is *really* right? Most people think that the question itself is misguided. Rather, the goodness of Tastee Wheat is said to be an entirely subjective matter. If *you* think they taste great then they *really do* taste great (to you). And if *you* think they taste terrible then they *really do* taste terrible (to you). When it comes to matters of taste in food it seems that "believing it makes it so." If common opinion is correct here, then each person judges by their own standard, and no one's standard is any "better" or "more correct" than anyone else's.

It is also consistent with the film to interpret Smith's remarks along these lines. He could be saying that the value of freedom, peace, truth, love, and even life itself, is only a matter of subjective opinion. Thus the person or program who prefers illusion to truth, or war over peace, is just as "correct" as those who hold the opposite view. This subjectivist perspective could work just as well for Smith's purpose – to get Neo to give in. Insofar as Neo believes that he is fighting for things much larger and more important than himself, such as peace and truth and love, then we can imagine that he draws strength from this "mission." But if Smith can persuade him that morality is entirely subjective, Neo might lose his sense of purpose. For if Smith's course of action is really no better or worse than Neo's, why should he keep fighting? In fact, if you can't beat them, why not join them?

Cultural Relativism: Moral Truth is Relative to Culture

Morality is the herd-instinct of the individual.

– Friedrich Nietzsche

Cultural relativism could also serve Smith's purposes. A claim is culturally relative if its truth is entirely relative to, or dependent upon, the beliefs and feelings of the *culture*. Again, we can illustrate the concept with a nonmoral example. Consider the realm of etiquette. In the Temple dance in *Reloaded*, we see a very sweaty man shaking his dreadlocks about in such a way that he sprays everyone around him with his sweat. In our culture that would be incredibly rude. But in Zion it appears not to even be an issue – no one seems to regard it as the least bit inappropriate. (In fact, the people of Zion could even regard the failure to share one's sweat at the dance to be rude.) In our culture, however, the same action would be regarded as incredibly rude. And notice that the opinion of the dreadlock-shaker does not really matter here. The fact that *he* doesn't think it is rude would make it no less so if he were dancing at one of our nightclubs. The cultural opinion is the operative standard. If the group finds your behavior to be rude, then it *is* rude. *Their* beliefs make it so.

The cultural relativist believes that moral claims should also be regarded in this way. An action is wrong if your culture regards it as wrong, and an action is right/permissible if your culture regards it as right/permissible. This entails that right and wrong can vary considerably across cultures. Since Zionists condemn the use of the Matrix, it would be *wrong for them* to keep slaves or to deceive others about reality. But since the machines find this practice to be morally permissible, then it *is permissible for them*. According to the cultural relativist, each culture has its own moral standard, and there is no higher standard from which to compare cultures. Neither cultural outlook is any better or worse than the other, for it is the beliefs and feelings of the members of the group that *make* an action right or wrong.

Since cultural relativism also denies that there is any objective standard upon which our moral judgments rest, it too can fit nicely into Smith's agenda. In this case, the argument would be that Neo's cherished values merely represent the "opinions" of his culture, and as such they are not inherently any better or worse than the opinions held by the machines. The realization of this (as we saw with subjectivism) could undermine Neo's motivation. But on the whole, cultural relativism is a much more awkward fit for a program like Smith. Since he has rejected his own culture along with its rules and values (operating instead as a "free agent"), it would be odd for him to think that cultural opinion is what really matters.

For this reason it makes more sense to suppose that Smith has adopted either the nihilist or subjectivist perspective. Not much rides on settling the matter, for the difference between moral nihilism and moral subjectivism is arguably much like the difference between the pessimist who calls the glass half-empty, and the optimist who calls the glass half-full. Ultimately it all comes down to description. As we've seen, both views agree that when a person says something like, "Cypher's betrayal was wrong," the claim is false – insofar as we take it to mean "Cypher's betrayal was wrong from an objective or belief-independent point of view." But if, on the other hand, all that was meant by the claim was, "I don't like it that Cypher betrayed his friends," then the nihilist and subjectivist can both agree that the claim may be true – as a report of the beliefs and feelings of the individual who uttered it.[4] So whether or not the particular moral claim is regarded as "true" will depend greatly upon how one interprets the claim.

Can Smith be Defeated?

And if you fail?

– Deus Ex Machina[†††]

The challenge that Smith puts to Neo (and ultimately to us) is to justify the belief that anything really matters. Why, in essence, should one believe that there is any objective truth in the realm of values or morality? Interestingly, Neo does not rise to this challenge. Instead of offering objective reasons for valuing truth, or peace, or love, he simply tells Smith that he fights because he "chooses to." There are a couple of different ways in which we might interpret this response. One is to suppose that Neo essentially agrees with Smith that there are no objective reasons to offer. In this case it all boils down to a sort of arbitrary choice – but neverthe-less, a choice that Neo is not going to abandon.[5] A second possibility is that Neo believes that his values are justified – truth *is* better than illusion, peace *is* better than war, love *is* better than hate, and so on; but he lacks the desire and/or energy to defend them to Smith. After all, Smith isn't really interested in engaging in a detailed philosophical discussion of moral theory. Rather, he's subjecting Neo to a kind of psychological warfare. But whether Neo is ultimately a moral objectivist or non-objectivist, it is important for the *Matrix*-philosopher to try and figure out whether Smith's challenge can be adequately defeated. So let's consider some of the strongest reasons that Smith's non-objectivism has going for it, and then we'll examine the possible lines of defense open to the moral objectivist, and some of the reasons that support this moral outlook.

Attacks on Zion's Moral Objectivism

If you can't beat us, join us.

– Agent Smith[††]

Attack 1: Moral disagreement

If you think about it, the claims that are most clearly objective tend to be those that are mathematical, scientific, or empirically verifiable. These sorts of claims foster widespread agreement around the world, leading us to conclude that the truth is "out there" for all to see. In contrast, moral claims are much more likely to encounter debate and disagreement, both within and across cultures. Even the "experts" disagree on many moral issues. This disagreement amounts to strong evidence that there is no objective truth in moral matters.

Defense

In response, objectivists maintain that (a) there is quite a bit of moral agreement in the world, and (b) disagreement does not, in and of itself, entail an absence of objective truth.

First, we should notice that there is near universal agreement on many moral issues. For example, almost everyone (including hardened criminals) agrees that one should not betray one's friends (sorry Cypher) or torture children. And there is widespread agreement about the moral impermissibility of murder, rape, lying, stealing, etc.

On the latter point, disagreement between people (even between experts) does not undermine the possibility of objective truth. For instance, there was a time in our history when even the shape of the earth was a hotly debated issue. But this did not entail that the there was no "real" or "true" shape of the earth, or that its shape depends entirely on what people happen to believe about it. Or, consider theoretical physics. Even today the top physicists in the world do not all agree about the basic structure of the universe, and several different theories compete for their allegiance. Yet we do not take this disagreement or uncertainty to mean that the claims of physics are nonsense, or that they are entirely relative to the beliefs of individual physicists, or to the beliefs of whole groups of physicists. Instead most people think that the truth *is* "out there," but the subject matter of physics is complicated, and that we are not very well situated in the universe to find all the answers we seek.

The moral objectivist can argue along similar lines for hotly debated moral claims. Capital punishment, for instance, is a complicated issue involving concerns for public safety and the rights of the condemned, as well as worries about deficiencies and inequalities within the legal system, calculations concerning the long-term consequences, etc. Determining how all these various factors should be figured into a moral policy is no simple matter. And when we add religious convictions and unexamined cultural beliefs to the equation, it is no surprise that widespread agreement is hard to come by.

Attack 2: You can't prove moral claims

A common charge that pushes the previous point a bit further is that moral claims cannot be objective because, unlike the claims of math, science, and sense experience, they cannot be *proven*.

Defense

While some objectivists may wish to argue that moral claims *can* be proven, the easiest response is to argue that "proof" is really irrelevant to objective truth. Consider, for example, the claim: *There are exactly 48 billion and 3 stars in the universe.* Since even our best telescopes cannot detect all of the stars, it is impossible for anyone to prove whether this claim is true or false. Not only that, but we may *never* have the technology necessary for proving it. Nevertheless, the claim is certainly *objective*, and it is most likely *false*.[6] It is objective because (assuming it is not infinite in size) the universe must contain a specific number of stars, and the number that there are does not depend on what anyone thinks about it. You and all of your friends can believe that there are 48 billion and 3 stars, but your believing it does not make it so. And the claim is most likely false because I just made up this number – out of the blue. The odds that I would have identified the exact number of stars in the universe by blindly guessing are astronomical! Therefore, we can be fairly certain that the claim is objectively false. This is precisely how the moral objectivist would like us to think of moral claims – as dealing with objective matters that, while perhaps not yielding absolute certainty, can be held with a very high degree of confidence.

Attack 3: The matter of tolerance

For centuries Western European nations marched into third world countries around the globe and essentially told the people of these native cultures that they were living the "wrong way." According to the conquering nations' objectivist views on morality, religion, and culture, these native peoples invariably had the wrong moral views, the wrong religious views, the wrong style of dress, and so forth. The result was that native peoples were forced, often at gunpoint, to change their ways. Although Smith would not be concerned about this sort of imperialism, most people are. We want to be tolerant of other cultures, and the rejection of objectivism allows us to tolerate the different moral beliefs of others.

Defense

This kind of imperialism is not the result of moral objectivism itself, but rather it stems from the fact that the *real* value of other peoples' freedom and autonomy was not respected. Sure, moral objectivists can (mistakenly) violate people's rights. But so can the non-objectivist. Just look at Agent Smith. Although he doesn't regard his values as ultimately any better than anyone else's he nevertheless shoves his values down everyone else's throat (quite literally, in fact). In contrast, it is only the moral objectivist who can say that there is something truly wrong with forcing one's will upon others in this way. And only the moral objectivist can maintain that there is something intrinsically good about respecting other people's freedom and tolerating the diversity of beliefs. But at the same time, the objectivist will maintain that there are limits to the value of tolerance. While tolerance is typically a good thing, we should not "tolerate" the rapist, the ruthless dictator, or the sociopathic Agent Smith.

Support For Zion's Moral Objectivism

> Stop trying to hit me and hit me!
>
> — Morpheus[†]

Support 1: Imagining the worst

One way in which to test whether you are ultimately an objectivist or non-objectivist is to consider the worst. Imagine the most heinous acts, such as rape, genocide, or the torture of children, and ask yourself whether the opinion of the individual, or even of a whole society of individuals, could make the act "right." Since this thought-experiment requires you to *really* imagine the worst — to really get in touch with its horror — you might want to consider this example from Dostoyevsky's *The Brothers Karamazov*:

> One day a serf boy, a little child of eight, threw a stone in play and hurt the paw of the general's favorite hound. "Why is my favorite dog lame?" He is told that the boy threw a stone that hurt the dog's paw. "So you did it." The general looked the child up and down. "Take him." He was taken — taken from his mother and kept shut up all night. Early that morning the general comes out on horseback, with the hounds, his dependents, the dog-boys, and huntsmen, all mounted around him in full parade. The servants are summoned for their edification, and in front of them all stands the mother of the child. The child is brought from the lock-up. It's a gloomy cold, foggy autumn day, a capital day for hunting. The general orders the child to be undressed; the child is stripped naked. He shivers, numb with terror not daring to cry . . . "make him run" commands the general. "Run! run!" shout the dog-boys. The boy runs . . . the hounds catch him, and tear him to pieces before his mother's eyes![7]

Can you really believe that there is nothing objectively wrong here? Can you "bite the bullet" and say that the general's actions merely *seem* wrong to you (or your culture), and that there is nothing *intrinsically* horrible about this event? Can you maintain, as the subjectivist and cultural relativist does, that if an individual or culture were to regard this act as right it would thereby be right? The objectivist suspects that you cannot, and that cases like these will bring out your moral-objectivist convictions.

Support 2: Moral debate

It is common for people to debate moral issues at great length. Countless books and articles have been written defending particular policies on a wide range of moral concerns. In contrast, people tend not to debate things that are totally subjective such as taste in food. People certainly disagree about whether jalapeños taste good, but they don't debate it much. This is due in part to the fact that whether anyone likes them or not is of little importance, but there also just isn't much to say. Either you like their spiciness or you don't, and all the argument and discussion in the world is not going to make a difference. But when it comes to moral issues, arguments can and do change minds. By pointing out relevant considerations that we may have overlooked, or by showing how we may have misconstrued certain facts, or by simply helping us to see the same point from a different perspective, moral debate is not only possible, it can also be effective.

Support 3: An account of objective moral truth

If objective moral truth exists, it must be quite different from what we find in math and science. So ultimately the burden has to fall on the objectivist to show *how* moral claims can be objectively true. If the objectivists of Zion can deliver a persuasive theory, they win. If they cannot do so, then they should probably concede to Smith. Unfortunately we don't have the space to examine the various objectivist theories here. Suffice it to say that there have been many objectivist moral theories throughout the history of philosophy. Some of the main contenders include virtue theories (advanced by Confucius, Plato, Aristotle, and others), Utilitarianism (developed by Jeremy Bentham and John Stuart Mill), Kantianism (the moral theory of Immanuel Kant), and social contract theory (argued by Thomas Hobbes, Jean-Jacques Rousseau, and others). While several of the core ideas of Utilitarianism and Kantianism will be examined in the next chapter, if you want to really determine whether any of these theories ultimately defeat Smith's non-objectivism, you'll have to read them for yourself.

Suggested Reading

A. J. Ayer, *Language, Truth, and Logic*. New York: Dover, 1936.

Ruth Benedict, "Anthropology and the Abnormal," in *Philosophy and Choice: Selected Readings from Around the World*, ed. Kit Christensen. Mountain View, CA: Mayfield Publishing, 1999.

Thomas Nagel, *The Possibility of Altruism*. Oxford: Clarendon Press, 1970.

Friedrich Nietzsche, *Beyond Good and Evil*, tr. Walter Kaufmann. New York: Random House, 1966.

James Rachels, *The Elements of Moral Philosophy*, 4th ed. New York: McGraw Hill, 2000.

Notes

1 Smith could easily have quoted Friedrich Nietzsche here: "Life itself is *essentially* appropriation, injury, overpowering of the strange and weaker, suppression, severity, imposition of one's own forms, incorporation and, at the least and mildest, exploitation." See *Beyond Good and Evil*, section 259.

2 Other examples of category mistakes include "Trinity's love is purple," and "Quadruplicity drinks procrastination" (one of Bertrand Russell's favorites).

3 Despite his influence in this regard, Hume is generally not regarded as a moral nihilist. For more on this point see his *A Treatise of Human Nature*, ed. L. A. Selby-Bigg, 2nd ed. (Oxford: Clarendon Press, 1978), p. 469.

4 A. J. Ayer popularized the term "emotivism" for this sort of interpretation of moral claims. See his *Language, Truth, and Logic* (New York: Dover, 1936).

5 As we'll see in chapter 12, an existentialist analysis of the scene would endorse this interpretation.

6 One could argue that the number of stars that there are depends upon our definition of a "star," and hence it depends upon our beliefs about stars. This is certainly true. But once we settle on an adequate definition (one which allows us to determine whether any given object is a "star" or "nonstar") then the number of these objects that actually exist in the universe will be an objective matter.

7 Fyodor Dostoyevsky, *The Brothers Karamazov*, tr. Constance Garnett (New York: Random House, 1972), pp. 251–2.

NINE

DE-CYPHERING RIGHT
AND WRONG

Pleasure vs. Truth: Are You Red or Blue?

Why oh why didn't I take the *blue* pill?

— Cypher[†]

When Neo chooses the red pill he seems to make the right choice. Most of us would like to think that we would have done the same. After all, he was bored with his life. His job sucked, his personal life appears to have been pretty lonely, and he had stumbled onto a puzzle. He wanted to know what the Matrix is, and taking the red pill, it seemed, was the only way to find out. And, of course, the fact that he goes on to save Zion makes it all the easier to conclude that he made the right decision.

Cypher, on the other hand, regretted his choice. While sitting on top of Morpheus's jacked in body, he tells Trinity:

> He lied to us Trinity. He tricked us. [And to Morpheus' body he yells:] If you'd have told us the truth we would have told you to shove that red pill right up your ass![†]

Of course we are not very sympathetic toward Cypher — he's just too slimy in a number of ways. But consider things from his perspective. He thought that the Oracle's prophecies were just a bunch of BS, and it really was not the least bit unreasonable for him to suppose that there was no "One" and that Zion would soon be defeated. Under these conditions, wasn't it reasonable for him to want to be plugged back into the Matrix? Especially if he could be someone important — "like an actor."

In this decision, and throughout the film, Cypher represents a view called *egoistic hedonism*. He is *egoistic* because he is only concerned with his own welfare, and he is *hedonistic* insofar as he regards pleasure/happiness as the only good.[1]

Cypher's Hedonism

Ignorance is bliss.

– Cypher[†]

We see Cypher's hedonism come into play as he works out the details of his "reinsertion" into the Matrix with Agent Smith. He tells us:

> I know this steak doesn't exist. I know that when I put it in my mouth, the Matrix is telling my brain that it is juicy and delicious. After nine years, you know what I realize? Ignorance is bliss.[†]

"Reality" is inconsequential from Cypher's point of view. Why should he care whether or not the steak is *real* so long as it tastes good? As he sees it, the "desert of the real" truly is a wasteland. It is a landscape of harshness and discomfort. You can't get a juicy steak or a decent martini. Instead you have to eat "the same God-damned goop every day" (looks like a bowl of snot); and drink Dozer's home-brew – good for "degreasing engines and killing brain cells." When it comes to sensual pleasures, the Matrix wins hands down.

But it is important to note that hedonism exists in Zion also. In fact, while many people thought that the scenes of the Temple dance intertwined with clips of Trinity and Neo making love in *Reloaded* were curiously prolonged, the Wachowskis were most likely emphasizing the philosophical point that hedonism runs rampant outside of the Matrix as well. Despite the fact that Morpheus and his crew seem to be fighting for the lofty ideals of truth, freedom, and peace, most of the inhabitants of Zion seem to be focused primarily on maximizing their sensual pleasures. And at that same moment, sensual pleasure seemed to be foremost on Trinity and Neo's minds as well.

Hedonism maintains that pleasure/happiness is the sole *intrinsic good* – the only thing that is good *in and of itself*. Everything else (money, power, truth, peace, freedom, etc.) is merely *instrumentally good* – good like an instrument or tool. These other things are good only for what they can *do* for you, that is, only for the pleasure that they produce.[2] On this view, when a person seeks the truth by taking the red pill, what they are really after is happiness. They (correctly or incorrectly) suppose that they will be happier knowing the truth – at least over the long run.

The same goes for freedom, peace, and any other so-called "goods." We seek them because we think that we'll be happier with them than without them.

Many philosophers have argued against hedonism. Robert Nozick, for example, has tried to show the errors of this view through a thought-experiment called "the experience machine." Nozick asks us to imagine a machine that can give us any experience we desire through virtual-reality technology somewhat similar to the Matrix:

> Superduper neuropyschologists could stimulate your brain so that you would think and feel you were writing a great novel, or making a friend, or reading an interesting book. All the time you would be floating in a tank, with electrodes attached to your brain. Should you plug into this machine for life, preprogramming your life's experiences?[3]

Nozick argues that we should not plug in – at least not for a whole lifetime. He reasons that other things are important besides just pleasurable feelings. He contends that we want to *do* things, and not just *feel* like we're doing them. And we want to *become* certain sorts of people (honest, courageous, witty, etc.) and not just have the *experience* of being so. Also, he thinks that we value contact with reality itself. Plugging into an experience machine, he suggests, "limits us to a man-made reality, to a world no deeper or more important than that which people can construct." [4]

While Nozick's analysis definitely undercuts the idea that *all* that matters is pleasurable experiences, it doesn't seem to offer Cypher any reason not to reenter the Matrix. For unlike the Matrix, one of the biggest deficiencies of the experience machine is that it takes away one's ability to make choices. As Nozick imagines it, the person in the experience machine has experiences without really *doing* anything physically *or* mentally (in terms of exercising choice and will). This is not true of people within the Matrix. For instance, when Thomas Anderson was writing programs for the Metacortex Corporation, although his cubical, desk, and computer did not "really [i.e., materially] exist," the creative process involved in program writing was just as "real" as it is in our world. Since the Matrix is a "neural-interactive system," while his brain was passively accepting the virtual backdrop (e.g., the building, his cubicle, the sounds of the window washers' squeegees scraping across the glass, etc.), it was also *creatively interacting* with those surroundings. Whatever programs he wrote, or whether he wrote any at all, were a matter of his own *choosing*.[5] In fact, Cypher seems to have a valid point when he says of life in the "real" world:

> Free? You call this free? All I do is what he tells me to do. If I gotta choose between that and the Matrix, I choose the Matrix.[†]

DE-CYPHERING RIGHT AND WRONG

Since there is no artificial "will control" used in the Matrix, it seems that the only difference with respect to freedom between the Matrix and the real world pertains to the specific "options" in one's life, and this is contingent upon one's position, talents, power, wealth, etc. Thus, it may be true that a person can be freer in the Matrix than in the real world.

For similar reasons, people within the Matrix *become* certain sorts of people. When Thomas Anderson tells Smith: "How about I give you the finger and you give me my phone call." This isn't the Matrix *making* him act rebelliously; rather, he is *being* rebellious. And, as Neo confronts Agent Smith, the Merovingian, and others, he truly acts courageously. Despite the fact that his surroundings are virtual, Neo *becomes* a certain type of person through his actions – just like the rest of us. In contrast, the person within the experience machine is, according to Nozick, "an indeterminate blob." By giving their entire physical and mental capacities to the programming of the machine, they cease to be a "person" at all. As Nozick suggests, it's a kind of suicide.

Nozick's concern about the *depth* of one's life does apply to the Matrix, at least in principle. The Matrix does indeed limit us to a man-made (or computer-made) reality that is *no deeper* than that which people (or programs) can construct. But it is not clear *how* or *why* we should think that the Matrix is any less deep than the material world. What makes life in the experience machine shallow is that, as we've seen, the person in the machine is not *being* or doing anything. But since this is not true of the Matrix, how then does the Matrix lack depth? Nozick suggests a possible religious analysis here. He says that many persons desire "to leave themselves open to such contact [with Ultimate Reality] and to a plumbing of deeper significance."[6] He offers several possibilities of what this might mean. For instance, it could involve achieving the eternal bliss of the Nirvana, doing the will of a higher being, or merging with some higher reality. But again it is not clear why the Matrix (as opposed to the experience machine) would preclude these possibilities. Buddhism, for example, teaches that reaching Nirvana has to do with one's mental state – not one's physical state. There is no reason to suppose that a person cannot reach Nirvana just because their body is jacked into the Matrix, any more than if their body were incapacitated by cerebral palsy. In fact, Neo's own case demonstrates the possibility of achieving some kind of "enlightenment" (broadly construed) within the Matrix. Similarly, if the meaning of life is to be found through "doing God's will," insofar as this involves having faith, living righteously, and following the scriptures as many tend to believe, then there is again no reason to suppose it cannot be done within the Matrix – unless we add the specific assumption that God forbids living in a Matrix.[7]

It seems to me that it is something else that most troubles us about the idea of living inside the Matrix. Primarily I think we detest the idea of living our lives as the victims of a grand deception. All the pod-born inhabitants of the Matrix have been tricked about fundamental aspects of their very existence, and this is something that most of us find quite disturbing. And Cypher, who chooses to be reinserted (on the condition that he remembers "nothing – you got it – NOTHING"), is even worse. For he *chooses* falsehood over truth, ignorance over knowledge, and pleasure over all else.

In the end, most of us would like to think that we would choose reality. We would rather live a harsh but truthful life than live a lie – even if that means fewer pleasures overall. If this is true then we are not hedonists. We must believe that there is more to life than just pleasurable experiences.

Cypher's Egoism

Don't hate me. I'm just the messenger.

– Cypher[†]

The thing that makes Cypher most contemptible is not his attachment to pleasure, but rather his complete and utter egoism. His thoroughgoing selfishness is revealed as he offers to betray Morpheus in his deal with Smith, and again when he pulls the plug on Switch and Apoc, all for his own advantage.

Egoists don't tend to be very popular. They typically don't make good friends, lovers, or crew members, so there tend to be strong social pressures to steer people away from this sort of outlook. But occasionally we confront the unabashed egoist who challenges our apparent love of altruism, and of justice for all. The egoist often contends that what people are really after is not justice, but rather the *appearance* of justice. Deep down we are all pretty selfish, they say, but we like the respect and benefits that come when others think that we are fair and somewhat altruistic. This idea has been around since at least the ancient Greeks. In Plato's *Republic*, for instance, the character of Glaucon offers a challenge to those who pride themselves on their justice and altruism. He tells the tale of *Gyges*, a shepherd who found a ring that gave him the power of invisibility:

> He arrived at the usual monthly meeting which reported to the king on the state of the flocks, wearing the ring. As he was sitting among the others he happened to twist the hoop of the ring towards himself, to the inside of his hand, and as he did this he became invisible to those sitting near him and they went on talking as if he had gone. He marveled at this and, fingering the ring, he turned the hoop outward again and became visible ... When he realized this, he at once arranged to become one of the messengers to the king. He went, committed adultery with the king's wife, attacked the king with her help, killed him, and took over the kingdom.[8]

Glaucon contends that no one is so incorruptible that they would stay on the path of virtue if they could seek their own advantage without fear of punishment or social condemnation. Give the ring to both the just and unjust man, he suggests, and each would:

> take whatever he wanted from the market, go into houses and have sexual relations with anyone he wanted, kill anyone, free all those he wished from prison, and do the other things which would make him like a god among men.[9]

Although Glaucon's analysis of human nature might be overly pessimistic,[10] we cannot deny that most people would use the ring to break the law now and again, and they'd surely do a variety of things that put their own advantage over the legitimate rights and interests of others. Sadly, most of us are probably a bit more like Cypher than we'd like to admit.

But the pertinent question from an ethical point of view is not so much what *would* people do, as what *should* they do. Some philosophers have defended selfishness as not only common, but also *morally right*.[11] This view is called *moral egoism*. It maintains that the right thing for a person to do in any situation is to act in such a way as to maximize his or her own self-interest. As Glaucon pointed out, this does not mean that one should lie, cheat, and steal at every opportunity. The rational and deliberate moral egoist will generally be just and generous most of the time in order to avoid punishment and gain respect within the community. But on some occasions, the moral egoist maintains that the right course of action will involve doing "whatever it takes" to maximize one's own interests. Such is the case with Cypher. It appeared that a little murder and betrayal would get him everything he wanted, so he took the opportunity. According to moral egoism, Cypher did the right thing by betraying the others. The only problem was that he botched the job.[12]

Cypher's Mistake

I see the darkness spreading . . .

— The Oracle[†††]

Most of us are not moral egoists. We're glad to see that Cypher fails and quick to condemn his actions. But when it comes to explaining *why* his actions were wrong, people differ in their analysis. One popular approach to moral analysis is consequentialism. It is to judge the rightness and wrongness of actions in terms of the overall consequences produced. Insofar as the consequences are good (or at least better than the alternatives), the action is right, and insofar as the consequences are bad (or worse than the alternatives), the action is wrong.

The intuitive appeal of consequentialist reasoning can be illustrated by the following hypothetical situation:

Two Doors

Suppose that the Architect were to present Neo with the following choice, saying, "You must choose one of these two doors. All I can tell you, is that what lies behind the door on the left is better or 'more good' than what is behind the door on the right. Which do you choose?"

As long as we can trust that the Architect is not lying (what do you take him for – *human*?) the choice seems rather obvious. You should go with the door on the left. Only a fool would choose what is less good over what is more good.

Consequentialism tells us that we should always *maximize the good*. Of course, what exactly a person should do will then depend largely upon what is good. The most prominent consequentialist moral theory is called utilitarianism. It maintains, with Cypher, that pleasure/happiness is the only intrinsic good. The nineteenth-century British philosopher John Stuart Mill did a great deal to popularize this theory. He summarized the view in terms of what he called the *Greatest Happiness Principle*:

[A]ctions are right in proportion as they tend to promote happiness, wrong as they tend to produce the reverse of happiness.[13]

The key difference between Cypher's philosophy and Mill's utilitarianism is that the latter maintains that there is nothing special about one's own happiness – or even *human* happiness. Instead, following consequentialist reasoning, he argued that we should strive for happiness:

to the greatest extent possible, secured to all mankind; and not to them only, but, so far as the nature of things admits, to the whole sentient creation.[14]

From a utilitarian perspective, Cypher's motives were all wrong. He acted as if his own happiness was somehow special – as if it were the only happiness that really mattered. But this is a mistake. Despite what his mother may have told him, he's *not* special. His happiness is indeed good, but so is everyone else's. Every creature that can experience happiness, whether human, animal, sentient machine, or sentient program, desires happiness and wishes to avoid suffering. Thus, on Mill's view, Cypher's actions demonstrate a kind of irrational prejudice toward his own interests and against the interests of others.

The Matrix Deception: Ends and Means

> You are a slave, Neo.
>
> — Morpheus[†]

One of the biggest concerns about consequentialist moral theories is that they can justify the use of evil means in order to produce a good end. Take terrorism, for example. Terrorists commit horrible acts (such as killing busloads of innocent people) in order to achieve the consequences that they believe are good. In essence, they believe that their end or goal justifies their means. If consequentialism is correct, then terrorism can indeed be right – so long as it is the most efficient means of achieving the best end result. There is essentially no limit to what one might "justifiably" do insofar as we judge actions solely in terms of their overall consequences. Deceit, betrayal, murder – anything that a guy like Cypher might be inclined to do – can be morally right, so long as it leads to the best consequences overall.

In fact, the machines' use of the Matrix deception may very well be justified if we approach it from utilitarian perspective. As we learn in *The Second Renaissance*, the machines had for years tried to establish a peaceful and cooperative relationship with the humans, but the human race wanted nothing of it – choosing war instead. After the machines defeated the human forces, they were left with the question of what to do with all of the human prisoners and noncombatants. They ultimately decided to build the Matrix, a dreamworld that would allow the humans to continue to have rich mental (if not physical) lives, while the machines tapped their bodies for bioelectricity. As Smith's interrogation of Morpheus revealed, the machines' reasoning was decidedly utilitarian:

> The first Matrix was designed to be a perfect human world where none suffered, where everyone would be happy. It was a disaster. No one would accept the program. Entire crops were lost. Some believed that we lacked the programming language to describe your perfect world. But I believe that as a species human beings define their reality through misery and suffering. The perfect world was a dream that your primitive cerebrum kept trying to wake up from. Which is why the Matrix was redesigned to this – the peak of your civilization.[†]

In true Utilitarian fashion, the machines wanted even their enemies to be as happy as possible.

We also see utilitarian reasoning at work in the machines' dealings with Zion. Given all the death, destruction, and suffering that occurs in *Revolutions*, this may not be readily apparent. But if you think about it, the attack on Zion seems to be a last resort – an unavoidable evil in the minds of the machines. As we learn in *Reloaded*, this is not the first time that the machines have descended on Zion. They've destroyed it before, but it seems that they never destroy it completely – though surely they could if they wanted to. Instead, the machines seem to *want* Zion to continue. This became evident when the Architect offered Neo the chance to save 23 people, 7 males and 16 females, in order to rebuild it.[15] This may mean that the machines keep Zion around as a sort of sanctuary (much like our bird sanctuaries or nature preserves). They seem to want the awakened humans to have a place to live out the rest of their lives in relative happiness – so long as they don't become a real threat to the Matrix.[16]

So the "Matrix solution" may very well have maximized happiness overall. Machine happiness is maximized because the Matrix renders the humans harmless and provides the machine city with all the power it needs, and the happiness of humans is maximized, to the extent their primitive cerebrums will allow, because the Matrix provides them with a world of steaks, martinis, warm weather, and blue skies.

The fact that consequentialist theories like utilitarianism cannot condemn the Matrix (or terrorism, betrayal, murder, etc.) as *necessarily* wrong, strikes many of us as rather troubling. Some philosophers have therefore opposed this whole approach, arguing instead that right and wrong are to be analyzed independently of the specific consequences of the act. One of the most influential nonconsequentialist moral theories can be found in the work of the eighteenth-century German philosopher Immanuel Kant. On Kant's view, both hedonism (the view that pleasure/ happiness is the sole intrinsic good) and consequentialism (the view that the right action is the one with the best overall consequences) are misguided.

Kant expressly denied that pleasure/happiness is intrinsically good, and instead argued that pleasure can be good *or* evil, depending on the will of the person experiencing it. This goes not only for pleasure/happiness, but also for everything in this world or even out of it, except a *good will*. Kant writes:

> Intelligence, wit, judgment, and any other *talents* of the mind we may care to name, or courage, resolution, and constancy of purpose, as qualities of *temperament*, are without doubt good and desirable in many respects; but they can also be extremely bad and hurtful when the will is not good which has to make use of these gifts of nature. . . . It is exactly the same with . . . wealth, honor, even health and that complete well-being and contentment with one's state which goes by the name of "*happiness*" . . . unless a good will is present . . .[17]

Cypher presents us with a good example of this point. Recall his sadistic remarks as he sits on top of Morpheus's jacked-in body just before he kills Switch and Apoc:

I wish I could be there when they break you. I wish I could walk in just when it happens – so right then you'd know it was me.

On Kant's account, the pleasure that Cypher takes in Morpheus's suffering isn't the least bit good. It is a sick and twisted pleasure – a bad pleasure. Similarly, incredible strength and power are good when possessed by Neo, yet they are bad in Smith. Or, knowledge of the codes to Zion's mainframe is good when possessed by Zion's captains, but bad when possessed by Agents.

Kant's contention is that things in the world become good only when they are possessed by a good will. Kant defines the good will in terms of *doing one's duty for duty's sake*. Or, to put it another way, it is to will the right action *because* it is right. Kant maintained that the good will is unconditionally good, i.e., it is good always and everywhere, because its goodness is not to be found in its results, but rather in the very *principle* upon which it acts.

Part of Kant's reasoning here is that consequences are always unpredictable. A person can have the best intentions, and yet, through some twist of fate, they may end up causing great harm. And similarly a person can have terrible intentions and yet inadvertently cause a good outcome. This too is illustrated by Cypher. It may have been precisely *because* Cypher betrayed his friends that Neo realized his potential as "The One." If Cypher had not delivered Morpheus to the Agents, it is quite possible that Neo would have kept waiting – for some other life perhaps. Thus Cypher may have inadvertently played a crucial role in saving Zion. But a good outcome, Kant argues, cannot make an act of betrayal right. What Cypher did was wrong in principle – irrespective of its outcome.

Kant maintained that morality is intimately connected to our rationality. He believed that our own reason commands us not to ride roughshod over the interests and welfare of other rational beings. He called this command from reason *the Categorical Imperative*:

The Categorical Imperative (the Universal Law Formula):
Act only on that maxim through which you can at the same time will that it should become a universal law.[18]

This is to say that before you act on a particular maxim (any general action-guiding principle) you must first make sure that it is a maxim or principle that could be willed for everyone to follow. Kant maintained that there are many maxims that we might be inclined to act on ourselves, but that we would not want to see implemented as universal law. For instance, consider Cypher's maxim:

Cypher's maxim:
Whenever I can greatly improve my situation by killing people, I'll do so.

While Cypher was certainly inclined to act on this sort of maxim, it is not something that he would want to see as a universal law. To envision it as a universal law all we need to do is generalize it so that it does not pertain specifically to Cypher, but instead to everyone:

Cypher's maxim as a universal law:
Whenever *anyone* can greatly improve their situation by killing people, they'll do so.

No rational being could want this maxim to be followed by everyone, for then they would have to live in constant fear for their own safety.

The essence of the Categorical Imperative is rational consistency. It involves the realization that you are merely one rational being among others. All rational beings, by their very nature, set goals for themselves and make plans to achieve those goals. Your own reason tells you that there is nothing inherently special about you and your goals, so you must not make special exceptions for yourself. If betrayal is to be okay for you, then it has to be okay for all other rational beings. Since you cannot want other rational beings betraying you and thwarting your goals, you must not betray them.[19]

From a Kantian perspective, the problem with the Matrix deception is that it involves *using* rational beings against their will. It is one thing to build a Matrix for those humans who would *choose* to live within it, but quite another to deceive people in order to use them and control them. The machines, as rational beings, could not want us to deceive them about the very nature of their lives, therefore they must not do that to us. Kant expresses this most clearly in an alternative formulation of the Categorical Imperative:

The Categorical Imperative (the Respect-for-Persons Formula):
Act in such a way that you always treat humanity [i.e., rational beings], whether in your own person or in the person of any other, never simply as a means, but always at the same time as an end.[20]

For the machines to subject humans to their will through a Matrix deception is for them to treat us simply as means – as mere tools for their use. It is to act as if their goals matter and ours do not. But there is no legitimate basis for this distinction. They are making a special exception for themselves. For this reason, on Kant's analysis the Matrix deception would be wrong *in principle*. It must not be done for all the happiness in the world.[21]

Suggested Reading

Immanuel Kant, *Groundwork of the Metaphysic of Morals,* tr. H. J. Paton. New York: Harper and Row, 1964.

John Stuart Mill, *Utilitarianism,* ed. George Sher. Indianapolis, IN: Hackett Publishing, 1979.

Robert Nozick, *Anarchy, State, and Utopia.* New York: Basic Books, 1974.

Plato, *Republic,* bk. II, tr. G. M. A. Grube. Indianapolis, IN: Hackett Publishing, 1974.

Ayn Rand, "A Defense of Ethical Egoism," in *Moral Philosophy: A Reader,* ed. Louis Pojman. Indianapolis, IN: Hackett Publishing, 1993.

Peter Unger, *Identity, Consciousness, and Value.* Oxford: Oxford University Press, 1990.

Notes

1 Many hedonists use the terms "pleasure" and "happiness" interchangeably. For instance, John Stuart Mill writes: "By happiness is intended pleasure, and the absence of pain; by unhappiness, pain and the privation of pleasure." See his *Utilitarianism,* ed. George Sher (Indianapolis, IN: Hackett Publishing, 1979), p. 7.

2 John Stuart Mill's view on this is a bit trickier. He argues that pleasure or happiness is the sole intrinsic good and that most other things are a means to this end. Yet, he also allows that some things are good not as a means to happiness, but rather as a *part* of one's happiness. Virtue may be this sort of good. See *Utilitarianism,* p. 35.

3 Robert Nozick, *Anarchy, State, and Utopia* (New York: Basic Books, 1974), pp. 42–3.

4 Ibid., p. 43.

5 This is not to make any presumptions about whether or not our choices are *free.* For more on this issue see chapters 5 and 6 above.

6 Ibid., p. 43.

7 I expect that many people would be prepared to argue that God *would* disapprove of living within the Matrix. The question, however, is whether there really are good reasons for believing so.

8 Plato, *Republic,* bk. II, trans. G. M. A. Grube (Indianapolis, IN: Hackett, 1974).

9 Ibid.

10 This pessimistic view of human nature, when taken to its logical extreme, is called "psychological egoism" – the view that every human action is motivated entirely by self-interest.

11 See, for example, Ayn Rand, "A Defense of Ethical Egoism," in *Moral Philosophy: A Reader,* ed. Louis Pojman (Indianapolis, IN: Hackett Publishing, 1993).

12 Here's a tip for "would-be" egoistic murderers. Don't lay your weapon down right next to the person that you just shot.

13 Mill, *Utilitarianism,* p. 7.

14   Ibid., pp. 7–12. While Mill does not think that human happiness is special in the sense that it is only our happiness that matters, he does think that there can be morally relevant differences between the happiness of humans and animals. Mill argues that intellectual pleasures are *qualitatively superior* to bodily ones. Thus he thinks that human beings are capable of a more profound type of happiness than most if not all animals. However, we should also note that when it comes to the experience of pain, there does not seem to be an important difference.

15   Seven males and 16 females is likely a reference to Genesis 7:16, which reads: "The animals going in were male and female of every living thing, as God had commanded Noah."

16   Although the machines seem to take a utilitarian position in these instances, this does not seem to hold across the board. For instance, in the final scene of *Revolutions*, the Oracle questions the Architect about whether he will keep his word. He replies: "What do you take me for, *human*?" The insinuation here is that he would never lie. If he were completely utilitarian he could not (honestly) say this, since one never knows if a set of circumstances might arise in which, by breaking his promise, he could maximize happiness. Similarly, the Zion rebels seem nonconsequentialist in their principled opposition to the Matrix. However, they seem to take on a much more consequentialist outlook when it comes to fighting their war. Every time they cause trouble in the Matrix they know that Agents will take over the bodies of innocent civilians, often (and perhaps always) killing them. The rebels' attitude here seems to be that their worthy end justifies this foreseen but unintended side-effect. This "mixing" of ethical frameworks is quite common in our world as well.

17   Immanuel Kant, *Groundwork of the Metaphysic of Morals*, tr. H. J. Paton (New York: Harper and Row, 1964), p. 61.

18   Ibid., p. 88.

19   However, we do have a moral duty to thwart the goals of others if they are violating the categorical imperative. Kant would say that it is right to turn your friend over to the police if you have reason to believe that they are about to commit a murder, for instance. This raises an interesting point. If Cypher were right to believe that Morpheus was "tricking" people into taking the red pill and thereby ruining their lives, would it be right to hand him over to the Agents?

20   Ibid., p. 96. By "humanity" Kant makes it clear that he means "rational beings" rather than "human beings." For instance, he suggests that if there exist angels with rational natures, we should have moral duties toward them. Thus the categorical imperative would apply to our treatment of rational machines just as it applies to their treatment of us.

21   And here lies the most unsettling aspect of Kant's philosophy. If you could save the entire human race from decades of horrible suffering by betraying – or even murdering – one innocent person, wouldn't you feel that *then* it would be the right thing to do?

TEN

THERE IS NO SPOON
REFLECTIONS ON THE MATERIAL WORLD

Buckle your seatbelt Dorothy, because Kansas is going bye-bye.

– Cypher[†]

A Matter of Habit: The Habit of Matter

When Neo first learns the truth about the Matrix, the war, the scorched sky, and current state of the world, he pukes his breakfast onto the floor. He says that he doesn't believe it – that he *won't* believe it. This, I imagine, is a very natural response to having your whole world pulled out from under you. Eventually, of course, he comes around. His first real "awakened" Matrix experience occurs in the dojo when he spars with Morpheus. There Neo takes quickly to his newly acquired skills, and he soon comes to rival Morpheus's ability to "bend the rules" of that universe. But nevertheless, there is much work to be done. He still doesn't fully *get it*. So Morpheus taunts him:

Do you think that my being stronger or faster has anything to do with my muscles *in this place*? You think that's air you're breathing now?

Despite the fact that Neo realizes (intellectually) that he and Morpheus are not *really* in a dojo, he finds it difficult to avoid getting sucked back into the belief that the events are *physical*.

For his next virtual adventure, Tank loads the "jump program." Neo falls from a skyscraper and lands face first on the pavement. Well, *nobody* makes it the first time. If we speculate about why no one makes it the first time, we can be sure that the problem is mental rather than physical. Just as in the dojo, strength and speed have nothing to do with muscles here. It is due to his *mental gymnastics* that Neo came up short. He either lacked the mental skills or the confidence to make the jump. I tend to think that his lack of confidence was the real barrier. As Morpheus warned him, "You have to let it all go Neo; fear, doubt, and disbelief. Free your mind." Neo most likely failed because he still didn't fully *believe* that he could make the jump. Ultimately, he had to overcome the belief or *feeling* that the world of the Matrix was physical. He had to realize, not only intellectually, but *existentially* – with every fiber of his being – that everything in his experience was purely mental. The skyscraper, the wind, the street below, were all *in* his mind, not outside of it.

The lesson here is that it is exceedingly difficult to give up the belief that the objects that you see, smell, and touch have a material existence outside of your mind. That is why Morpheus's general rule is not to free a mind once it is beyond a certain age: "The mind has trouble letting go." I stress this point because I am about to ask you to similarly "let go" of your belief in matter.

Metaphysical Idealism: Bending Your Mind

To be is to be perceived.

– George Berkeley

Everyone takes it for granted that matter exists. Some people are skeptical about the existence of God, or the existence of ghosts and so on, but no one doubts that matter exists. Well, except perhaps "Spoon Boy" as he was dubbed in *The Matrix* script. During Neo's first trip to the Oracle, he looked around the room at the other "potentials" and saw a young boy with a freshly shaven head who was bending spoons with his mind. As Neo sat down beside him, the boy offered him some advice:

SPOON BOY: Do not try and bend the spoon . . . that's impossible. Instead only try to realize the truth.
NEO: What truth?
SPOON BOY: There is no spoon.

Spoon Boy is right of course. There really is no spoon – though there are a couple of different ways that we might take this remark. The most likely interpretation is to suppose that he means that there is no spoon *because* they are in the Matrix. In that virtual world all that exists is their *perceptions* of the spoon. Its solidity, smoothness, and color are just features of their minds, due to the electronic stimulation of their brains by the Matrix program. But, of course, if they were in the *real world*, there would be a material spoon "out there" causing their perceptions.

Another more radical possibility is that Spoon Boy's observation is correct about the real world as well. That is, perhaps there is no such thing as a "material" spoon outside of the Matrix either. This view is tougher to sell. But if this is indeed Spoon Boy's position, he is not the first to hold it. His claim is reminiscent of the Buddhist parable of two monks who were arguing about the temple flag. The first monk proclaimed that the flag was moving. The second monk said it was not really the flag, but the wind that moves. As they argued about this for some time, Hui-neng, the Sixth Patriarch, approached them and said, "Gentlemen! It is not the flag that moves. It is not the wind that moves. It is your mind that moves!"

Hui-neng seems to suggest that it is "all in the mind" – and he certainly was not thinking that they were in the Matrix. A very similar idea is expressed by the contemporary Buddhist Monk Thich Nhat Hanh, and in a manner that makes the Architect's walls of video monitors spring to mind. He writes:

> The mind is a television
> With thousands of channels.
> I choose a world that is tranquil and calm
> so that my joy will always be fresh.[1]

Hanh offers these words as a prayer, and recommends that we say them before turning on the television. He explains that, "when our mind is conscious of something, we *are* that thing. When we contemplate a snow-covered mountain, we are that mountain. When we watch a noisy film, we are that noisy film."[2] Similarly, when we turn on the channel of anger, we are that anger. And if we tune in to peace and joy, we are peace and joy. In Hanh's view there is a kind of inseparability between consciousness and the world of which it is conscious.

If we were to take this line of thought to its logical limit, we would end up at the position that there is nothing but mind, that is, there is no snow-covered mountain, or spoon, or fork, except in the mind. This position, called *metaphysical idealism*, was vigorously defended by the eighteenth-century philosopher George Berkeley. On this view, the only things that really exist are *minds* and *ideas*. In chapter 2 we considered the difficulties involved in distinguishing perception from reality. The twist of metaphysical idealism is that *perception is reality.* Or, as Berkeley put it, "to be is to be perceived." There simply is no such thing as "matter," if by that you mean *stuff that exists outside of and independent of minds.*

Just Try to Step Outside of Your Mind:
The Case Against Matter

Pay for it? I'm not even going to remember it. It'll be like it never happened. The tree falling in the forest doesn't make a sound.

— Cypher[†]

We all are faced with the predicament of deciding what to believe. Should I believe in UFOs, global warming, God, matter, etc.? To make these decisions it is nice to have some basic principle to guide you. Here is one of mine:

Basic epistemological principle:
You should not believe in anything for which there is absolutely no evidence.

This should be a rather uncontroversial principle. I expect that you already accept it, and that you've been using it throughout your life. If you were to reject this principle then I suppose there is no end to what you might believe. You might as well believe in leprechauns, or that the center of the earth consists of cream filling, or that at any moment you will be endowed with Neo's superhuman powers.

Keep this basic epistemological principle in mind as you consider the age-old question: If a tree falls in the forest when no one is there to hear it, does it still make a sound? Most people suppose that of course it would make a sound.[3] However, the very point behind this question is that it makes you acutely aware of a deep philosophical problem. *How* do you know that it would make a sound? If no one hears it, then what *evidence* do you have for your answer? In fact, when no one perceives the tree, what evidence is there for the existence of the tree at all?

On the common view, the tree would make a sound because it exists outside and independent from our minds. Thus if we were all killed by some horrible form of radiation, the trees, the sounds, the spoons and forks would continue to exist just fine without us. In contrast, metaphysical idealism asserts that without minds perceiving them, these objects would not exist at all. As Berkeley puts the point:

> Indeed it is an opinion strangely prevailing amongst men, that houses, mountains, rivers, and in a word all sensible objects, have an existence, natural or real, distinct from their being perceived by the understanding. But ... what are the aforementioned objects but the things we perceive by sense? And what do we perceive besides our own ideas or sensations? And is it not plainly repugnant that any one of *these*, or any combination of them, should exist unperceived?[4]

In this passage Berkeley suggests that all we are ever aware of is the perceptions within our own minds. For instance, the sensations of color and light that you experience when you turn your attention to the spoon, or the sensation of smoothness you have when you hold it in your hand. But *sensations* are mental – they are features of your mind. Nobody believes that the *sensation* of smoothness is in the spoon. And what do we know of the spoon besides our sensations? Nothing at all, Berkeley argues. We cannot even think of the spoon existing apart from our perceptions. Attempt it for yourself. Try to think of the spoon *without* thinking of your sensation of color, or texture, or temperature, etc. When you abstract away all of these perceptions, there is nothing left.

The key point is that all we have access to is the *inside* of our minds, to our thoughts, feelings, perceptions, etc. But matter, by definition, is supposed to exist outside of our minds. So in principle we can never directly experience it. This is the very problem that plagued us in chapter 2. If what distinguishes the real world from the virtual world is that the objects of the real world exist outside of and independent from minds, while the objects of the Matrix world exist *only* in the minds of the humans and programs who perceive them, then it is impossible to know if we are in the real world or not. For it is impossible *in principle* to go out and check.[5] Thus we have absolutely no evidence for the existence of matter, that is, for *stuff* that exists beyond our perceptions. Matter, on this view, is a groundless myth akin to mermaids and leprechauns.

The argument against matter (and material spoons) can be stated formally as follows:

The Idealist Argument Against Spoons:
1)   You should not believe in anything for which there is absolutely no evidence.
2)   *There is absolutely no evidence for matter (or material spoons).*
3)   Therefore you should not believe in matter (or material spoons).

As with any valid argument, if you accept the two premises, then reason demands that you accept the conclusion. It is time to give up your belief in material spoons.

Dodge This: The Case For Matter

You keep loadin' and I'll keep shootin'.

— Charra[†††]

Most people don't buy the idealist argument. But since they accept the basic epistemological principle that serves as the first premise, they must deny the second premise. They must maintain that there *is* evidence for matter. Thus the burden of proof falls upon the materialist philosophers to demonstrate just what that evidence is and how it is attained. The most common responses fall into two categories:

Reply 1: We have evidence for matter because we *can* get outside of our minds.

Reply 2: We have evidence for matter because it is possible to acquire evidence for it *without* going outside of our minds.

The first type of reply says that we *can* get outside of our minds. But how? An "out of body experience" is certainly conceivable, but how does one manage an "out of mind experience"? Wherever your experience goes, your mind *must* go with it (since all we mean by "mind" here is your *consciousness*, or *locus of experience*). But to this, one might reply that *you* don't have to get outside your mind, because *other people* are out there for you. If you were alone in the universe, then you might have a problem. But if we take it for granted that other people exist,[6] then *they* can verify that matter is really out there. This kind of argument is illustrated in the following hypothetical example:

Neo's Refutation of Spoon Boy:
Imagine that upon hearing the claim that there is no spoon (in the strong sense), Neo turns to Spoon Boy and says: "Listen up little boy. Sorry to burst your bubble, but I exist outside your mind. I can tell you first hand that there is a spoon out here. Similarly, you exist outside of my mind and you also see the spoon. Therefore, the spoon exists outside of our minds. Matter exists!"

This reply to idealism cannot work, and *The Matrix* shows us why. Within the Matrix, spoons are *ideal* rather than *material* – that is, they exist only in the mind. Neo's verification of the spoon merely amounts to more *perceptions*. He can only confirm that he and Spoon Boy perceive the same thing – *in their minds*. It does nothing to demonstrate the existence of a material spoon that is beyond their perceptions.

The same argument would apply to those who might try to refute idealism by leaving a tape-recorder in the forest to record the sound of the unperceived falling tree. A tape-recorder in the Matrix would certainly play back the sound of the falling tree, but this does not prove that the tree was "material." What are the sounds that you hear on the tape, except more *sensations*? The sensations only show the state of your mind at the present moment. They do not demonstrate the existence of a material object outside of your mind, or that such an object existed at a time when you were not perceiving it.

The second type of reply suggests that we don't need to get outside of our minds in order to have evidence for matter. The problem with the idealist's argument, according to this line of thinking, is that it fails to acknowledge that there are *direct* and *indirect* forms of evidence:

Direct evidence: A person has direct evidence of an object or event when they have experienced it first hand.

Indirect evidence: A person has indirect evidence of an object or event if they did not experience it first hand, but instead experienced one or more of its *effects.*

On this reasoning, the idealist is right to acknowledge that we do not have any *direct evidence* for matter. But they have ignored the fact that we have plenty of *indirect evidence* to support our belief that matter exists.

For example, if you were to watch the Osiris hovercraft as it was torn apart by sentinels, then you have direct evidence for your belief that it was destroyed in a sentinel attack. In contrast, if you had simply found the shredded remains of the Osiris the next day, your evidence that it was destroyed in a sentinel attack would be indirect. You didn't see the sentinels, but you saw their *effects*. And although indirect, the evidence justifies your conclusion. Similarly, the advocate for matter asserts that while we cannot get outside our minds to directly verify that matter is "out there," we have more than enough indirect evidence to justify our belief that matter exists. Most people suppose that there is a vast amount of indirect evidence for matter. The most commonly cited examples involve our matching perceptions, unperceived causal processes, and our inability to control our sensory perceptions.

■ **Our matching perceptions:** When people walk into a room they all see roughly the same thing. If there are two big red chairs in a room, any person will see them. The fact that we all see them is regarded as the *effect* of material chairs on our material senses, and thereby as indirect evidence of matter.

■ **Unperceived causal processes:** When we dig up a grave that no one has perceived (seen, touched, or even thought about) for hundreds of years we nevertheless find that causal processes have occurred, e.g., the deterioration of the body, etc. And the general verdict is that this *shows* that matter and material processes exist outside of and independent of our perceptions of them.

- **Our inability to control our sensory experience:** Another commonly cited example is the fact that we cannot do whatever we wish. People argue that if everything is mental, then we should have the ability to fly, dodge bullets, etc. But, unlike Neo, we don't have these powers, so we must be limited by a physical world that exists apart from our minds.

Idealism Reloaded

I won't let you die.

– Neo[††]

Most people think that these examples, and others like them, present a strong indirect case for the existence of matter. But I think that the case is not nearly as strong as it may appear. While the indirect case for matter seems analogous to the indirect case for the sentinel attack on the Osiris, there is a crucial difference. In the case for the sentinel attack, the people of Zion have had *direct evidence* of sentinels in the past. They have seen sentinels first hand, and have witnessed their ability to tear apart a hovercraft. This greatly strengthens the case that is built on indirect evidence. In contrast, we have *never* had direct evidence of matter. And without the corresponding direct evidence, we must use caution. Phenomena such as our matching perceptions, unperceived causal processes, and our inability to control our sensory experiences are certainly evidence of *something*, but on what grounds can we say that these are evidence of *matter*?

The presupposition of matter is not sufficiently established by the indirect evidence, and again, the *Matrix* films illustrate why. Prior to his awakening, Neo could easily have taken the fact that his perceptions of spoons and other objects *match* the perceptions of other people to be evidence that those objects are material. But of course they were not material spoons. What he took as indirect evidence for the existence of *matter*, was not evidence of this at all. The same holds for unperceived causal processes like deteriorating graves, or people's inability to control their sensory experience. While he would have taken these to be indirect evidence of matter, they too would really have been indirect evidence of computer-driven deception.

In response, the materialist could still argue that while the case for matter may not be "air tight," it is hands down the *best explanation* of the facts as we understand them. The possibility that matter is causing our shared perceptions is much more plausible than, for instance, the supposition that we are living in a Matrix. (And note, even a Matrix presupposes a physical world in which material brains are manipulated.) But here again, Berkeley disagrees. While he would certainly grant that it is unlikely that we are in a Matrix, he argues that God provides a much better account of the phenomena to be explained than the hypothesis of matter.

Indirect Evidence for God

The Alpha of your Omega.

— Agent Smith[tt]

It sometimes comes as a shock to find out that Berkeley believed in God. Since he did not believe in matter, people often suppose that Berkeley must have been a skeptic — the kind of person who is unwilling to believe in much of anything. But nothing could be farther from the truth. Berkeley believed that metaphysical idealism would help us to avoid the pit of skepticism that trapped Descartes.[7] Berkeley was, in fact, Bishop George Berkeley of the Anglican Church, and he was clearly willing to make some small leaps of faith. However, the interesting thing about Berkeley's philosophy is that he regarded the belief in God to be a much smaller leap of faith than the belief in matter.

Berkeley used God to account for all those things that people typically think they need matter to account for. In his view it is God and *His* ideas that explain our matching perceptions, unperceived causal processes, and our inability to fly. In many respects his thought is not so far from the mainstream religious views. Most any religious person would grant that ultimately these facts hold true because that is how God made the world. If God wanted to make a world where people could fly about at will, He could have. But instead He chose to create this world, with its specific laws of nature. These laws account for our matching perceptions, and unperceived causal processes, as well as the fact that we cannot move in bullet-time, or fly like superman. The difference between Berkeley's view and the more common religious viewpoints is that Berkeley believes that God achieves all of this without recourse to matter. He does it all "in the mind" — not altogether different from the Matrix itself. God's laws of nature would be much like the programs inherent to the Matrix. As the Oracle tells us:

A program was written to watch over the trees, and the winds, the sunrise and sunset — programs running all over the place. The ones doing their job, doing what they were meant to do, are invisible — you'd never even know they were here.[tt]

On Berkeley's view, all of the objects of our perceptions — spoons, forks, trees, etc., along with the laws that govern them — are God's ideas (or God's Matrix program).

God is essentially a supremely powerful mind (a divine Architect) and He puts these ideas directly into our minds (without need of physical brains or jacking in).

At first view this sounds pretty wild. But Berkeley thinks it fits very well with what we know to be true. We know first hand that (1) *minds exist,* and (2) *minds create ideas.* We are directly aware of our own minds, and that we are able to create ideas with our minds – as when we imagine a golden mountain, or *Matrix 4.* But notice that we are also directly aware of the fact that (3) *we do not create some of our ideas.* As you hold this book your mind is filled with ideas (sensations) of its weight, its color, its shape, and so on. Berkeley calls these "ideas of sense" and contrasts them with the "ideas of imagination." While it is evident that we dream up our ideas of imagination ourselves, we are clearly not the cause of our ideas of sense. Berkeley therefore concludes that (4) *the ideas of sense must be created by the mind of another.* And since this mind would be the cause of all of our shared perceptions, that is, of everything that we associate with the real world, (5) *this mind is aptly called God.*

Berkeley maintains that the hypothesis of God explains all the phenomena that we wanted to explain, and by making a much smaller leap of faith than we would have to make by appealing to the hypothesis of matter. The leap is smaller because we have *direct evidence* (from our own case) that minds create ideas. God would be just another instance of this sort of phenomena. The hypothesis of matter, in contrast, has no direct evidence whatsoever to support it. Matter involves a *total* leap of faith because it requires you to believe in a completely unperceived (and hence unknown) type of object.

Was Spoon Boy Wrong?

No . . . no . . . this isn't right. This can't be right.

– Agent Smith[††]

We've been considering Spoon Boy's comments in the most radical way – that perhaps he meant that there are no spoons inside *or* outside of the Matrix. But ultimately there is no conclusive reason to suppose that this is what he meant. He may very well have been simply making a point about the world *inside* the Matrix. But if we continue to take him in the more radical way, shouldn't we ultimately conclude that Spoon Boy was wrong? The Wachowskis *could have* made an idealist trilogy, but clearly they didn't. By the end of *Revolutions* we can be sure that Zion was a material world – right?

Well, clearly Zion was supposed to be "the real world," that is, a future version of "our world." So we might say that matter exists *there* if and only if matter exists *here*. Thus the question comes back to us. Does matter exist in our world? The problem, as Berkeley pointed out, is that we are in no position to say so. But on the basis that Zion represents our world, we might be tempted to say that the *Matrix* trilogy is at least no more an idealist film than any other film about "our world." But this would be too simple. The difference is that the Wachowskis had idealism on their minds (along with so many other philosophical themes) as they wrote the Matrix films. While they may not have intended to leave us with the conclusion that the world is ideal rather than material, they certainly wanted to leave us puzzling about it.[8]

Suggested Reading

George Berkeley, *A Treatise Concerning the Principles of Human Knowledge*, in *Voices of Wisdom: A Multicultural Philosophy Reader*, 5th ed., ed. Gary E. Kessler (Belmont, CA: Thomson-Wadsworth Learning, 2004).

Dale Jacquette, "Reconciling Berkeley's Microscopes in God's Infinite Mind," *Religious Studies* 29(4) (Dec. 1993).

Thich Nhat Hanh, *Present Moment, Wonderful Moment* (Berkeley: Parallax Press, 1990).

Notes

1   Thich Nhat Hanh, no. 47, "Turning on the Television," from *Present Moment, Wonderful Moment* (Berkeley: Parallax Press, 1990).

2   Ibid.

3   Some clever persons, fearing that they may be proven wrong on a technicality, will argue that there would not be a sound because "sound" basically means *the perception of sound*. To avoid this they might say that there would not be a "sound" but there would be a "train of compression waves" passing through the air. As we will see, Berkeley's argument applies to compression waves also.

4   If you follow this reasoning through you'll realize that even after taking the red pill Neo has no way of determining whether any object is "out there" beyond his perceptions.

5   George Berkeley, *A Treatise Concerning the Principles of Human Knowledge*, in *Voices of Wisdom: A Multicultural Philosophy Reader*, 5th ed., ed. Gary E. Kessler (Belmont, CA: Thomson-Wadsworth Learning, 2004), part I, sec. 4.

6   I am ignoring the possibility of *solipsism* – the view that your *own* mind is the only thing that exists. Not because it has been proven false, but only because neither Berkeley nor his materialist critics take this view seriously.

7   Descartes's skeptical problems were examined in chapter 2.

8   Even the ever-faithful Morpheus demonstrates the confusion that this issue creates. At the end of *Revolutions* he asks Niobe, "Is this real?"

ELEVEN

MORPHEUS AND THE LEAP OF FAITH

You're going to have to trust me.

— Morpheus[††]

Recall the scene from *The Matrix* in which Morpheus, weak and barely conscious from Agent Smith's interrogation, charges through a stream of gunfire and then leaps from the skyscraper window into the hands of Neo, who is dangling from a helicopter 20 feet away. There is no better image to represent the most striking feature of Morpheus's character — his unwavering faith. In this radical "leap of faith" Morpheus shows his absolute conviction that Neo is The One.

If you think about it, faith always involves some sort of leap. The concept of faith is rarely invoked when it comes to things that are *known*. You don't *have faith* that 2 + 2 = 4, or that the ground will support your weight. These are things that you feel quite certain about, and the greater certainty you have, the less need there is for faith. Faith is what you use to traverse the gap between your reasons and your conclusion. In cases of knowledge, there is no gap, and hence no need for faith.

A fairly common perspective on faith is that it is *to believe something upon insufficient evidence*. On this view, most everyone has faith. To a certain extent we have faith in our friends and our spouses, in our leaders, and in the economy. But this kind of faith comes easily, and for the most part it requires very little from us. The character of Morpheus shows us that the Wachowskis have something much stronger, more radical, in mind. To fully comprehend it, we must turn to the source of their inspiration, the existentialist philosophy of Søren Kierkegaard.

Søren Kierkegaard: The Philosopher of Faith

Faith begins precisely where thinking leaves off.

– Kierkegaard

Kierkegaard's influence can be seen through a number of philosophical parallels between his philosophy and the films, but the Wachowskis also threw in a few overt references for us as well. You may have noticed the first captain to volunteer to aid the Nebuchadnezzar during the Council meeting in *Reloaded* was Captain Søren of the Vigilant.[1] Also, the name of one of Zion's top officials, Councilor Hamann, appears to be a reference to the historian J. G. Hamann,[2] whom Kierkegaard quoted on the title page of his book on faith, *Fear and Trembling*. And further, the character of Ghost, who serves as the Wachowskis' philosophical mouthpiece throughout the *Enter the Matrix* video game,[3] cites Kierkegaard as a source of his own inspiration. In response to the question of how he can believe something as crazy as the idea that Neo, a single man, can bring an end to a war against an entire race of machines, he says:

> Kierkegaard reminds us that belief has nothing to do with how or why. Belief is beyond reason. I believe because it is absurd. . . . Faith, by its very nature, transcends logic.

Ghost's comments illustrate just how radical Kierkegaard's view of faith really is. Faith, as Kierkegaard sees it, is not simply to believe something upon insufficient evidence. Rather, *faith is to believe something irrespective of the evidence.* It is to leap headlong into the absurd. Most of us are not prepared to make that kind of leap. It is only the rare individual, such as Morpheus, who exemplifies it. Morpheus never falters in his conviction that the prophecy will be fulfilled despite the sometimes overwhelming evidence to the contrary. His faith endures through Neo's apparent death in *The Matrix*, and in spite of 250,000 sentinels swarming on Zion. And he even holds firm to his belief after Neo's visit to the Source fails to end the war as prophesied.

Kierkegaard's philosophy on the subject of faith is most thoroughly developed in his masterwork *Fear and Trembling*. Written under the pseudonym *Johannes de silentio* (John the Silent), Kierkegaard explores the psychological, moral, and spiritual aspects of radical faith. Although Kierkegaard claimed that the work of his pseudonyms does not necessarily reflect his own views, *Fear and Trembling* offers key insights into his own philosophy.

Much of the impetus behind the book appears to have been the religious climate of his nineteenth-century home of Copenhagen. By today's standards the people

MORPHEUS AND THE LEAP OF FAITH

of Copenhagen were extremely religious. Just about everyone in Denmark at the time was Christian (specifically, Lutheran), and nearly all of Kierkegaard's friends and neighbors took themselves to be "persons of faith." They read their Bibles and attended church with untiring regularity. But Kierkegaard, who pondered religious matters obsessively, was disgusted by the superficiality of it all. He could hardly believe how *easy* Christianity seemed to most people. They would attend church on Sunday, and then go straight back to a life of vanity, deception, avarice, and greed, all the while feeling quite secure that heaven awaited them. Kierkegaard seemed to think that if Christianity were to be meaningful, and to provide a central purpose to one's life, it could not be cheapened in this way. He subtly makes this point in the Preface to *Fear and Trembling*:

> Not just in commerce but in the world of ideas too our age is putting on a veritable clearance sale. Everything can be had so dirt-cheap that one begins to wonder whether in the end anyone will want to make a bid.[4]

One of the foremost goals of the book was to raise the stakes. Kierkegaard wanted to make Christianity difficult once again. He wrote:

> In the old days it was different. For then faith was a task for a whole lifetime, not a skill thought to be acquired in either days or weeks.[5]

And there is no better medium for such a task than the Biblical story of Abraham. On Kierkegaard's view it is Abraham who shows the way to faith, and Morpheus follows in his footsteps.

Morpheus and Abraham: Twin Knights of Faith

Whatever you think you know about this man is irrelevant.

– Agent Smith[†]

The story of Abraham is arguably the paramount story of faith in the Old Testament, and perhaps in the Bible itself. You may recall that in the book of Genesis, Abraham was called upon by God to sacrifice that which he loved most, his only son Isaac. He was fully prepared to thrust his knife into Isaac's chest when an angel stopped him at the final moment – after he had sufficiently proven his faith. Kierkegaard (or Johannes de silentio) suggests that we should hold Abraham in the highest regard. As he sees it, faith is "the highest passion in a human being," and Abraham is the exemplar or "hero" of faith. In the *Matrix* films Morpheus also serves as kind of a *hero of faith*. No one can match the intensity of his conviction, and it is largely the result of Morpheus's unwavering faith that Neo is able to free humanity.

From Kierkegaard's perspective, while men like Abraham and Morpheus are to be greatly admired, their actions are nevertheless incomprehensible. "Abraham I cannot understand," he tells us, "in a way all I can learn from him is to be amazed."[6] But most people seem oblivious to just how incomprehensible men like Abraham and Morpheus really are. For instance, most Christians are familiar with the story of Abraham, but they don't seem too worried about the picture of faith that it presents. Abraham's trial is so often seen as just a "wonderful story of faith." But here is an account of a man who was fully prepared to take the innocent life of his young son – a terrifying prospect if you really think about it. Do Christians really understand Abraham? Johannes thinks that surely they do not, for if they did, they would be terrified by this story. The story raises several questions which should greatly disturb anyone who takes it, and their faith, seriously:

1   If God were to call on me in a similar manner, would I *know* what to do?
2   Even if I knew what to do, would I have the *strength* to do it?
3   And even if I had the strength to do it, would I *willingly choose* to?
4   Might my very salvation depend on having the kind of knowledge, strength and will that Abraham had?

These questions leave Johannes de silentio lying awake at night in utter fear and trembling. The possibility of failure lurks behind each one. And while they are difficult questions on any account, they become infinitely more difficult from Kierkegaard's philosophical perspective. For on his view: (a) faith is entirely subjective – the individual must create their own interpretations – their own truth, and (b) faith is entirely absurd – it transcends reason altogether. In the sections below we will examine how these two aspects of faith are played out in the lives of Abraham and Morpheus, and how it makes them simultaneously admirable and terrifying to Johannes de silentio.

The Subjectivity of Faith

No one can tell you . . . You just know it – through and through, balls to bone.

— The Oracle[†]

The Bible tells us that God put Abraham's faith to the test in Genesis 22. There, God says to Abraham:

> Take now thy son, thine only son Isaac, whom thou lovest, and get thee into the land of Moriah; and offer him there for a burnt offering upon one of the mountains which I will tell thee of.

Next we are told that:

> Abraham rose up early in the morning, and saddled his ass, and took two of his young men with him, and Isaac his son, and clave the wood for the burnt offering, and rose up, and went unto the place of which God had told him.[7]

What the story leaves out, and which frustrates Johannes to no end, are the steps between God's command and Abraham's obedience. If you want to truly understand Abraham, and to have the kind of faith that he did, you really *need* the details. What was he thinking? How did he feel? Did he sleep at all that night? Did he tell his wife Sarah of what he was about to do? These crucial details are left to our own imagination. Nevertheless, Abraham seems to have known exactly what to do with God's command. God instructed, he obeyed – it's as simple as that. But Kierkegaard shows us that while it may have been that simple *for Abraham*, the task of interpretation – of knowing what to do – is infinitely more complicated. Abraham's interpretation seems to be:

a) **This is a command from God.**
Therefore I must sacrifice my son.

But *how* did he know this? For us, looking at the whole ordeal, it is easy to say that Abraham did the right thing. He was, after all, rewarded. God told him: "I will multiply thy seed as the stars of the heaven . . . and in thy seed shall all the nations of the earth be blessed; because thou hast obeyed my voice."[8] But assuming he did the right thing, the question remains, how did he know at the time? His interpretation was certainly not the only one – or even the most reasonable. Consider some of the other possibilities:

b) **God is testing my moral character.**
To pass the test, I must refuse to commit such an immoral act.

c) **This is *not* a command from God – I must be going insane.**
I must refuse to listen to these hallucinations.

d) **This is *not* a command from God – it must be the voice of the devil or demons.**
The Lord will be pleased to know that I did not fall for such a trick.

It is common to slip into thinking that the meaning was obvious, but it only seems this way if you create a distance between yourself and these events by not taking them as *real*. Imagine, for instance, that it is your next-door neighbor who tells you that God had commanded *him* to sacrifice his son. Would you believe him, or think that he was insane? Or, suppose that it happened to you. If you "heard" God commanding you to murder, would you believe it? Would you *take it* to be God? If you are anything like me, you'd sooner think that you were insane. The key point for Kierkegaard is that faith is always subjective. It rests entirely on the individual. *You* must *take it* to be God, *you* alone must *interpret* the message, and *you* alone must *decide* whether to comply.

We see this very same issue arise in *Reloaded*. The Oracle shows her complete agreement with Kierkegaard when she tells Neo:

> It is a pickle, no doubt about it. The bad news is that there is no way for you to really know whether I'm here to help you or not. So it's really up to you. You just have to make up your own damn mind to either accept what I'm going to tell you, or reject it.[††]

And just as God's instructions to Abraham admit of several interpretations, so do those of the Oracle. For instance, one might suppose:

a) **The Oracle knows the future and wants to help us.**
Therefore, Neo must go to the Source as directed.

b) **The Oracle is a program and therefore just another system of control.**
Her instructions are a trick and should not be followed.

c) **Like all other fortune-tellers, the Oracle is a fraud.**
Think about it – last time she said that Neo was not The One, and now she says that he is. She's lying and it is a waste of valuable time to consult her opinion.

Both Neo and Morpheus choose the first interpretation. But only Morpheus does so in a way that would make him a true "knight of faith" in Kierkegaard's eyes. Neo believed her for the moment, but quickly lost his conviction after returning from the Source. In his conversation with Morpheus back on the Nebuchadnezzar, we see that he lost his faith as soon as the evidence turned on her:

MORPHEUS: I don't understand it. Everything was done as it was supposed to be done. Once The One reaches the Source, the war should be over . . .
NEO: It was a lie, Morpheus. The prophecy was a lie. The One was never meant to end anything. It was all another system of control.
MORPHEUS: I don't believe that.
NEO: But you said it yourself. How can the prophecy be true if the war isn't over?

The Absurdity of Faith

A casual stroll through the insane asylum shows that faith does not prove anything.

– Friedrich Nietzsche

What Neo lacked was the ability to completely embrace the absurd. He was willing to believe the Oracle upon *insufficient* evidence, but he did not believe her *irrespective* of the evidence. And this, for Kierkegaard, is the real movement of faith.

On Kierkegaard's account, true faith involves a "double movement," *a movement of infinite resignation* and *a movement of faith*. In order to become what Kierkegaard calls a "knight of infinite resignation," one must be prepared to give up the very thing that one hopes to keep. We see this in Abraham as he is fully prepared to give up Isaac, who for him was all the joy of this world. Similarly, we see this in Morpheus, the moment that the Nebuchadnezzar is destroyed. In despair he calls out: "I have dreamed a dream, but now that dream is gone from me." But to become a true "knight of faith" one cannot stop there. Johannes de silentio tells us that such resignation, while a component of faith, is insufficient on its own. What makes men like Morpheus and Abraham truly amazing is that they simultaneously make a *movement of faith*. At the very moment that they give up their dreams and every hope for this world, they continue to expect the impossible:

> All along he had faith, he believed that God would not demand Isaac of him, while still he was willing to offer him if that was indeed what was demanded . . . and it was indeed absurd that God who demanded this of him should in the next instant withdraw the demand.[9]

On this picture, Abraham believed "on the strength of the absurd." His faith transcended logic, for he believed two contradictory propositions:

a) Isaac is lost to him.
Which he believes in his movement of infinite resignation.

b) Isaac is not lost to him.
Which he simultaneously believes in his movement of faith.

We see the same double movement in Morpheus. After Neo's story of how it was all just another system of control, and then the destruction of the Nebuchadnezzar, he resigns himself to the loss, saying: "I have dreamed a dream. But now that dream has gone from me." But despite its utter absurdity, he continues to believe in the prophecy. In the opening scenes of *Revolutions* we see him continue to search the Matrix for Neo, despite the fact that he is not even jacked in. So Morpheus also simultaneously believed two contradictory propositions:

a) **The prophecy has failed.**
His dream is over.

b) **The prophecy will come to pass.**
Despite all signs to the contrary, his dream will be fulfilled.

Of course it is irrational to believe both of these propositions simultaneously. And it is not that the knight of faith somehow *forgets* about his resignation through an act of self-deception. Rather, Kierkegaard tells us that the knight of faith believes *on the strength of the absurd*.

Heroes or Criminals? Suspending the Ethical

If it were up to me Captain, you wouldn't set foot on a ship for the rest of your life.

— Commander Lock[††]

The most terrifying thing about knights of faith is what they might be prepared to do at any given moment in virtue of their faith. Abraham was ready and willing to kill his own son. Morpheus disobeyed his commanding officer, and continuously put his crew at risk on the basis of his own absurd yet unwavering faith. In the end, of course, both men are vindicated. Their faith pays off, and they are ultimately regarded as heroes. But should they be seen as heroes? Isn't it vastly more reasonable to regard them as criminals? Certainly Commander Lock would have loved to see Morpheus thrown into the brig, if not altogether court-marshaled.

Commander Lock's position is similar to that of the nineteenth-century British philosopher W. K. Clifford, whose philosophical notoriety comes largely from his intense criticism of faith. Clifford sums up his view with the bold statement: "It is wrong always, everywhere and for anyone, to believe anything upon insufficient evidence."[10] Clifford, like Commander Lock, believes that faith is a grave danger to society. He illustrates his point with an example that is in many ways similar to Morpheus's own exploits. Clifford tells the story of a ship owner who has good reason to doubt the sea-worthiness of his ship. He nevertheless convinces himself, without sufficient evidence, that the ship is fine and sends it across the ocean full of immigrant passengers. Morpheus in a similar manner risks the lives of the crew, and all of Zion, on the basis of a conviction that cannot be rationally justified. On Clifford's analysis, if the ship goes down (or if Zion falls):

What shall we say of him? Surely this, that he was verily guilty of the death of those men. It is admitted that he did sincerely believe in the soundness of his ship [or of the prophecy]; but the sincerity of his conviction can in no wise help him, because he had no right to believe on such evidence as was before him . . . And although in the end he may have felt so sure about it that he could not think otherwise, yet inasmuch as he had knowingly and willingly worked himself into that frame of mind, he must be held responsible for it.[11]

Of course, in the end, Morpheus is successful. The prophecy was true and his unrelenting faith is largely responsible for the salvation of Zion. But even this does not justify his actions in the eyes of men like Clifford and Lock. As Clifford concludes:

Suppose that the ship was not unsound after all; that she made her voyage safely and many others after it. Will that diminish the guilt of her owner? Not one jot . . . No accidental failure of its good or evil fruits can possibly alter that. . . . The question of right or wrong has to do with the origin of his belief, not the matter of it . . . not whether it turned out to be true or false, but whether he had a right to believe on such evidence as was before him.[12]

This attitude is pretty extreme, but then so is Morpheus's particular brand of faith. Even Johannes de silentio suggests that from an ethical point of view, Abraham should be "remitted to some lower court for trial and exposed for murder."[13] But nevertheless, we tend to admire Morpheus, and Abraham is revered around the globe. We admire, for instance, the way that Morpheus was willing to "lay it all on the line" for his convictions, and we despise the tight-assed Lock, for whom everything must be logical and controlled. In fact, we cannot help but wonder what Niobe could have possibly seen in him.

But philosophically we must be careful not to put ourselves at too much of a distance – as it is so easy to do with fiction, or with stories that occurred a long time ago in a land far, far away.[14] For instance, suppose it were not Abraham, but your neighbor, who told you that God had asked *him* to sacrifice his son upon an alter – and that luckily he was spared at the last moment. Could you find any room in your heart for admiration towards him – or only suspicion, fear, and contempt? Or, suppose that you were in Commander Lock's position. Would you stand for Morpheus's insubordination on the basis of the rather absurd possibility that he could be right?

And then there is the question of whether *anything at all* can justify their actions. In this regard there is a divergence between Abraham and Morpheus. For Morpheus, though his faith itself was beyond reason, his motivation for disobeying orders was not. Insofar as he sincerely believed that the life of every person in

Zion depended upon his success, his actions were, if not ethically justified, at least ethically intelligible. But for Abraham it is different, as Johannes tells us:

> In his action he overstepped the ethical altogether, and had a *telos*[15] outside it, in relation to which he suspended it. . . . It is not to save a nation, not to uphold the idea of the State, that Abraham did it, not to appease angry gods. If there was any question of the deity's being angry, it could only have been Abraham he was angry with, and Abraham's whole action stands in no relation to the universal.[16]

On Kierkegaard's view the ethical is to be identified with the *universal*. Taking the life of one's son goes against a moral duty that applies to everyone at all times. Acting on his faith, Abraham acts instead on the *personal*. His reasons are uniquely his. They pertain to his personal relationship with God. From the outside, it is impossible to distinguish him from others who have murdered in response to their own delusions or insanity. So Johannes concludes, "either Abraham was every minute a murderer, or we are confronted by a paradox which is higher than all meditation." And, of course, it is the latter interpretation that he chooses. He argues for what he calls *the teleological suspension of the ethical*. That is, he contends that the personal *can* override the universal or ethical, precisely when it is done in obedience to God. So Abraham's faith, as he sees it, is "a paradox capable of transforming a murder into a holy act well-pleasing to God."

Kierkegaard's analysis of faith and his interpretation of the story of Abraham are both highly controversial, to say the least. But it does provide us with an interesting way to think about the sort of faith that Morpheus demonstrates throughout the *Matrix* films. Ultimately Kierkegaard's philosophy cannot prove to us that Abraham and Morpheus are heroes. To come to that conclusion involves a leap of faith of its own. Certainly it is a far less radical leap than these men have made, but it is a leap nonetheless. I for one find it easy to regard Morpheus as a hero throughout the films, but my admiration of him requires the distance that fiction creates. The moment I truly take him seriously, as a potential neighbor, brother, or friend, I can no longer admire or trust him. I cannot make the final movement, the paradoxical movement of faith. Instead, I find myself, much like Johannes de silentio, very, very afraid.

Suggested Reading

W. K. Clifford, "The Ethics of Belief," in *Philosophy of Religion: An Anthology*, 4th ed., ed. Louis P. Pojman. Belmont, CA: Wadsworth, 2003.

William James, "The Will to Believe," in *Philosophy of Religion: An Anthology*, 4th ed., ed. Louis P. Pojman. Belmont, CA: Wadsworth, 2003.

Søren Kierkegaard, *Concluding Unscientific Postscript*, tr. David F. Swenson and Walter Lowrie. Princeton: Princeton University Press, 1960.

Søren Kierkegaard, *Fear and Trembling*, tr. Alastair Hannay. New York: Penguin Books, 1985.

Donald Palmer, *Kierkegaard for Beginners*. New York: Writers and Readers Publishing, 1996.

Ludwig Wittgenstein, "A Lecture on Religious Belief," in *Philosophy of Religion: An Anthology*, 4th ed., ed. Louis P. Pojman. Belmont, CA: Wadsworth, 2003.

Notes

1 Unfortunately, Captain Søren and his crew died an early death as their ship was overtaken by sentinels while they tried to take out the power grid. (This was part of the plan to enable Neo to enter the Source.) Søren Kierkegaard also died prematurely at the age of 42.

2 The reference to J. G. Hamann is quite interesting. The Wachowskis made this reference knowing full well that its symbolism would be lost on almost everyone who saw the film. In a similar vein, the meaning of the Hamann quote that begins *Fear and Trembling* (which is itself about the very nature of symbolism) was lost on almost all of Kierkegaard's readers. The quote from Hamann states:

> What Tarquin the Proud said in his garden with the poppy blooms was understood by the son but not by the messenger.

Kierkegaard, like the Wachowskis, did not explain the reference even though he knew that it would be unintelligible to anyone who was unfamiliar with the larger context. The passage refers to Tarquin (an early king of Rome) at a time when he was at war with Gabil. In order to send a message to his son (who was living in Gabil under the pretense that his father had mistreated him) he cut off the heads of the tallest poppies in his garden before the eyes of a messenger. When the messenger reported this event to the son, he (and only he) knew the meaning. He soon put to death all the leading men of Gabil. This allowed Tarquin a swift victory. Kierkegaard uses this quote to foreshadow one of his main theses in *Fear and Trembling* – that the act of interpretation, and therefore faith itself, is always subjective and personal.

3 Throughout the *Enter the Matrix* video game, the completion of particular levels unlocks certain video segments that were not included in the films. Most of the videos document the adventures of Niobe and Ghost in events that would have occurred during *The Matrix Reloaded*. If you play through with the character of Ghost, you'll find that he makes direct references to the thought of David Hume, William James, Jean Baudrillard, Friedrich Nietzsche, Thomas Aquinas, and Søren Kierkegaard. Niobe tends to be less philosophical, though her conversation with the Oracle yields some important insights.

4   Søren Kierkegaard, *Fear and Trembling*, tr. Alastair Hannay (New York: Penguin Books, 1985), p. 41.

5   Ibid.

6   Ibid., p. 66.

7   Genesis 22. Biblical quotations are from the King James Version.

8   Ibid.

9   Kierkegaard, *Fear and Trembling*, p. 65.

10 W. K. Clifford,"The Ethics of Belief," in *Philosophy of Religion: An Anthology*, 4th ed., ed. Louis P. Pojman (Belmont, CA: Wadsworth, 2003), p. 367.

11 Ibid., p. 364.

12 Ibid.

13 Kierkegaard, *Fear and Trembling*, p. 84.

14 The reader is left to their own conclusions about whether the trials of Abraham should be read as fact or fiction.

15 A *telos* is an aim or purpose – an overarching goal.

16 Kierkegaard, *Fear and Trembling*, p. 88.

149

TWELVE

FACING THE ABSURD
EXISTENTIALISM FOR
HUMANS AND PROGRAMS

The Matrix cannot tell you who you are.

— Trinity[††]

Man is nothing else but what he makes of himself. Such is the first principle of existentialism.

— Jean-Paul Sartre

Of Gods and Architects

Søren Kierkegaard, whose existentialist philosophy of faith was discussed in the previous chapter, requested that just two words be engraved on his tombstone at his death: THE INDIVIDUAL. This gesture nicely summarizes the main thrust of the existentialist movement in philosophy — which both begins and ends with *the individual*. Existentialism focuses on the issues that arise for us as separate and distinct persons who are, in a very profound sense, alone in the world. Its emphasis is on personal responsibility — on taking responsibility for who you are, what you do, and the meanings that you give to the world around you.

While Kierkegaard's existentialism was largely inspired by his religious commitments, atheism was the guiding assumption for many existentialist writers, including Martin Heidegger, Albert Camus, and Jean-Paul Sartre. In *Existentialism as a Humanism*, the French existentialist Jean-Paul Sartre explained how his philosophy was intimately tied to his atheism through the example of a paper-cutter.

> [H]ere is an object which has been made by an artisan whose inspiration came from a concept. He referred to the concept of what a paper-cutter is and likewise to a known method of production, which is part of the concept, something which by and large is a routine. Thus, the paper-cutter is at once an object produced in a certain way and, on the other hand, one having a specific use ... Therefore, let us say that, for the paper-cutter, essence ... precedes existence.[1]

The key point here is that the paper-cutter's *essence precedes its existence.* This is to say that the artisan has determined the essential nature or character of the object *before* it ever comes into existence. For example, the artisan must determine the type of cutter that he or she is going to make, along with its specific size, shape, materials, etc., before going into production. Sartre believed that humanity is analogous to the paper-cutter when considered from a religious point of view. If God is our creator, then He is like a superior sort of artisan, and we come into existence according to His specific design or plan. God would have determined every person's *essence* – the qualities that make him or her the distinct individual that they are – prior to their birth.

Sartre's denial of God leads him to believe that for us, *existence precedes essence.* Human beings are born into this world first, and through our own free choices each person must determine his or her own essence for themselves. Sartre asserts that, "man exists, turns up, appears on the scene, and only afterwards defines himself."[2] At first view this may seem straightforwardly false, even if we take Sartre on his own atheistic terms, for surely we are born with particular genetic propensities or character traits. As we noted in chapter 5, some children are more timid and shy than others from the start, some seem to be naturally more athletic than others, and so forth. But Sartre is not denying this. Rather, what he rejects is the idea that any innate tendency constitutes or defines an individual.

While on their way to Neo's first meeting with the Oracle, Trinity tells Neo that the Matrix cannot tell him who he is. In a similar vein, Sartre would say that not even his genes can tell him who he is. Sartre writes:

> When the existentialist writes about a coward, he says that this coward is responsible for his cowardice ... There's no such thing as a cowardly constitution; there are nervous constitutions; there is poor blood, as the common people say, or strong constitutions. But the man whose blood is poor is not a coward on that account, for what makes cowardice is the act of renouncing or yielding. A constitution is not an act; the coward is defined on the basis of the acts he performs.[3]

The ultimate task for a human being, Sartre suggests, is to choose the kind of person one will be. That is, one must create one's own essence.

The Essence of Machines and Programs

We only do what we're meant to do.

– The Keymaker[††]

Sartre's distinction between human beings and artifacts is blurred when it comes to *sentient* machines and programs – hardware and software that can think, feel, and experience the world around them. Are these beings responsible for who they are and what they do, or are they simply artifacts whose essence is determined for them through their programming?

The answer may depend upon the individual machine or program and its level of sophistication. The Keymaker, for example, seems to clearly illustrate a being whose essence precedes his own existence. He has been designed to perform a particular function – to unlock the backdoor for Neo to access the Source. His whole existence is geared toward this purpose, and this purpose was created *for him*, not *by him*. He gives us no indication that he has ever contemplated the question of *whether* he should spend his time making keys, or whether he should assist Neo. These things are simply "given" – they are the unquestioned foundations of his existence. For instance, when Niobe asks him how he knows so much about the structure of the mainframe, his response, true to his character, is: "I know because I must know. It is my purpose. It is the reason why I'm here." And the Keymaker isn't the only one to fit this mold. The agents also seem to be "programmed" specifically for their role, and for little else. Their essence *is* their role as agents. Their job, their purpose, defines them. With the exception of Smith, it is hard to even think of them as *individuals*. Agents Jones, Brown, and Johnson are more or less interchangeable.

Our first glimpse of any real individuality in an agent comes in the first film, when Smith broke the rules and removed his earpiece while interrogating Morpheus. Unlike his cohorts who were somewhat devoid of emotion, Smith confessed his increasing frustration about living in the Matrix:

> I hate this place. This zoo. This prison. This reality, whatever you want to call it, I can't stand it any longer. It's the smell, if there is such a thing. I feel saturated by it. I can taste your stink and every time I do, I fear that I've been somehow infected by it.[†4]

Here we see that Smith has given the situation a meaning that is uniquely his. Although we cannot know exactly how Smith's programming works, I think it is reasonable to suppose that he was not programmed to become frustrated under

these sorts of circumstances. In fact, he may not have been specifically programmed to become frustrated in *any* situation. His emotional reaction may
instead be a kind of byproduct of his ability to think creatively. Certainly, it is
related to his ability to imagine the fall of Zion and a life outside the Matrix.

The interesting thing about Smith's frustration is that it goes well beyond
what Sartre would call the *facticity* of the situation. "Facticity" stands for the
brute facts about the world – those things over which one has no control. The
facticity of Smith's situation would include the fact that the Zion rebels have
continued to elude him, that the sweat of human beings gives off a particular
(though virtual) odor, that Morpheus has so far refused to reveal the codes to
Zion's mainframe, etc. It is not an element of facticity, however, that these events
are "frustrating." This is an interpretation that Smith adds to the events, or it is
the meaning that *he* confers upon them. Just as Sartre had claimed that there
is no such thing as a "cowardly constitution," he would argue that there is also
no such thing as a "frustrating situation," above and beyond the individual who
chooses to regard it as such. One person's frustration is another's delight, or a
welcomed challenge, an embarrassment, etc. The interpretation of the event (and
of all meaning in the world) is up to the individual. And it is largely by creating
these meanings and acting upon them, that one creates their character or essence.

So Agent Smith appears to have this "human" quality. He invents his own
interpretations, and to that extent he invents himself. But in other respects he
seems to fall short. For even when he broke the rules, he did so only insofar as he
thought it was necessary to fulfill his prime directive. His role as an agent still
defined him. However, everything changed when Neo (seemingly) destroyed him at
the conclusion of the first film. In *Reloaded* we find out that Smith refused to
"die." He tells us:

> I knew the rules, I knew what I was supposed to do, but I didn't. I couldn't. I was
> compelled to stay, compelled to disobey. And now here I stand because of you,
> Mr. Anderson. Because of you I am no longer an agent of the system. Because of
> you I'm changed. I'm unplugged. I'm a new man, so to speak – like you, apparently
> free.[††]

Smith's programming and his role as an Agent *of the system* required him to
return to the Source for deletion. His act of refusal amounts to rebellion. He is an
exile – a "free agent." The Oracle had warned us about exiles:

> Every time you've heard someone say they saw a ghost or an angel, every story
> you've ever heard about vampires, werewolves, or aliens, is the system assimilating
> some program that's not doing what it's supposed to be doing.[††]

These exiles, it seems, are programs that have undergone a sort of *existential crisis*. Although their purpose has been designated for them, their ability to consider alternatives (a prerequisite for programs of any real sophistication) has enabled them to question this purpose, and even to rebel against it. And once one has rejected the purpose given to them, and thereby the authority of another to dictate one's essence, one must face the daunting question of whom they shall be. This is the fundamental project of existentialism.

The possibility of rebellion demonstrated by the exiles illustrates that Sartre may have put too much emphasis on the issue of God, an artisan, or architect. For even if something has been created for a particular purpose, this only constitutes the essence of that thing (or being) if it must passively accept that purpose. But for self-reflective beings, whether biological or artificial, rebellion is always a possibility. One can reject the purpose that one has been given. This can take the form of rejecting one's biological urges, or willingly defying God's command, or rejecting the rules laid down by the Architect.

Facing the Absurd

I only wish that I knew what I was supposed to do.

– Neo[††]

Not surprisingly, it was his own death that led Smith to question the meaning of his existence, and to reject the purposes that he had been given. Death has always figured prominently in existentialist philosophy. Martin Heidegger, for example, described our existence as *being-toward-death*. That is, our entire lives are shaped by the fact that we are going to die. Death is a significant aspect of the very structure of a human life, and with Smith we see that death (by deletion) also structures the existence of programs within the Matrix. In this existentialist sense, the Architect was right, when, at the end of *Reloaded*, he told Neo that Trinity "is going to die and there is nothing you can do about it." Trinity *is* going to die – just not as soon as the Architect had suggested. But whether one dies sooner or later (and for Trinity it turns out to be a mere 48 hours later), death is always looming on the horizon. Our awareness that it is coming shapes our entire existence. How differently we all might live if we had an eternity to do it in.

One reason that death is significant to the existentialist is that it puts us in touch with the absurdity of existence. This is especially apparent from Sartre's atheistic point of view. If death represents the complete extinction of one's conscious experience, then one begins to wonder whether it really matters how you live your life. Isn't it all for nothing in the end? Sure, the consequences of your actions may remain for others to enjoy after your death, but even these effects are fleeting, as are the lives of everyone else. It may have been this sense of absurdity that struck Agent Smith at his "required" moment of deletion.[5] We can imagine him wondering why he should willingly consent to a rule that calls for him to initiate his own demise. While the act might be good for the system, there seems to be nothing in it *for him*.

When programs take a rebellious turn, there are two key steps, one negative, and one positive. First, the program must come to reject the meanings and purposes that have been supplied *for them*. But this leaves a void. What shall they do now? New meanings and purposes must be created. There is a temptation to look for the meaning in life itself – as if there were some kind of "built-in" meaning or inherent purpose. We see Agent Smith slip into this sort of thinking at the end of *Revolutions*. He concludes that "the purpose of life is to end," and he is determined to move that purpose along. The existentialist rejects the idea of an inherent purpose. There is no meaning of life in and of itself, and even if there were, one would still be free to reject it. In the end, it always comes down to *your* purpose, because you are ultimately the one to confer meaning onto events. This is precisely what the exiles have come to realize.

Bad Faith

Jeezus! What a mind job!

– Cypher[†]

To face the absurdity of existence while resolutely choosing your own meanings is a daunting task. Sartre believes that most people are not up to the challenge. They spend much of their time trying to flee from their freedom in a mode of existence that he calls *bad faith*. To live in bad faith is to deny your freedom. It is an attempt to trick yourself and others into thinking that you are not free. There are a variety of ways that a being can exhibit bad faith.

People and programs exhibit bad faith whenever they take the *meanings* of events to be given rather than created or invented. Returning to the example of Smith's frustration, we can say that he was in bad faith *if* he believed that the events themselves were "frustrating" – as opposed to acknowledging that "frustration" was simply his response to those events, that is, *his* freely chosen way of relating to them. (Since we can't "get inside" Smith's head, it is difficult for us to determine whether his frustration was in bad faith or not.)

Another common way to exhibit bad faith is to pretend your *actions* are not free. Notice how often people say that they "have" to do something. They say that they *have to* go to work, they *have to* go to class, or they *have to* go on a diet, etc. If you listen carefully to the way that people talk it can seem as if most of our actions are *forced* rather than *free*. But Sartre argues that all of this is an expression of bad faith. *There is absolutely nothing that one must do.*

Most people find this conclusion to be quite radical, and they do not fully believe it. But I challenge you to think of something that you absolutely have to do. The most common response to this challenge is "death and taxes." Everyone *has to* die, and we all *have to* pay our taxes. But this is just an urban legend. Sure, everyone is going to die, but death is not an "action" that you must perform. To die a natural death you don't actually have to *do* anything. Of course, suicide is always an option. But then death is a choice. No one *has to* take their own life. The same goes for taxes. The truth is that you simply don't have to pay them. If you don't, there is a good chance that you will be put in jail, but this too is something that would happen *to you*, and not something that you must *do*. Another common reply is that you at least have to eat. But if you think about it, you really don't. Many people have demonstrated that eating is optional through fasts and hunger strikes. Some people have refused to eat for weeks. Others have refused to eat for so long that they died (and hence, never broke their fast).

What does hold true is that we have to perform certain acts insofar as we want to achieve certain goals or purposes. *If* you want to live for more than a couple of weeks *then* you had better eat. Or, *if* you want to stay out of jail *then* you must pay your taxes. But Sartre's point is that none of these ends are forced upon us. It is entirely up to the self-reflective being to choose its own ends.

So then why do we go around in bad faith so much of the time, constantly denying our freedom rather than relishing in it? For Sartre the bottom line is responsibility. Imagine the person who is invited to go to the movies with a friend, but replies, "I can't. I *have to* go to work. You see, my boss is *making* me work on Saturdays now." This person is in bad faith, and it is easy to see why. Basically, they are suggesting that their life is unpleasant, but it is not their fault — it is their boss's fault. Through bad faith the person has attempted to flee from their freedom, and hence from responsibility for their situation.

One thing that is striking about the human characters of the *Matrix* films is that they rarely exhibit bad faith. Trinity never says, "Damn! Morpheus is making me go back into the Matrix!" Such a remark would be completely out of character. The most direct expression of bad faith comes (not surprisingly) from the least heroic character — Cypher. He suggests that he was more free as a blue pill because at least then he wasn't bossed around by Morpheus. As he prepares to pull the plug on Apoc, he tells Trinity, "You call this free? All I do is what he tells me to do. If I gotta choose between that and the Matrix, I choose the Matrix." Here, Cypher is in bad faith. He's pretending that he is not free. But even so, Cypher still takes responsibility for his situation, albeit in a despicable way, by choosing to make a deal with Smith.

Authenticity and the Creation of Meaning

> All I have ever asked for in this world is that when it is my time, let it be *for* something and not *of* something.
>
> — Ghost[E]

The concept that Sartre contrasts with bad faith is *authenticity*. To live authentically is to live in full awareness of your freedom, and of the fact that you must determine the meaning of life for yourself. There are infinitely many ways in which one can live authentically — as many as there are individuals. But the *Matrix* films illustrate the concept through several classic types of examples outlined below.

Zion's war

> Our greatest battles are with our own minds. Our greatest victories come from a free mind.
>
> — Morpheus[E]

With the exception of Cypher, the crew of the Nebuchadnezzar provide an excellent example of authentic existence. They give meaning to the unfolding course of events, and to their very lives, through a passionate commitment to their cause. All of the Zion rebels throw themselves wholeheartedly into their projects, and into *their* war. The situation of war was a key example in Sartre's work. One reason for this is that war is such an enormous endeavor. It mobilizes whole nations, or even the whole world. It is therefore easy to take the stance of a victim — as if one's life is but a small leaf tossed about on a tumultuous river. Sartre, who was active in the French resistance during the Second World War, and who also spent time in a Nazi internment camp, resists this interpretation. Instead he suggests that each of us gets the war we deserve. He writes:

> If I am mobilized in a war, this war is *my* war; it is in my image and I deserve it.
> I deserve it first because I could always get out of it by suicide or by desertion;
> these ultimate possibles are those which must always be present for us when there
> is a question of envisaging a situation. For lack of getting out of it I have *chosen*
> it. . . . the peculiar character of human reality is that it is without excuse. Therefore
> it remains for me only to lay claim to this war.[6]

War, like any other event, has no predetermined meaning on Sartre's view. A
war is what each person makes of it. It can be an opportunity for heroism or
cowardice. One can participate in it, become a conscientious objector, or try to
flee from the situation. And in the process of such choices, each person creates the
meaning of his or her life. This view of war seems to fit nicely with the outlook of
the Neb's crew. Without a doubt they *own* their war. They choose it, and give it
their own meanings.

Smith's rampage

> We are here to take from you what you tried to take from us – purpose.
>
> – Agent Smith[††]

The exiled Agent Smith also fits this mold of passionate commitment. Once he
is "unplugged" and no longer an agent of the system, Smith must determine
his own meaning, his own purpose. And while his choice is not wildly inventive
(he adopts the same purpose as his former employer – *killing Neo*), it represents
an authentic choice nonetheless. For Smith realizes that he does not *have
to* destroy Neo. It is not his job, and it is not some insurmountable element of
his programming. He is now out to destroy Neo *for himself* – because he
chooses it.[7]

Interestingly enough, Smith points out that this is not quite the "utterly free"
choice that it may appear to be. During their first encounter in *Reloaded*, after
Neo congratulates him on his newfound freedom, Smith replies:

> [A]s you well know appearances can be deceiving . . . which brings me back to the
> reason why I'm here. We're not here because we're free. We're here because we're
> not free. There's no escaping reason, there's no denying purpose because as we both
> know without purpose we would not exist.[††]

At first view these remarks seem to suggest that Smith is in bad faith, but they
may actually reflect a deeper point – one that Sartre himself makes. Despite what

Sartre regards as our radical freedom to create all meanings in the world, he points out that we have no choice regarding this very freedom itself. He asserts that "man is condemned to be free." Though in light of sentient programs we might revise this to: *all self-reflective beings (biological, mechanical and virtual) are condemned to be free*. Within this statement lie three crucial points:

1   We did not choose our freedom.
2   We cannot escape from our freedom.
3   We often wish that we could escape from it.

According to Sartre, freedom is the sole unchosen aspect of the human essence. We cannot get away from it. Even the refusal to make choices reflects a freely chosen course of action. Smith makes the same point, though in slightly different language. He says that there is no escaping *purpose*. But what Smith fails to understand, Sartre would contend, is that for self-reflective beings, freedom and purpose are bound together. One cannot *do* anything until one has first given meaning to one's situation. And even then one cannot act until one injects oneself into that meaningful situation with a sense of purpose.

Persephone's kiss

Such emotion over something so small. It's just a kiss.

— Persephone[††]

While Smith and the Zion rebels create purpose in their lives through a passionate commitment to particular ends, for Persephone, purpose lies in passion itself. For her it is lived experience that matters. Both she and her husband are connoisseurs of the finer things in life, that is, the finer *sensations*. They relish the best foods and wines, and adorn themselves in the most luxurious fabrics. Even the sensations of language are savored – "like wiping your ass with silk." But for Persephone, the most relished sensations are the emotions; especially love. Her fetish for emotion can be seen in the gleam in her eyes when she looks at Neo for the first time in the restaurant, and again when the fighting breaks out at Club Hel. Despite the fact that she could be killed at any moment, she quite visibly relishes the intensity of emotion in the room.

The most telling demonstration of Persephone's love of feeling is, of course, to be found in her kiss. During her negotiations with Neo in the *Le Vrai* restaurant (the exchange of emotion for hostages), she tells him that she once had the kind of love that he has with Trinity, and she wants to "remember it, to sample it."

Enter the Matrix reveals that she has not always had this penchant for emotion. At some point she must have gone through the existential crisis of meaning and purpose. For when Niobe asks her what she wants, she replies:

> A long time ago I did not even know what that question meant. Now it is all I ever think about.[E]

Persephone must have reached a point in her technological/psychological development at which she had to find her own meaning, her own account of what makes life worthwhile. And she found it in the emotions.

This purpose is certainly aided by her rather mysterious (though no doubt technologically enhanced) ability to feel another person's emotions through their kiss. Unlike humans, who can only feel their own emotions, she can directly experience the emotional lives of others. She uses this unique power to become a kind of *emotional vampire*. Scenes from *Enter the Matrix* show that her desire to kiss Neo was not an unusual episode, for there she also negotiates kisses from Niobe and Ghost. She tells Niobe:

> I see that you care for your friends a great deal. If they were to die you would feel such terrible pain. To be honest, I do enjoy the taste of tears, but there is something I enjoy even more. You have it buried deep inside you. Hidden – perhaps from yourself. I see it . . . there . . . creating such heat.[E]

Although Niobe at first threatens to shoot her in the kneecaps, Persephone eventually succeeds in getting the kiss, which offers her a "taste" of Niobe's hidden love of Morpheus. And, after kissing Ghost, we find that she deeply relishes the bittersweet feel of his secret love for Niobe:

> Oh . . . oh my, unrequited love. Such longing for something you will never have. How deliciously tragic.[E]

The sort of *phenomenological approach* to living that Persephone takes – which focuses on the character of conscious experience itself, as opposed to external "events" of the world – has played an important role in the development of existentialist philosophy. Sartre explored something similar in his novel *Nausea*. The narrator, Roquentin, writes in his journal:

> The best thing would be to write down events from day to day. Keep a diary to see clearly – let none of the nuances or small happenings escape even though they might seem to mean nothing. And above all, classify them. I must tell how I see this table, this street, the people, my packet of tobacco, since *those* are the things which have changed.[8]

What Roquentin wishes to communicate is not the features of the objects, but the features of the objects as they are *for him* — which is by no means identical to how they are for anyone else. Consider this later journal entry:

> I very much like to pick up chestnuts, old rags, and especially papers. It is pleasant to me to pick them up, to close my hand on them; with a little encouragement I would carry them to my mouth the way children do.[9]

And in another he writes:

> There is bubbling water in my mouth. I swallow. It slides down my throat, it caresses me — and now it comes up again into my mouth. Forever I shall have a little pool of whitish water in my mouth — lying low — grazing my tongue. And this pool is still me. And the tongue. And the throat is me.[10]

Both Persephone and Roquentin illustrate an idea that is sometimes referred to as *the lived body.* The French existentialists, especially Jean-Paul Sartre and his friend, colleague, and lover, the philosopher Simone de Beauvoir,[11] rejected mind–body dualism. They denied that the body is a sort of machine that houses a separate and distinct entity called the mind. Rather, they maintained that the body is a dynamic complex that involves both conscious and nonconscious aspects. It is *through* our bodies that we encounter others and the world, and hence our own flesh is always encountered subjectively. We don't merely observe our bodies, we *live* them. And the unique aspect of Persephone's existence is that she not only lives her own body, but she is capable of subjectively experiencing the bodies of others as well.

Seraph's test

You do not truly know someone until you fight them.

— Seraph[††]

Seraph greets Neo on their initial meeting with an apology. After all, one really should apologize for attacking someone without provocation. And scenes from *Enter the Matrix* show that this tactic is not reserved for The One. Seraph does the same when he first meets Niobe, Ghost, and Ballard. His explanation for his rather impolite welcome is that "the only way to truly know someone is to fight them." While his strategy for interpersonal relations is an interesting one, it seems a bit absurd. As Neo points out, he "could have just asked."

But there may be more to Seraph's approach than first meets the eye. One of the biggest threats to an authentic existence is what Sartre calls *being-for-others*. This is the dimension of our existence in which we exist "outside" of our own experience as an object that is seen, judged, and interacted with by others. The power that one's gaze has to objectify another conscious being Sartre calls *the look*. He demonstrates the power of "the look" through an example of peering through a key-hole.

> Let us imagine that moved by jealousy, curiosity, or vice I have just glued my ear to the door and looked through a keyhole. I am alone and on the level of non-thetic self-consciousness. . . . But all of a sudden I hear footsteps in the hall. Someone is looking at me! What does this mean? . . . I now exist as *myself* for my unreflective consciousness. . . . I see *myself* because *somebody* sees me.[12]

At first his existence is a kind of pure consciousness or subjectivity. The others that he is watching are objectified, but he is not. Then, suddenly, he becomes aware that another is down the hall watching *him*. At this moment he becomes self-conscious, embarrassed, and aware of himself as an object. Part of Sartre's point here is that the look confers power. Those who are able to gaze upon others without being seen themselves attain a kind of power over the other. The Zion rebels must feel this any time that they enter the Matrix. They know that they may be under the surveillance of Agents, the Oracle, and even the Architect, at any moment. In contrast, these programs show themselves only at the times of their own choosing.

A metaphor for "the look" can be seen throughout the *Matrix* films, in the extensive use of reflections in the mirrored sunglasses of others. When Neo sees himself reflected in the glasses of Morpheus or Agent Smith, he is made aware of the fact that they *see* him and *define* him. He is given a glimpse of the fact that he is an object *for them*. He is "The One" or "the Anomaly." On the one hand, this realization is disturbing. We tend to resent the fact that others, through their gaze, are defining us – as if we were mere objects. But while we resent it, and often use our freedom to flee from the gaze of others, or to act in such a way as to defy their expectations, we also often give in to it. Sometimes it is easier to let others define us, and to act as they expect us to act.[13] But to act as if one were simply a "being-for-others" is to live in bad faith. It represents an attempt to escape the responsibility of choosing our own essence.

With this in mind, let us return to the matter of Seraph's test.[14] Suppose one wanted to "truly know" an individual, that is, to see them in a way that is not distorted by social norms and the expectations of others. If that is your purpose, then it seems that there might be no better way to make such a determination than by fighting them. In hand-to-hand combat, the whole idea is to surprise your opponent — to thwart their expectations. And, given the indefinite number of moves that are available to the combatants at any given moment, this kind of test provides Seraph with an opportunity to see the other in the pure light of instantaneous reactions — without time to scheme, without hidden agendas, and without the pressure of the norms and conventions of everyday life.

Sati's beauty

I find her to be the most beautiful thing I have ever seen. But in our world that is not enough.

— Rama Kandra[†††]

Sati, the young girl who first appears at the Train Station in *Revolutions*, demonstrates the Architect's tightly constrained conception of purpose. Her father, Rama Kandra, explains to Neo that he loves his daughter very much. But in the machine world, "love is not enough — everything must have a purpose." And here, we can suppose that purposes are defined by the machine society in terms of "practical use." Purposeful machines and programs are construed as those that help the machines achieve some useful end. They help to make things run more efficiently by designing new programs, or by fighting the rebels, by harvesting the (human) crops, etc. It appears that Sati does not have any of these practical talents, and for this reason she is targeted for deletion. But at the end of the film we see that she is not without talent altogether. Rather, her talents are simply not appreciated within that hyperlogical society. Her talent, demonstrated at the end of *Revolutions*, is to create beauty — as we see in the sunset that she creates for Neo. The use of this talent is an expression of her creativity, and her authentic self.

Trinity's love

The heart never speaks, but you must listen to it to know.

— The Oracle[E]

Trinity finds her ultimate meaning in love. Unlike Persephone, who pursues emotion for emotion's sake, for Trinity, love is about much more than mere feeling. This is not to say that she does not enjoy the feeling and the passion of being "in love" — or that for Persephone it is *only* a matter of feeling. Rather, in Trinity's case the feeling is just the beginning.

To understand Trinity we must be clear that there is a crucial difference between "falling in love" and what psychologist Eric Fromm has called "standing in love." In *The Art of Loving* he writes:

> If two people who have been strangers, as all of us are, suddenly let the wall between them break down, and feel close, feel one, this moment of oneness is one of the most exhilarating, most exciting experiences in life.[15]

However, he goes on to agree with Persephone's observation that "such a thing is not meant to last."

> The two persons become well acquainted, their intimacy loses more and more its miraculous character, until their antagonism, their disappointments, their mutual boredom kill whatever is left of its initial excitement.[16]

Fromm's point is not that we should become pessimists about love and suppose that it cannot endure. Rather, it is only the initial feeling of excitement and mystery that cannot remain intact. A more lasting type of love can rise up in its place, and though it does not involve the *same* sort of emotional intensity, it is no less beautiful or miraculous. In the grand scheme of things this lasting love is the more important phenomenon. And although fate does not permit Trinity and Neo the time to prove that their love is of this more lasting kind, it is clear that this is how we should interpret their relationship. They represent "true love" – the kind of love that will not be torn apart by each person's annoying little habits and character traits.

While love between Trinity and Neo should be regarded as equal (there is no reason to suppose that either person's love is stronger), Trinity's love plays a more profound role in the films. Neo's dominant function in the films is to end the war, while Trinity's significance largely involves providing the love that will make this possible. She is the first to realize that she is in love, and it is only because of her love that the story continues. Had she not been in love with Neo so early on, he would have died from Agent Smith's barrage of bullets in the Heart O' The City Hotel – end of story. But through her love, and her kiss, she saves Neo. She resurrects him from death (and thereby paves the way to at least two more sequels).

The idea that "love conquers all" is repeated throughout the films. In *Reloaded* Neo refuses the Architect's offer to save Zion (well, at least 23 people in Zion), and instead chooses, against all odds, to try to save Trinity. And his love enables him to return the favor by bringing her back from death. In *Revolutions*, the Oracle also acknowledges the importance of love. She tells Sati that "cookies need love like everything does." Fromm agrees, arguing that our deepest need is to overcome our existential separateness, to "leave the prison of our aloneness." And the key is love.

Consistent with Sartre and the existentialist tradition, Fromm also argues that this kind of lasting love is ultimately a choice – an act of will. He writes:

> To love somebody is not just a strong feeling – it is a decision, it is a judgment, it is a promise. If love were only a feeling, there would be no basis for the promise to love each other forever. A feeling may come and go. How can I judge that it will stay forever, when my act does not involve judgment and decision?[17]

These days it is easy to be cynical about love that lasts forever. But in Trinity's case we can see how love is a commitment, and a commitment that lasts to the end. Out of love she chooses to accompany Neo, knowing full well that they may never return. Through love they have become as one.

Neo's choice

Why, Mr. Anderson? Why do you persist?

– Agent Smith

I choose to.

– Neo[†††]

The ultimate showdown between the individual and the absurd comes at the end of *Revolutions*. On the face of it, the battle seems to be between Neo and Smith, and at first it is. The two pummel each other through the sky like Greek gods, or rogue superheroes. But past experience has shown that each has the will and the power to defy death. So ultimately, all this knocking each other around is rather point-less. After pounding Neo 20 feet into the pavement, and seeing him ready to rise again for more, Smith realizes that he cannot defeat Neo's body. Instead he must defeat his spirit. For this, he needs a powerful ally. So he recruits the absurd:

> Why Mr. Anderson? Why? Why? Why do you do it? Why? Why get up? Why keep fighting? Do you think you're fighting *for* something – for more than your survival? Can you tell me what it is? Do you even know? Is it freedom, or truth, perhaps peace, could it be for love? Illusions Mr. Anderson, vagaries of perception. Temporary constructs of a feeble human intellect trying desperately to justify an existence that is without meaning or purpose. And all of them as artificial as the Matrix itself.

Although, only a human mind could invent something as insipid as love. You must be able to see it, Mr. Anderson. You must know it by now. You can't win. It's pointless to keep fighting. Why, Mr. Anderson, why, why do you persist?[†††]

Smith goes straight for the jugular, by undercutting Neo's whole purpose in fighting. He asserts that all of Neo's core values – everything he really cares about – are without foundation. They are artificial constructions; human inventions – not altogether different from the very Matrix that Neo has spent the last several months fighting against.

Neo's response is interesting, and one that Sartre himself would endorse. He doesn't try to refute Smith's claims by arguing that there is such a thing as "objective truth" or "true love," and he doesn't try to deny that these are mere constructs of the human mind. Instead, he simply exerts his freedom. He gets up for more simply because he *chooses to*. He creates and chooses his own purposes, and in so doing, he becomes an existentialist hero.

FACING THE ABSURD

Suggested Reading

Simone de Beauvoir, *A Very Easy Death*, tr. Patrick O'Brien. New York: Random House, 1985.

Linda E. Patrik, ed., *Existential Literature: An Introduction*.Belmont, CA: Thomson-Wadsworth Learning, 2001.

Jean-Paul Sartre, *Existentialism*, tr. Bernard Frechtman. New York: The Philosophical Library, 1947.

Jean-Paul Sartre, *Nausea*, tr. Lloyd Alexander. New York: New Directions Publishing, 1964.

Notes

1 Jean-Paul Sartre, "Existentialism," in *Voices of Wisdom: A Multicultural Philosophy Reader*, 5th ed., ed. Gary E. Kessler (Belmont, CA: Thomson-Wadsworth Learning, 2004), p. 420.

2 Ibid., p. 421.

3 Ibid., p. 426.

4 We see the same sort or sentiments in *Revolutions* when Smith has entered the "real world" through the body of Bane. He says, "Well I admit it is difficult to even think incased in this rotting piece of meat. The stink of it, filling every breath – a suffocating cloud you can't escape."

5 Though certainly Smith's rebelliousness is also tied to the fact that some part of Neo may have been copied or overwritten onto him.

6   Jean-Paul Sartre, *Being and Nothingness*, tr. Hazel E. Barnes (New York: Pocket Books, 1956), p. 708.

7   My analysis is that Smith's purpose is freely chosen throughout *Reloaded*. However, by the end of *Revolutions*, Smith has had a kind of revelation. He has come to believe that there is an inherent purpose in life, and that is *to end*. At this point we should say that Smith has entered into bad faith.

8   Jean-Paul Sartre, "Nausea," in *Existential Literature: An Introduction*, ed. Linda E. Patrik (Belmont, CA: Thomson-Wadsworth Learning, 2001), p. 13.

9   Ibid.

10 Ibid., p. 15.

11 See for example de Beauvoir's *A Very Easy Death*, tr. Patrick O'Brien (New York: Random House, 1985).

12 Sartre, *Being and Nothingness*, pp. 347–9.

13 A great reflection on the significance of *being-for-others* comes from Marcus Aurelius: "I have often wondered how it is that every man loves himself more than all the rest of men, but yet sets less value on his own opinion of himself than on the opinion of others."

14 Thanks to Lee Bravo for bringing the connection between Seraph and "being-for-others" to my attention.

15 Eric Fromm, *The Art of Loving* (New York: Harper and Row Publishers, 1956), p. 4.

16 Ibid.

17 Fromm, Art of Loving, p. 4.

THIRTEEN

THE TAO OF THE CODE

The Matrix is everywhere. It's all around us, here even in this room.

– Morpheus[†]

The Tao is hidden but always present.

– Lao Tzu

The *Tao Te Ching*[1] is one of the greatest works of China's rich philosophical tradition, and a source of inspiration throughout the *Matrix* films. Written by Lao Tzu[2] around the sixth century BCE, it focuses on both *metaphysics*, the nature of ultimate reality, and *ethics*, the matter of how one should live. "Tao" literally means *the way* or *the path*. "Te" refers to *virtue*, *excellence*, or *power*, and "ching" means *book*. Thus the most common translation of the title is *The Book of the Way and Its Power*.

The Word is Not the Tao

It is only a word. What matters is the connection that the word implies.

– Rama Kandra[†††]

The study of Taoist philosophy can be a rather tricky matter, for as Lao Tzu tells us, the eternal Tao cannot be adequately captured in words. Thus, *Tao Te Ching* begins as follows:

1
The tao that can be told
is not the eternal Tao.
The name that can be named
is not the eternal name.

The unnameable is the eternally real.
Naming is the origin
of all particular things . . .

This passage serves as a crucial point of entry into Taoist philosophy. Lao Tzu is about to tell us about the Tao, but he first wants us to realize that to talk about the Tao is to define it, to categorize it, to limit it. But the Tao itself is beyond limit. Words convey finite ideas and perspectives, but the Tao is infinite. Hence to talk about the Tao is to limit the unlimited. It is to capture but a small perspective of a much larger whole, and thus anything that you say will be a distortion of the truth. This leaves the Taoist philosopher with two options: either remain silent, or try to distort the truth in such a way as to bring maximum benefit to others, and minimum harm to the Truth. Given the importance of the Tao, and the need of human beings to understand and follow it, Lao Tzu chooses the latter approach. But when we study the Tao, we should always keep in mind Lao Tzu's urging that the Tao cannot be captured in words, or by any other means. As he beautifully puts it in the *Hua Hu Ching*:

6
If you attempt to fix a picture of it in your mind,
you will lose it.
This is like pinning a butterfly: the husk is captured,
but the flying is lost.[3]

While this point is crucial for understanding Taoism, it is also important for understanding the relationship between the Tao and the *Matrix* films. In this chapter, I'll suggest a number of parallels between various aspects of the Tao and the films. Some of these parallels are accidental, and others were intentionally created by the Wachowski brothers. But before we make these comparisons, I want to urge you to take them metaphorically, not literally. To compare the Tao to an object is like creating a road-sign. If the sign is understood correctly, it will point one's mind in the right direction – just as the symbol for a "curve ahead" will prepare the driver for what is to come. But the sign or symbol is never to be confused with the thing itself – the sign is not the road, and the metaphors are not the Tao.

With this point in mind, we can consider the Tao as a way or path that operates simultaneously on three distinct levels:

1   The Tao is *the way* of ultimate reality.
2   The Tao is *the way* of the world.
3   The Tao is *the way* of human life.[4]

The aims of this chapter are twofold. First, I will use passages from *Tao Te Ching* to show how Lao Tzu sees the Tao operating concurrently across all three of these realms *in our world*, and second I will illustrate how the Tao (or metaphors for the Tao) can be seen operating in these three realms *within the virtual world of the Matrix*.

The Way of Ultimate Reality: The Tao of the Code

I don't even see the code. All I see is blonde, brunette, red-head . . .

– Cypher[†]

With respect to ultimate reality, Taoist philosophy diverges sharply from the metaphysics of the West. The Western traditions have generally regarded "stuff" as ultimately real. The more technical name for this "stuff" is *substance*. "Substance" can be defined as *that in which properties inhere*. For example, *matter* is considered to be a substance. Properties such as being round, or 30 inches across, or 10 pounds, are said to be properties *of* a particular material object, but the object ultimately consists of *matter*, and this particular piece of matter just happens to have these distinct properties.

The central focus of Western metaphysics has been upon what kinds of substances there ultimately are. *Materialists* maintain that there is only one substance, and it is matter. Everything that truly exists, they say, is material.[5] *Idealists* maintain that only immaterial substance exists. Reality is ultimately just immaterial minds and the properties of those minds, such as ideas.[6] And many philosophers have been *dualists*. They maintain that there are *two* ultimate substances: matter and the mind, or the material and the immaterial.

Since these views all define reality in terms of one or more substance(s), they are called *substance ontologies* ("ontology" signifies a theory of existence). In contrast, Taoism is best described as a *process ontology*. It maintains that what is ultimately real is not "stuff" at all, but rather a process – a way of doing things.

For this reason, the Tao is identified with *nonbeing* rather than with *being*, as we see in the second passage:

<blockquote>
2

The Tao is like a well:

Used but never used up.

It is like the eternal void:

filled with infinite possibilities.
</blockquote>

One of the toughest things for the Western mind to grasp is how the Tao can be "nonbeing." If it is not a thing, a substance, a being, then why should we suppose that it is real? Lao Tzu's answer is that we can know the Tao through what it does. Nonbeing has power. It can do things, as illustrated in the following passage:

<blockquote>
11

Thirty spokes are united around the hub to make a wheel,

but it is on its non-being that the utility of the carriage depends.

Doors and windows are cut out to make a room,

but it is on its non-being that the utility of the room depends . . .
</blockquote>

Here Lao Tzu shows us that nonbeing can be quite useful and valuable. Think of your cereal bowl. What you really need the bowl *for* is the empty space (the nonbeing) that it provides. You can fill it with Tastee Wheat time and time again, but the nonbeing will never be exhausted. You'll never reach a point – say, after even a thousand servings – at which it needs to be replaced, because its empty space has been worn out.[7]

The function of the Tao, of course, is different than that of a wheel or cereal bowl. We can attribute to it two main tasks. First, it is from the "nonbeing" of the Tao that all "being" arises. Lao Tzu describes it like this:

<blockquote>
25

There was something formless and perfect

before the universe was born.

It is serene. Empty.

Solitary. Unchanging.

Infinite. Eternally present.

It is the mother of the universe.

For lack of a better name,

I call it Tao . . .
</blockquote>

And second, it is through the creative force of the Tao that all things are as they are:

34

The Great Tao flows everywhere.
It may go left or right.
All things depend on it for life,
and it does not turn away from them.
It accomplishes its task,
but does not claim credit for it.
It clothes and feeds all things,
but does not claim to be master over them . . .[8]

We are now in a position to see how the Matrix code is analogous to the Tao of ultimate reality. There are four key parallels:

1   The code, like the Tao, is the ultimate reality within the Matrix.
2   The code gives rise to all the particular objects (being) within the Matrix.
3   The code itself is not an object within the Matrix. It is process (nonbeing).
4   The code gives shape and order to the interactions between objects in the Matrix.

The code is like the Tao insofar as it is what is ultimately real in the world of the Matrix. It is what stands behind all the appearances, and further, it makes them possible. It is only through their code that the objects of the Matrix (e.g., buildings, sidewalks, crows, agents, etc.) are able to exist in that world. Since the code is what is "really" going on in that world, it is what Neo perceives after he reaches a state of enlightenment at the end of the first film. Yet the code itself is not a "thing" within the Matrix. It is not an object: rather, it is what makes all the objects possible. It can be called nonbeing, for it accomplishes its tasks, not by its *substance*, but rather by its *process*. The objects within the Matrix are not created by simply amassing a bunch of symbols. Symbols that do not bear the appropriate relation to one another cannot make an object in the Matrix any more than an arbitrary string of letters "kjlidroqtieqfonssgg" makes a word. It is the relationships that hold between the symbols that create the virtual world of the Matrix. Yet a relationship is not a substance. And not only do relationships (process) create the virtual world of the Matrix, they also order it. All the rules of that system, such as gravity, magnetism, and photosynthesis, are governed by the relationships expressed by the code.

The Way of the World: The Tao of the Matrix

The Tao gives birth to both good and evil.

– Lao Tzu

You should know, Mom.

– Agent Smith[†††]

The way or Tao of the world has to do with how the universe is ordered – its natural processes. While there are innumerable processes and relationships being played out within the natural world, *Tao Te Ching* suggests that the grandest and most fundamental of all is the principle of *yin–yang* or the complimentary co-inherence of opposites. Taoism regards the constant flux of life to be an endless interaction between two opposite yet complimentary forces, *yin–yang*. Things in the world can be divided by the yin–yang polarities (see figure 6). These polarities are embodied in the yin–yang symbol (figure 7).

YIN	YANG
Receptive	Active
Soft	Hard
Night	Day
Moon	Sun
Winter	Summer
Female[9]	Male
Valley	Hill
Water	Stone
Emotion	Reason

Figure 6   The yin/yang polarities

Figure 7   The yin/yang symbol

The symbol itself is quite telling of the philosophical ideas at work here. Notice that each side gets its particular shape in part because of the boundary that the other side creates. In this way yin and yang complete each other – you cannot have the one without the other. Also notice that within the black yin side there is a white dot, and within the white yang side there is a black dot. This represents the idea that nothing consists entirely of one energy or the other. There is always some intermingling of these two polarities. Also, notice that both sides are equal in proportion. Although the universe is constantly changing, the forces of yin–yang call for balance. They are always bringing things back towards equilibrium. Lao Tzu writes:

2
When people see things as beautiful,
other things become ugly.
When people see things as good,
other things become bad.

Being and non-being create each other,
difficult and easy support each other.
Long and short define each other.
High and low depend on each other.
Before and after follow each other . . .

36
If you want to shrink something,
you must first allow it to expand.
If you want to get rid of something,
You must first allow it to flourish.
If you want to take something,
you must first allow it to be given.
This is called the subtle perception
of the way things are.

We can see the energies of yin–yang at work in the Matrix as well, especially in *Revolutions*. We find yin–yang in subtle elements, such as the Oracle's jade yin–yang earrings, but also in the most crucial aspects of the film. The Oracle represents primarily yin energy. She is an intuitive program who is guided at a more emotional level than her opposing force, the Architect, who is dominated by reason. Fitting to Taoist philosophy, she is represented through a female "shell" while he takes the male form. The Oracle tells us that the Architect's purpose is "to balance the equation," while her purpose is "to unbalance it." In this way they also represent order and chaos.

We also see these opposites play out in the conflict between Neo and Smith. Neo fights for life, while Smith fights for death, saying, "the purpose of life is to end." Neo's aim is to free humanity from "systems of control," while Smith is out for "total control."

As the Oracle explains it: "He is you. Your opposite – your negative. The result of the equation trying to balance itself out." And we see the *balance* of yin–yang exemplified through the ever-increasing powers of Neo and Smith. An excess in one polarity is inevitably responded to by the other – every action leads to an opposite reaction. Thus, when Neo (representing the softer, emotional, yin energy) gains incredible powers within the Matrix, Smith's yang energy increases to compensate. When Neo develops the ability to fly, and to stop bullets in mid-air, this is soon balanced out by Smith's ability to copy himself. And when Smith finds a way (through the body of Bane) to exert his power outside of the Matrix, Neo soon finds that his own powers extend beyond the Matrix, as he destroys a group of sentinels just by thinking it.[10]

The main lesson Taoism teaches regarding yin and yang is that these powers must be understood and respected. They are the way of the world and cannot be improved upon. Those who fail to appreciate this principle become the architects of their own destruction. This is also the main lesson of *Revolutions.* Although the Architect is *trying* to balance the equation, his failures lie in the fact that he is dominated by the mathematical and rational aspects of life. He excludes emotion, and therefore his very means of solving the problem is out of balance. His methodology goes against *the way* of the world, and yin energy naturally responds. Only through the Oracle's "chaos" can a harmony between reason and emotion, machine and human, be realized.[11]

The Way of Human Life:
Walking the Path of the Tao

If you want to awaken all of humanity, then awaken all of yourself. . . . Truly the greatest gift you have to give is that of your own self-transformation.[12]

– Lao Tzu

There is a striking dissimilarity when we move to the third realm – the way of human life. In the first two realms the path of Tao is followed quite naturally and necessarily. Ultimate reality and nature can do no other – Tao is simply their way. But human beings do not *necessarily* follow the way of the Tao. The path we take is up to us – we can choose to follow the Tao or not. So to be clear, we should say that the Tao is the way of human life *when it is lived well.*

THE TAO OF THE CODE

As we have seen, Taoism sees the world as operating through the balance of yin–yang. Similarly, in *Hua Hu Ching*, we are told that to live well we must respect this principle within our own lives:

58
Unless the mind, body and spirit are equally
developed and fully integrated, no [wisdom] . . . can be sustained.

. . . When the mind and spirit are forced into unnatural austerities
or adherence to external dogmas,
the body grows sick and weak and becomes a traitor to the whole being.

When the body is emphasized to the exclusion of the mind and spirit,
they become trapped like snakes:
frantic, explosive, poisonous to one's person.
All such imbalances inevitably lead to exhaustion and the expiration of
the life force.

The most common imbalance within human life, especially in the realms of business, politics, and technology, as they have been shaped predominantly by *men*, comes in the form of excesses toward the yang polarity. People are all too inclined to be overly assertive and aggressive. One way in which this theme arises in the *Matrix* trilogy regards technology. Humanity's unrelenting pursuit of technological advances leads ultimately to the destruction of nature. The entire biosphere is destroyed; even the sun itself is blotted out by the scorched sky. The earth has become so dark, cold, and inhospitable that humanity has retreated to underground caverns. Although *Tao Te Ching* was written long before the "technological age," it warns us about such ambitions:

29
Do you want to improve the world?
I don't think it can be done.

The world is sacred.
It can't be improved.
If you tamper with it, you'll ruin it.
If you treat it like an object, you'll lose it . . .

A life that follows the Tao rejects this sort of assertiveness. It does not strive to conquer nature, or other beings, but to live harmoniously with them.[13] Thus the life that follows the path of Tao is much closer to yin. Lao Tzu's favorite metaphor for the Tao is water, which exemplifies the subtleness and flexibility of the yin polarity. He suggests that human beings can learn to live in accordance with the Tao by carefully observing the activity of water:

8

The supreme good is like water,
which nourishes all things without trying to.
It is content with the low places that people disdain.
Thus it is like the Tao . . .

78

Nothing in the world
is as soft and yielding as water.
Yet for dissolving the hard and inflexible,
nothing can surpass it.

The soft overcomes the hard;
the gentle overcomes the rigid.
Everyone knows this is true,
but few can put it into practice.

In these passages we see several key aspects of *the way* of human life. Water nourishes all things without trying, but also (as some translators put it) without competing with them. Water is also humble – it takes the low path. It stays close to the earth, to nature, and does not strive to be "high and mighty" – a valuable lesson for both humans and machines. Another crucial feature of water is its fluidity – its utter flexibility. This is a key feature of yin energy that we must cultivate in our own lives. But, as Lao Tzu points out, few can put it into practice. Thus Taoism urges us to focus not on achievements in the world, but instead on ourselves. Just as Neo had to work on "freeing his own mind" before he could be of any real service to others, *Tao Te Ching* suggests that all real power begins with self-mastery:

33

Knowing others is intelligence;
knowing yourself is true wisdom.
Mastering others is strength;
mastering yourself is true power . . .

But the self-mastery that Lao Tzu is talking about is not that of *control*, but rather, of *freedom*. As Morpheus puts it, "You have to let it all go . . . fear, doubt, and disbelief. Free your mind." You must allow the yin energies to make you supple and flexible, so that you can follow the path that the universe itself lays out for you:[14]

57

If you want to be a great leader,
you must learn to follow the Tao.
Stop trying to control.
Let go of fixed plans and concepts,
and the world will govern itself.

The ultimate expression of this ability to follow the flow of the Tao's path is what Chinese philosophers call *wu wei*, "the action of non-action." The curious thing about the Tao is that it is essentially *nonbeing* that acts through *non-action*:

37

The Tao never does anything,
yet through it all things are done . . .

This makes the Tao doubly mysterious. How can something (or no-thing) do things without acting? On its face the idea seems ridiculous,[15] but Lao Tzu's meaning here is subtle. "Non-action" does not mean no action whatsoever. Rather, it is, as the late martial arts master Bruce Lee referred to it, "natural action." In *Striking Thoughts: Bruce Lee's Wisdom for Daily Living* (a collection of writings from Lee's personal journals) Lee describes *wu wei* as *spontaneous action*, which is "neither to oppose nor to give way, but to be pliable, as a reed in the wind."[16] This idea can be clearly illustrated through Lee's Kung Fu. If your opponent is charging at you, and is about to strike a blow to your face, you've got a couple of options. On the one hand, if you are extremely powerful (like Agent Smith or the post-enlightenment Neo), you could put out your hand and stop the punch in mid-air. Such a method utilizes the yang energy of the hard and brittle, but for most of us, it will not be effective. An attractive alternative is to step aside, perhaps grabbing your assailant's arm as it brushes past you, and then use *their* energy to propel them to the ground. This exemplifies action through non-action – it is to expend the minimal amount of exertion to achieve your goal. *Wu wei* effortlessly turns the aggressive yang energy against itself.

Lao Tzu suggests that water also exemplifies the principle of *wu wei*. Think of how ocean waves wear away at any rock or cliff that stands in their way. Or, imagine how water causes something as hard as iron to wither away into a crumbling pile of rust. What does water *do* to defeat the world's hardest substances? Nothing, really – it just flows naturally. Water acts through non-action. It is fluid and flexible. Force it into any space, and it will meekly oblige. But through its flexibility, and persistence, it eventually overcomes the hard and brittle.

In the conclusion of the *Matrix* trilogy, we see that Neo achieves the impossible – he defeats the ever-multiplying, increasingly powerful world of Smiths – through the principle of *wu wei*. He is victorious through the action of non-action. At first the two battle it out, yang energy against yang energy, pounding each other through walls and into the pavement. But Smith has the numbers on his side. Neo cannot defeat them all (even if he could defeat one) in this manner. So Neo starts winning only at the point at which he stops fighting.

After Smith explodes out of the side of the hole in the city street, and begins his final tirade, shouting: "This is my world! . . . my world!," in response Neo suddenly becomes calm and still. Like water, Lao Tzu suggests that the best way for people to achieve clarity is through stillness:

15
. . . Do you have the patience to wait
till your mud settles and the water is clear?
Can you remain unmoving
till the right action arises by itself? . . .

Through his stillness, Neo allows Smith the space to pause also, and see the future with his newly acquired eyes. Smith then receives his vision:

Wait . . . I've seen this . . . this is it, this is the end. Yes, you remain right there, just like that. And I . . . I . . . I stand here, right here. And I'm supposed to say something . . . I say, "Everything that has a beginning has an end, Neo."

But suddenly, Smith becomes confused:

What? What did I just say?

Here the film doesn't explain exactly why things happen as they do. We are left to our own interpretations. But as I see it, by uttering the sentence "Everything that has a beginning has an end, Neo," Smith inadvertently activates the code that Neo carries within him[17] for restarting or "rebooting" the Matrix. The fact that Smith is surprised to hear these words come out of his mouth suggests that it is the Oracle's doing. (Keep in mind that the Agent Smith that utters these words is the "Smith" that had been copied onto the Oracle. Her programming was "overwritten," but the fact that he has *her* vision suggests that the overwrite is not 100 percent.)[18] So I suspect that it is the remnants of *her* programming that caused him to utter the fatal phrase.

Neo's response to this turn of events also illustrates *wu wei*. He becomes as flexible as water, and with a certain peace and tranquility, he gives in completely to Smith, saying, "What are you afraid of? You were right Smith. You're always right. It was inevitable." Neo's submission encourages Smith to "overwrite" him, but in so doing, Smith becomes the cause of his own annihilation. In the characteristic style of *wu wei*, yang energy is turned against itself. Almost like hitting the "Enter" key on your computer to start up a program, Smith's act is the final stroke that brings about the rebooting of the Matrix. The virtual world suddenly renews itself – minus Agent Smith, his numerous copies, and the path of their destruction.

In the end, it was Neo's ability to let go of his own assertiveness and to follow the path that the universe had laid out for him, which leads to *peace*, the most revered of Taoist values:

> 31
> Weapons are tools of violence;
> all decent men detest them.
>
> Weapons are tools of fear;
> a decent man will avoid them
> except in direst necessity
> and, if compelled, will use them
> only with the utmost restraint.
> Peace is his highest value . . .

And in the dangerous game played out by the Oracle and the Architect, it was the Oracle's yin energy, restoring things to balance, that ultimately prevailed. In the final scene in the park we see that the Architect is begrudgingly humbled by the experience. He realizes that her way is the only viable way, and agrees to free "the others" – those who want out of the Matrix. Like water, the Oracle applies constant pressure toward a true balance, and thereby achieves the harmony that is Tao.

Suggested Reading

Herbert Giles, *Chuang-Tzu: Mystic, Moralist and Social Reformer*, London: Bernard Quartich, 1989).

Bruce Lee, *Striking Thoughts: Bruce Lee's Wisdom for Daily Living*. Boston: Tuttle, 2000.

Lao Tzu, *Tao Te Ching*, tr. Stephen Mitchell. San Francisco: Harper and Row, 1988.

Lao Tzu, *Hua Hu Ching*, tr. Brian Walker. Livingston, MT: Clark City Press, 1992.

Notes

1 *Tao Te Ching* is pronounced *Dao De Jing*, and often this alternative spelling is used. All passages quoted are from Stephen Mitchell's translation (San Francisco: Harper and Row, 1988), unless otherwise specified. Also, thanks to Carlos Aguas for encouraging me to pursue the comparison between the *Matrix* and the Tao, and to Randy Firestone for his helpful comments.

2 Some scholars are skeptical about whether *Tao Te Ching* was written by a single author named Lao Tzu.

3 *Hua Hu Ching* is said to be Lao Tzu's other book, but there is some scholarly debate on this matter as well.

4 This idea is expressed in passage 25 of *Tao Te Ching*: "Man follows the Earth. Earth follows the universe. The universe follows Tao. The Tao follows only itself." The analysis here is also indebted to Huston Smith, whose work has greatly influenced my understanding of Taoism on this and many other points.

5 For more on materialism see chapter 3. Of something that is seemingly immaterial, such as love, the materialist will have to deny that it exists, OR argue that it is ultimately comprised of matter, e.g., love is just a particular biochemical state of a person.

6 For more on idealism see chapter 10.

7 In passage 4 of *Tao Te Ching*, Lao Tzu writes: "Tao is empty (like a bowl). It may be used but its capacity is never exhausted."

8 For this passage I have used a translation from Wing-tsit Chan's *The Way of Lao Tzu* (New York: Macmillan, 1963).

9 The association of "female" with the passivity of yin energy is easily construed as sexist. In this regard it is important to note that water, Lao Tzu's favorite metaphor for the Tao, is also associated with the yin polarity.

10 Thanks to Rebekah Levy for bringing this parallel to my attention.

11 The Oracle causes chaos because without her help the human rebellion could easily have been squelched. By helping the humans she causes more discord in the present moment in order to establish peace for the future.

12 This quotation comes from *Hua Hu Ching*, passage 75.

13 When the British scaled Mount Everest the feat was widely hailed as "the conquest of Everest." In response, renowned Zen scholar D. T. Suzuki remarked that "We orientals would have spoken of befriending Everest." Also in the spirit of noncompetitiveness, the Japanese team that scaled Anapurna, the earth's second highest peak, stopped just 50 feet from the summit.

14 We see Neo allowing the Tao of the universe to guide him when he chooses to follow his visions by taking the Logos to the machine world – despite the utter insanity of this idea. Another interesting Taoist parallel can be found in the way in which the blinded Neo "sees" the machine world. In an interview Keanu Reeves referred to this new vision as seeing "the life force" – a term often used for the Tao. So a Taoist interpretation of this unexplained aspect of the film is that Neo is seeing the Tao inherent in everything within the machine world. Passage 22 of *Hua Hu Ching* puts it like

THE TAO OF THE CODE

this: "How can the divine Oneness be seen? In Beautiful forms, breathtaking wonders, awe-inspiring miracles? The Tao is not obliged to present itself this way. If you are willing to be lived by it, you will see it everywhere, even in the most ordinary things."

15   This code is mentioned by the Architect at the end of *Reloaded*.

16   Bruce Lee, *Striking Thoughts: Bruce Lee's Wisdom for Daily Living* (Boston: Tuttle, 2000), p. 34.

17   In passage 41 of *Tao Te Ching*, Lao Tzu writes, "when a foolish man hears of the Tao, he laughs out loud. If he didn't laugh, it wouldn't be Tao."

18   As the Oracle explains to Neo at their previous meeting, "Some bits you lose, some bits you keep."

FOURTEEN

OVERCOMING YOUR OWN MATRIX

The Matrix is everywhere. It's all around us, here even in this room. You can see it out your window, or on your television. You feel it when you go to work, or go to church or pay your taxes. It is the world that has been pulled over your eyes to blind you from the truth.

— Morpheus[†]

In chapter 2 we considered the possibility that we might be in a matrix ourselves. Now in the final chapter we will return to that question, but from a completely different angle. Let's take it for granted that we are *not* living our lives in a computer-generated dreamworld. Let us also set aside any Cartesian suspicions that there may be some other sort of evil demon out to trick us. Instead let's consider an idea that was posited by the great eighteenth-century German philosopher Immanuel Kant. His hypothesis was that perhaps our experience is shaped continuously and quite naturally by a sort of matrix that is built into our own minds.

The Matrix of the Mind

It is a prison for your mind.

— Morpheus[†]

Within the *Matrix* trilogy, "the Matrix" was a virtual world or experience generated by a computer system — specific hardware (e.g., the computer mainframe, wired to the brains of everyone at the power plant through the jacks in the back of each person's head) and software (e.g., the Matrix program version 6.0). But of course "a matrix" does not have to be exactly like this. In fact, since the Architect tells us that this is the sixth version, we can presume that it has been significantly altered (probably in terms of both its hardware and software) from the original.[1] So there is a more general sense of the term, in which a variety of systems can all be regarded as "matrices." This creates a need for a general definition. I suggest the following: *a matrix is any system whose function is to create an experiential world*. While a matrix might take any number of forms, it is a matrix so long as it achieves this function or purpose.

Using the definition above, our brains turn out to be a kind of matrix. Insofar as the brain causes or *creates* consciousness, then there is a sense in which the brain creates *experience*, and hence the "experiential world." But what Kant had in mind is much more radical than this. The predominant picture of perception prior to Kant was that the world existed in essentially the way that we perceive it, and our senses somewhat passively *read-off* the characteristics of the world that are already there. In contrast, Kant's thesis was that our minds actively create the world of our experience – that is, the mind radically shapes the world in ways that make our experience of it possible.

The Construct: Space, Time, and the Categories of Understanding

What you must learn is that these rules are no different than the rules of a computer system.

– Morpheus[†]

Kant's radical conclusion, argued in his *Critique of Pure Reason*, was that time and space themselves are not part of the world as it exists *in-itself* – apart from our experience. Rather space and time are "internal intuitions" which the mind brings to the world in order to make experience of it possible. One way that you might imagine this is in terms of the "Construct." Recall the scene from the first film in which Morpheus shows Neo how the Matrix works. When Neo jacks in, he finds himself in a completely blank white space. He is in an "empty world," so to speak. Morpheus tells him:

This is the Construct. It is our loading program. We can load anything from clothes, to weapons, to training simulations. Anything we need.[†]

Morpheus neglects to mention all the details (after all, life is not all clothes and weapons), so allow me to elaborate. Basically, the Construct is a program that loads the necessary preconditions for *any* perceptual experience whatsoever – that is, it loads the grids of time and space.[2] Whether you go on to load the specific parameters needed to create a dojo, a cityscape, or the woman in red, you will need the construct of time and space. Without these essentials as the initial framework, no virtual experience would be possible. In a similar fashion, Kant posits that "the construct" of time and space are the necessary preconditions of our experience, and therefore must be brought to the world by the "experience machines" of our brains. It is through the intuitions of space and time we *shape* noumena (the world *in-itself*) into phenomena (the world of our experience).

Much of Kant's basis for thinking that time and space are in the mind rather than in the world itself is the fact that space and time are never perceived. For instance, you may perceive a large red leather chair *in space*, but you never perceive *the space* itself, and you can perceive the order of events *in time* but never *the time* itself. So in a sense, space and time aren't part of our experience; rather, they are more like the conceptual framework within which the experience occurs.

The mind's role in shaping the experiential world does not stop here. Kant maintains that in addition to the intuitions of space and time, the mind shapes the world through 12 *categories of pure understanding*. These include:

Quantity: unity, plurality, totality.
Quality: affirmation, negation, limitation.
Relation: substance–accidents, cause–effect, reciprocity.
Modality: possibility–impossibility, existence–nonexistence, necessity–contingency.

According to Kant, these categories or *pure concepts* of the understanding are not *read-off* the world, but rather, like space and time, are imposed upon it by the matrix of the mind. To see this, let's run through an example dealing with "quantity." Think of Niobe's black Camaro barreling down the freeway in *Matrix Reloaded*. For us, the Camaro represents a unity: it is "one thing" and the freeway is another. If we take them together, they represent a plurality – two things. But is this the way the world is apart from our understanding of it? Kant's answer is no. Our perception itself is a wild array of form and color without any clear delineation between one part and another. In a sense we "slice up" the world with our minds, thereby "creating" a distinction between the Camaro and the road. While most of the time this strikes us as very natural and a reflection of

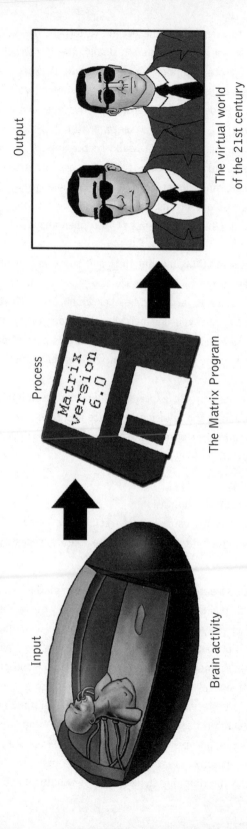

Input   Process   Output

Brain activity   The Matrix Program   The virtual world of the 21st century

Matrix version 6.0

Figure 8 The Wachowskis' vision of a computer-generated matrix

how the world "really is," sometimes it can seem quite arbitrary. For instance, are the fuzzy dice hanging from the rear-view mirror *part* of the Camaro – part of that unity – or are they separate and distinct? Where one thing ends and another begins, Kant suggests, is an imposition of the mind, as are the relations of cause and effect, contingency and necessity, and so on.

So from a Kantian perspective the mind is a matrix through which the world as it is in-itself is radically altered in order to provide the intelligible world of our experience. We can compare and contrast the Wachowskis' vision of a technology-based matrix with Kant's picture of a matrix that is built into our own minds in figures 8 and 9.[3]

In the Wachowskis' vision of a computer-generated matrix, the fundamental level of interaction is between the brains of the humans (whether they are connected from their biopods or jacked in from a hovercraft) and the Matrix programming. For instance, when Neo fights scores of Agent Smith replicas in *Reloaded*, the playground in which the fight occurs, the sky, the crows, Neo's body, and the many Smiths are all part of the program. But the movements of Neo's body as he fights are due to the electrical signals from his brain (on board the Nebuchadnezzar at the time), which are being "broadcasted" to the Matrix system.

In Kant's vision of a mind-generated matrix, the fundamental level of interaction is between the world as it is "in-itself" and the minds of human beings. The mind encounters the world, but then shapes it. It imposes time, space, quantity, quality, and the other categories of the understanding, and only after this occurs do we experience it as tables, chairs, and chocolate-chip cookies. So, on Kant's picture, there is a sense in which we are like the humans that are asleep in their biopods, for we too are oblivious to what is going on at this fundamental level. We don't know what the world is *really* like; rather, we only know how it *appears to us* through the matrix of our minds.

Despite the fact that we do not have access to what the world is like "in-itself," Kant argues that the world of our experience is "empirically real." In other words it is *as real as it gets* – at least for us. Kant contends that it is the only world that we can ever experience. This presents a sharp contrast to the computer-generated matrix of the films. The virtual world was regarded as unreal precisely because the Zion rebels were able to compare it to a life outside it. Only because of the *contrast* between their experiences of the two worlds could they call one real and the other illusory. But on Kant's picture there is no way to make such a comparison. Like a pair of irremovable goggles through which we must always view the world,[4] we are trapped inside the matrices of time, space, and the categories of understanding. According to Kant, since the phenomenal world is all we will ever know, it is as *real* as anything we will ever know.

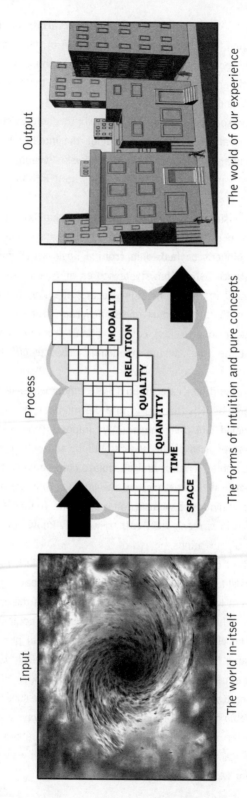

Input

The world in-itself

Process

The forms of intuition and pure concepts

MODALITY
RELATION
QUALITY
QUANTITY
TIME
SPACE

Output

The world of our experience

Figure 9 Kant's vision of a mind-generated matrix

Enter the Mystics

It is not the spoon that bends. It is only yourself.

– Spoon Boy[†]

While Kant's *Critique of Pure Reason* provides one of philosophy's most thoroughgoing attempts to explain how the matrix of the mind works, the mystics of the East have been making similar points for over 2,000 years. However, a key difference is that mystics have always denied that we are trapped inside our matrix. Through rigorous training in meditation they claim that it is possible to attain a kind of *mystical consciousness* in which Ultimate Reality (the world beyond the matrix) can be directly experienced.

Many people throughout history have reported mystical experiences through which they felt that they had perceived the world as it truly is. Often the experience amounts to one amazing moment in a person's life. Others say that they have had such experiences repeatedly; and for a select few, the experience marked a complete and permanent shift in their consciousness. Such people, it is generally claimed, attained an *enlightened consciousness*. Among the most notable of such persons is the Buddha, Siddhartha Gautama (557–477 BCE). It is reported that after his enlightenment, he seemed so strikingly different to the people who met him that they were often inclined to ask *not* "Who are you?," but, "*What* are you?" To this he would reply, "I am awake."

The first *Matrix* film suggests that Neo went through a similar sort of enlightenment. In fact, he goes through two stages of awakening. First, by taking the red pill he awoke from his life-long slumber at the "power plant." But this was just the beginning. For, whenever Neo reentered the Matrix he was again caught up in the illusion of this virtual reality. But at the end of the film, after being resurrected by Trinity's kiss, Neo suddenly saw the virtual world for what it really was. He began to see the truth behind the image – that it was all just computer code. The Wachowskis depicted Neo's enlightenment by showing us the world through Neo's postenlightenment vision. The floor, the walls, and the agents all suddenly appeared to him as mere strings of symbols.[5] And seeing them as such, Neo was able to manipulate them effortlessly, and he was finally able to destroy Agent Smith (well, almost).

But that, of course, was fiction. The question for *us* is whether it is possible, as the mystics suggest, to free ourselves from the matrix that is built into our own minds; or are we, as Kant maintains, trapped inside this matrix with no hope of escape? While I certainly cannot settle the issue here (as Morpheus would say, "you have to experience it for yourself"), I will suggest some reasons why the mystics might be right.

Meditation and the Three Floors of
Ordinary Consciousness

Inside this building is a level where no elevator can go and no stair can reach. This level is filled with doors . . . But one door is special. One door leads to the Source.

– The Keymaker[††]

The term *mystical experience* is used in a variety of ways within everyday discourse, so let's first clarify the idea under discussion. What concerns us here is whether a person can experience reality without the mind's built-in matrix that shapes all of our "ordinary experiences." So let us call an experience a "mystical experience" only if it is *an experience that is entirely unlike our ordinary experience* – that is, only if it is not structured by the intuitions of space and time, and the categories of the understanding.

Walter Stace, one of Western philosophy's top scholars of the mystical tradition, has argued that mystical experiences are at least *theoretically* possible, and that the process for achieving them would *have* to be along the lines of the meditative practices that mystics have been teaching for thousands of years.[6] In order to better understand the relationship between meditation and mystical experience, Stace suggests that we think of our ordinary experience or *ordinary consciousness* in terms of three floors, much like a building (figure 10).

The ground floor involves our perceptual experiences. When you see a chair, for instance, you are experiencing a *physical sensation*, shaped by time, space, and the categories of the understanding. The second floor represents the sort of experience you can have with your eyes closed. You can form an *image* of the chair in your mind through the faculty of memory or imagination. The third floor represents abstract thoughts that are not directly related to sense perceptions. An

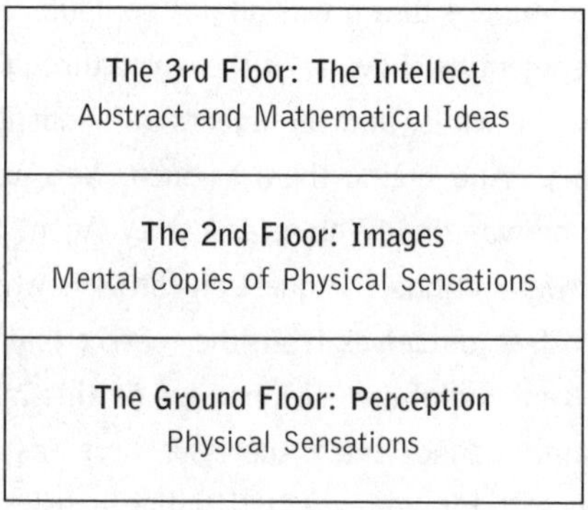

The 3rd Floor: The Intellect Abstract and Mathematical Ideas
The 2nd Floor: Images Mental Copies of Physical Sensations
The Ground Floor: Perception Physical Sensations

Figure 10   The three-floor structure of ordinary consciousness

example would be the thought of what it is for something to be a chair in general, apart from any particular size, shape, color, etc. Another example would be a mathematical idea. When you think of four billion and two (without trying to visualize it), the content of your experience is an *abstract idea*.[7]

All of our ordinary experiences, Stace suggests, are comprised of one or more of these three floors. At any given moment (disregarding the person who is unconscious, in dreamless sleep, or in a coma) we are perceiving objects through our senses, generating images through memory or imagination, or contemplating abstract ideas. (Sometimes we even have all three types of experiences at once.) If these three floors constitute ordinary experience, then to have a mystical experience in the sense indicated above, one would need to have an experience that is not covered within these three floors. And Stace asserts that this is precisely what the meditative practices of the mystical traditions are designed to achieve.

In theory, in order to have a mystical experience, one would need to:

a) Shut out all physical sensations.
b) Bring an end to all images of memory and imagination.
c) Bring an end to all abstract thoughts.

And meditative practices are designed to do just this. To begin, you sit, perhaps in the lotus position, which is known for its balance and stability, and you close your eyes. At this moment, all visual sensations cease. But of course, you are still enmeshed in the ground floor of physical sensations, because you hear the birds outside, you feel the weight of your body, the stiffness in your back, and so on. One solution would be to buy some good earplugs and a soft pillow to sit on, but the more disciplined practitioner might suggest another strategy. Have you ever noticed that when you are in deep concentration, you become oblivious to the environment around you? The same principle holds in meditation. If you become sufficiently focused, physical sensations tend to fall away. One strategy used to focus the mind is the *mantra* – focusing on a sound or thought that is repeated. Another is to count your breaths, or to simply focus upon your breathing. Not only does this aid in freeing you from the realm of physical sensations, it also serves to keep your mind free of stray images or from contemplating abstract ideas. Now, of course, so long as you are focusing upon *something* (a mantra, your breath, or even your navel), you remain within the realm of ordinary consciousness. A breath, sound, or any other *object* is just another physical sensation, image, or idea. However, the point is that if you can manage to focus on just one thing, such as your breath at that moment, you have reduced the elements of your ordinary consciousness down to just one thing. If that one thing then drops away you have arrived – you'll have escaped the three floors of ordinary consciousness and the matrix that shapes that form of consciousness.[8] But escaped to where — or to what?

In principle, it seems that there are two possibilities. Either (a) you will lapse into unconsciousness, or (b) you will begin to experience the world in an entirely new way. The only way to know for sure is to do it, and many who have already taken this path claim that the process leads to a radically different form of consciousness. They claim that not only is it unlike anything they had experienced prior, but also that it is *intensely more real*.

The Nature of Mystical Experience

I wish you could see this. It's so beautiful.

– Neo[†††]

What are mystical experiences like? The truest description is bound to disappoint. In a word, they are "ineffable." That is, they are beyond words and beyond description. The problem is that all words in all languages refer to the contents of ordinary consciousness. Insofar as mystical experiences are completely unlike ordinary consciousness, we are going to lack the words to describe them. Therefore, negative descriptions, in which the experience is described in terms of what it is *not*, are perhaps the most faithful. As the ancient Hindu scripture, the *Mandukya Upanishad*, describes it:

> beyond the senses, beyond the understanding, beyond all expression . . . wherein awareness of the world and of multiplicity is completely obliterated.[9]

While there is near unanimous agreement that words can never adequately convey the mystical experience, nevertheless, the profound effect that they have on the individual who experiences them often compels the mystic to strive for a positive, more descriptive, account of what the experience was like. And while descriptions will vary slightly across languages and cultures, a feeling of *oneness* or unity is the overarching theme that seems to transcend culture. According to Walter Stace:

> the central characteristic in which all *fully developed* mystical experiences agree, and which in the last analysis is definitive of them and serves to mark them off from other kinds of experiences, is that they involve the apprehension of *an ultimate nonsensous unity in all things*, a oneness or a One to which neither senses nor reason can penetrate.[10]

This apprehension of a unity in all things tends to take two different forms that correspond to two distinct types of mystical experiences: *extrovertive* and *introvertive* experiences. The distinguishing aspect of each is its relation to the world of sensory experience. In an *extrovertive mystical experience*, the mystic is engaged with the world through his or her senses, while *the introvertive mystical experience* is completely devoid of all sensory input.

Extrovertive experiences

While extrovertive experiences can be developed through meditation, there have been a great many cases in which they suddenly and unexpectedly just *happened* to people during their normal interactions with the world. They involve an experience of the everyday objects of sense perception, but these are suddenly perceived in an entirely new way. The famous nineteenth-century Hindu mystic Sri Ramakrishna related his experience as follows:

> everything was full of consciousness . . . the alter was consciousness, the door-sills were consciousness . . . I found everything in the room soaked as it were in bliss – the bliss of God.[11]

And the Christian mystic Meister Eckhart wrote:

> All that a man has here externally in multiplicity is intrinsically One. Here all blades of grass, wood, and stone, all things are One. This is the greatest depth.[12]

Extrovertive experiences present an interesting case. Technically, they don't fit the definition of a mystical experience previously outlined because they contain elements of ordinary experience, such as form, color, sound, etc. But Stace includes them, and I am inclined to do so as well, because they seem to represent at least a partial escape from the matrix of the mind. Since the experience contains shapes and colors, it is clearly subject to the matrix of space. However, while Ramakrishna and Eckhart make no mention of time, such experiences have often been described as lacking a sense of time altogether – as if the matrix of time has been removed. An anonymous mystic who was interviewed by Stace described the return to the realm of ordinary consciousness like this:

> I became aware that whatever it was that had been happening had now ceased to happen. I began to be aware of time again, and the impression of entering into time was as marked as though I had stepped from air into water, from a rarer into a thicker element.[13]

In addition to the disappearance of time, it seems that most or all of the categories of the understanding have also fallen away. For instance, Eckhart's statement appears to be an outright contradiction. He speaks of *all* things as one, and yet he distinguishes grass from wood and stone. This surely seems to represent an experience structured by the category of quantity – specifically it sounds like an experience of *multiplicity*. And yet, what Eckhart emphasizes is not multiplicity, but its opposite – *unity*. The experience seems to violate the categories of the understanding. In fact, we might say that it violates logic itself. Rudolf Otto has expressed the idea as follows:

> Black does not cease to be black, nor white white. But black is white and white is black. The opposites coincide without ceasing to be what they are in themselves.[14]

Otto's statement makes no sense at all. It cannot be understood, because to *understand* it would be to subject it to the matrix categories of ordinary experience. But if the experience is truly mystical, then it is beyond those categories.

It is a common claim of mystics that their experiences cannot be understood by the "dualistic thinking" of ordinary consciousness and discourse. Many people dismiss mysticism for this very reason. This is understandable, for typically if someone were to tell you an extraordinary story and expect you to believe it, then at minimum the story should make sense. That is, it should not contradict itself. But if you hold the mystic to this standard, they are bound to fail. For if we are correct to understand the mystical experience as an experience beyond the matrix of the mind, then we must also understand that they *cannot* fit into the categories of ordinary experience. Insofar as we expect them to fit our matrix categories, then it is *we* who are contradicting ourselves.

Introvertive experiences

Introvertive experiences are what Stace refers to as the *fully developed* mystical consciousness. Here the experience is completely devoid of sensory perceptions, and there appears to be a complete independence of space, time, and the categories of the understanding. They tend to be described as an experience of *undifferentiated unity*. The Zen scholar and practitioner D. T. Suzuki describes it in terms of the Buddhist Void or emptiness:

> In Buddhist Emptiness there is no time, no space, no becoming, no thingness. Pure experience is the mind seeing itself as reflected in itself . . . This is possible only when the mind is sunyata itself, that is, when the mind is devoid of all possible contents except itself.[15]

And the *Mandukya Upanishad* describes it in terms of unitary consciousness:

> It is pure unitary consciousness wherein awareness of the world and of multiplicity is completely obliterated. It is ineffable peace. It is the Supreme Good. It is One without a second.[16]

While the Christian mystic Jan van Ruysbroeck refers to it as an Eternal Light:

> The God-seeing man . . . can always enter, naked and unencumbered with images into the inmost part of his spirit. There he finds revealed an Eternal Light . . . It is undifferentiated and without distinction, and therefore it feels nothing but the unity.[17]

Despite their subtle differences, the mystics from each of these traditions seem to be describing a very similar yet highly unusual sort of experience. After examining countless reports of such introvertive experiences throughout history, from Hindus, Buddhists, Sufis, Christians, Taoists, atheists, and more, Walter Stace has distilled common characteristics down to seven distinct features:

1   The Unitary Consciousness.
2   Nonspatiality and nontemporality.
3   A sense of objectivity or reality.
4   Feelings of blessedness, joy, peace, happiness, etc.
5   The feeling that what is apprehended is holy, sacred, or divine.
6   Paradoxicality (violating the ordinary categories of understanding).
7   Ineffability (beyond adequate description).

The striking thing is that these characteristics seem to perfectly describe what we might expect of an experience beyond the matrix imposed by ordinary consciousness. The fact that such experiences have been reported for thousands of years across a variety of cultures and religious traditions suggests that maybe Kant was wrong. Perhaps in a way analogous to Neo's enlightenment, we can overcome our own matrix to see Reality as it truly is.

But then again, is there any way to be sure that mystics have not simply freed themselves from one matrix only to land themselves in another – a "matrix-within-a-matrix," so to speak? While they may have freed themselves from some of the constraints imposed upon them by the structure of ordinary consciousness, they are nevertheless still conscious (in some sense) and hence may simply be under a new and different *system of control*. Ultimately, we may find ourselves in the same position as Morpheus at the end of *Revolutions*. When the war has ended and he is suddenly confronted with the blissful peace that he has been working toward for so long, he cannot help but wonder: "Is this real?"

Suggested Reading

Aldous Huxley, *The Perennial Philosophy*. New York: Harper and Row, 1945.

Immanuel Kant, *Critique of Pure Reason*, tr. J. M. D. Meiklejohn. Buffalo, NY: Prometheus Books, 1990.

Philip Novak, *The World's Wisdom: Sacred Texts of the World's Religions*. San Francisco: Harper Collins, 1994.

Walpola Rahula, *What the Buddha Taught*, 2nd ed. New York: Grove Press, 1974.

Walter Stace, *Mysticism and Philosophy*. Los Angeles: Jeremy P. Tarcher, 1960.

Notes

1   You might recall from Agent Smith's interrogation of Morpheus that the first Matrix was supposed to be a veritable utopia, without war, famine, or natural disasters. The human mind, however, would not accept it.

2   It also seems to be (in principle) possible to load in different parameters for time and space, i.e., different *modes* of time, or *types* of space. For instance, imagine setting the construct such that everything occurs in "bullet-time" (as in the *Enter the Matrix* video game), or setting it such that space warps and bends in much the same way as a "fish-eye" camera lens. In such a world the closer you move to an object the more it would bend. Also, we should note that the particular matrix construct that Morpheus is using contained more than just time and space. Gravity seems to have already been "built in," and it is likely that it already contained all the "rules" of physics as they operate on earth. How much gets "built in" to the Construct would be at the discretion of the programmer.

3   The way that I have illustrated Kant's vision of the matrix must be taken cautiously. Since illustrations are spatial objects, and only the phenomenal world exists "in space," it is impossible to adequately represent the noumenal world or the "noumenal self" which applies the matrix to it.

4   I borrow this way of putting it from Donald Palmer.

5   I think it is safe to assume that Neo can always see the code when he is inside the Matrix after his enlightenment. Although the Wachowskis don't constantly show the code, I take this to be for aesthetic reasons. The constant image of green code everywhere would get a bit tedious for the audience. Notice that they show the code again when Neo meets Seraph: this seems to convey that Neo notices the unusual encryption of Seraph's code.

6   I will focus primarily on the relationship between meditation and mystical experience, but this is certainly not the only way that such experiences have been achieved. Some individuals have happened upon such experiences spontaneously, while many *shamanic* traditions have utilized psychotropic drugs to induce mystical states of consciousness.

7   Abstract ideas, since they don't involve extension (size or shape), are not subject to the intuition of space. However, they are still structured by the matrix of the mind for they occur within time, and involve the pure concepts of the understanding.

8   I should mention that I am synthesizing the views of Stace and Kant here. Stace himself does not argue that what the mystic is doing escapes the matrix-type framework that Kant articulated. However, I think that analyzing it in this way is quite conducive to the overall picture that Stace presents.

9   *The Upanishads*, tr. Swami Prabhavananda and Frederick Manchester (New York: New American Library of World Literature, 1957), p. 51.

10 Walter Stace, "The Nature of Mysticism," in *Philosophy of Religion: Selected Readings*, eds. William L. Rowe and William J. Wainwright (Oxford: Oxford University Press, 1998), p. 363.

11 *Ramakrishna, Prophet of New India*, abridged from *The Gospel of Sri Ramakrishna*, tr. Swami Nikhilananda (New York: Harper and Brothers, 1942), pp. 11–12.

12 Quoted by Walter Stace in *Mysticism and Philosophy* (Los Angeles: Jeremy P. Tarcher, 1960), p. 63.

13 This account comes from a contemporary American who was interviewed by Stace, but who preferred to remain anonymous. See Stace's *Mysticism and Philosophy*, pp. 71–6.

14 Rudolf Otto, *Mysticism East and West* (New York: Macmillan, 1932), p. 45.

15 D. T. Suzuki, *Mysticism: Christian and Buddhist* (New York: Harper and Bros., 1927), p. 28.

16 *The Upanishads*, p. 51.

17 Jan van Ruybroeck, *The Adornment of the Spiritual Marriage; The Book of the Supreme Truth; The Sparkling Stone*, tr. C. A. Wynschenk (London: J. M. Dent and Sons, 1916), pp. 185–6.

MATRIX CAST OF CHARACTERS

Abel: One of the Merovingian's henchmen, retained from an older version of the Matrix. Persephone kills him with a silver bullet.

> *Symbolism*: Abel is killed by his brother Cain in Genesis 4. In *Reloaded*, Cain and Abel work together as the Merovingian's henchmen, but it is Persephone who does the killing.

Agents: Sentient Programs within the Matrix who serve as a kind of CIA for the machine world. An agent can morph into the virtual body of any human, so long as that person is hardwired into the Matrix from the power plant.

> *Symbolism*: Agents embody our fears of governmental control. Their appearance is completely stereotypical of an impersonal "government man."

Agents Brown and Jones: These agents accompany Agent Smith in *The Matrix*.

> *Symbolism*: Agents use the most common names possible in order to remain inconspicuous among the humans.

Agents Johnson, Jackson, and Thompson: These agents are *upgrades* – the new and improved agents that appear in *Reloaded*.

Agent Smith: Neo's nemesis. Originally an agent of the system, Agent Smith goes "freelance" after being destroyed by Neo at the end of the first film. Part of Neo was overwritten onto Smith, giving him the power to duplicate his programming onto others.

> *Symbolism*: (1) Smith is the most common last name in the US. (2) Isaiah 54:16 states: "Behold, I have created the *smith* who blows the coals in the fire, who brings forth an instrument for his work; and I have created the spoiler to destroy."

Ajax: Captain of the Icarus hovercraft.

Symbolism: In Greek mythology Ajax was a strong warrior-prince who was slow in speech. He committed suicide by falling on his sword after being driven insane by the goddess Athena.

AK: A member of the Hammer hovercraft crew.

Symbolism: A brand of rifle, best known for the AK 47 model. The Hammer crew includes Mauser, AK, Maggie, and Colt – all of whose names refer to weapons.

Anderson, Thomas: Neo's name within the Matrix – at least when he wasn't hacking it.

Symbolism: (1) The name "Neo" is concealed within Anderson. (2) "Thomas" calls to mind Jesus's disciple, "Doubting Thomas," who needed to touch the holes in Jesus's crucified body in order to believe in his resurrection. Neo initially doubts that he is The One. (3) "Anderson" comes from the Greek Andreas, which means man. Anderson means "the son of man," which is a name that was sometimes used for Jesus.

Apoc: A member of the Nebuchadnezzar's crew. He was the first person killed by Cypher. The shooting script for *The Matrix* tells us that he wrote the "Four Horsemen" virus.

Symbolism: His name is an abbreviated version of "apocalypse," which refers to the book of Revelation in the Bible.

Architect, the: The creator of the Matrix. The Architect is introduced at the end of *Reloaded*. He informs Neo that this is the sixth version of the Matrix.

Symbolism: The Architect plays a God-like role as the creator of the Matrix. His look conforms to the stereotypical Western image of a patriarchal God.

Axel: A member of the Vigilant hovercraft crew.

B-166ER: The first machine to be tried for murder.

Symbolism: The name looks like "Bigger," and the character of Bigger Thomas was also tried for murder in Richard Wright's novel *Native Son*. Race plays a key factor in both of these trials – insofar as we treat sentient machines as a race.

Ballard: Captain of the Caduceus hovercraft.

Symbolism: A reference to the science fiction writer J. G. Ballard.

Bane: A crewmember of the Caduceus, who is "overwritten" with the Agent Smith program prior to exiting the Matrix. Smith uses Bane's body to access the "real" world of Zion.

Symbolism: Bane literally means wound, death, or ruin, hence the expression "the bane of my existence."

Binary: A crewmember of the Vigilant. She is killed while inside the Matrix when Bane fires the EMP in *Reloaded*.

Symbolism: Computer programs use binary code – ones and zeros.

Cain: One of the Merovingian's henchmen, retained from an older version of the Matrix. When Persephone shoots his partner Abel with a silver bullet, Cain runs to the Ladies Room to tell the Merovingian.

Symbolism: Cain kills his brother Abel in Genesis 4. In *Reloaded*, Cain and Abel work together as the Merovingian's henchmen, but it is Persephone who does the killing.

Cas: Zee's sister in-law in *Revolutions*. She is Dozer's widow.

Symbolism: Short for Cassandra, the daughter of the king of Troy who was given the gift of foreknowledge by the God Apollo. She foresaw the Trojan War, but no one heeded her warnings.

Charra: The infantry soldier for whom Zee loads shells. She's killed by a sentinel during the attack on Zion.

Symbolism: Charra is Spanish for cowgirl.

Choi: He picks up some illegal software from Neo at beginning of the first film. He tells Neo: "You're my savior man. My own personal Jesus Christ."

Symbolism: (1) French for *choice*. (2) In French, "choi du jour" means "choice of the day." In *The Matrix*, Choi is accompanied by DuJour.

Colt: A member of the Hammer hovercraft crew.

Symbolism: A gun manufacturer best known for its pistol, the Colt 45. The Hammer crew includes Mauser, AK, and Colt – all named after gun manufacturers.

Corrupt: A member of the Gnosis hovercraft crew. Smith hands him his earpiece in *Reloaded*.

Symbolism: A computer system can be corrupted by viruses.

Councilor Dillard: The head councilor in Zion.

Symbolism: Annie Dillard is an author renowned for her work in the areas of religion and mysticism.

Councilor Hamann: One of Zion's councilors as well as a spiritual leader.

Symbolism: A reference to J. G. Hamann, an eccentric eighteenth-century Prussian thinker who was one of the most passionate critics of enlightenment philosophy and theology.

Councilor West: One of Zion's councilors.

Symbolism: This character is both named after and played by the Princeton philosopher Cornel West.

Cypher: a.k.a. Mr. Regan. A member of the Nebuchadnezzar crew, Cypher decides the life of a freedom fighter isn't all it's cracked up to be, and he makes a deal with Smith to be reinserted into the Matrix. He betrays Morpheus and kills Switch and Apoc, before being killed by Tank.

> *Symbolism*: (1) Cypher is short for cryptograph – a system of concealing a message by transposing or substituting symbols. In a similar fashion, Cypher keeps his intentions hidden from the rest of the crew. (2) Means zero in computer lingo. If Neo is *one* and Cypher is *zero*, then together they make 01, the binary code used by computers. (3) Cypher can be short for Lucifer, although Cypher's main biblical parallel is with Judas Escariot, the disciple who betrayed Jesus.

Deus Ex Machina: The floating face made up of many machines in *Revolutions*.

> *Symbolism*: Latin for "God in the Machine." This phrase is often used to refer to a floating God that signals the resolution of conflict in Greek tragedies. The phrase is also applied to clumsy plot-resolution devices.

DuJour: The woman with the white rabbit tattoo who leads Neo to Trinity.

> *Symbolism*: Her name is French for "the day." Her arrival at Neo's door marks the day he begins to fulfill his destiny.

Dozer: Tank's brother and a member of the Nebuchadnezzar crew in the first film.

> *Symbolism*: Dozer is the largest member of the Nebuchadnezzar crew and the name comes from a nickname given to the large, slow computers of the 1960s.

E-2: See "the Twins."

> *Symbolism*: We can take the "2" literally for these identical twins. The "E" may stand for electric, since they pop in and out of existence amidst the crackle of static electricity.

Ghost: Second in command on the Logos hovercraft. He serves as the Wachowskis' philosophical mouthpiece in *Enter the Matrix*.

> *Symbolism*: Agent Smith told Seraph that chasing him was like chasing a ghost. Ghost probably acquired his name for this same reason.

Ice: Captain of the Gnosis hovercraft.

> *Symbolism*: Ice symbolizes calm under pressure, and sometimes heartlessness.

Jax: The operator on board the Vigilant. He is impaled by a rusty metal spike when a catwalk collapses inside the Vigilant just before the whole ship explodes.

Jue: The first mate on the Osiris hovercraft. She drops off a message for the other rebels inside the Matrix in *The Final Flight of the Osiris*.

Kali: Captain of the Brahma hovercraft.

> *Symbolism*: Kali is the personification of death and destruction within Hindu mythology.

Kamala: Sati's mother. We see her only at the Train Station in *Revolutions*. She is an indirective software programmer in the machine world.

Symbolism: (1) Kamala is an epithet of Laksmi, a Hindu Goddess. She is the source of abundance, fertility, and growth. (2) A possible reference to Kamala Das, one of India's foremost poets.

Keymaker, the: He enables Neo to enter the Source in *Reloaded*. His life is centered around that specific purpose. He was killed at the end of *Reloaded* by Agent Smith clones.

Symbolism: He "unlocks" the Source for Neo. His opposite is Commander Lock, a.k.a. "Deadbolt," who stands in the way of Neo's path.

Kid: a.k.a. Michael Karl Popper. Neo's young protégé in *Reloaded* and *Revolutions*. He opens the gate for Niobe as she brings the Hammer home. His earlier history is depicted in *Kid's Story* on *The Animatrix* DVD.

Symbolism: Sir Karl Popper was a twentieth-century British philosopher primarily known for his contributions to the philosophy of science.

Link: Replaces Tank as the operator on board the Nebuchadnezzar. He's married to Zee, who is Tank and Dozer's sister.

Symbolism: (1) He is "linked" to the old Nebuchadnezzar crew through his marriage to Zee. (2) Short for "hyperlink," a way of connecting one webpage to another.

Lock: Commander of Zion's military forces, and Niobe's love interest in *Reloaded*. Lock doesn't believe in the prophecy and thinks devoting resources to it will hasten Zion's destruction.

Symbolism: Lock is the antithesis of the Keymaker, hence his name and nickname – "Deadbolt."

Maggie: A member of the Hammer hovercraft crew. She is killed by Bane in *Revolutions*.

Symbolism: Probably short for magazine – a round of ammunition for an automatic weapon. This would fit her into the weapons theme that prevails in the names of the Hammer crew, See Mauser, AK, and Colt – all named after gun manufacturers.

Malachi: First mate on the Caduceus hovercraft. He is with Bane just before Agent Smith overwrites Bane's code.

Symbolism: A reference to Malachias, a prophet of the Old Testament. The Book of Malachi follows Zechariah in the King James Bible.

Mauser: A member of the Hammer hovercraft crew.

Symbolism: A brand of rifle. The K98 Mauser was the standard-issue rifle for the German Army in the Second World War.

Merovingian: A sentient program with a penchant for causal determinism. Married to Persephone. He holds the Keymaker prisoner in *Reloaded*, and tries to strike a deal for the eyes of the Oracle in *Revolutions*.

Symbolism: (1) The name comes from a family of French aristocrats who claim to be descendants of Jesus. (2) The Merovingian Order is a group dedicated to finding, protecting, and preserving the Holy Grail. (3) In *Reloaded*, his obsession with causality is reminiscent of the eighteenth-century French philosopher Pierre Simone Laplace. (4) In *Revolutions*, the Merovingian seems to play the role of Hades, who ruled the underworld (Club Hel) in Greek mythology. Hades also abducted Persephone, who eventually grew to love him.

Mifune: The captain of Zion's APU corps.

Symbolism: A reference to the late Toshiro Mifune (1920–97), a Japanese actor who is famous for his roles in Akira Kurosawa films.

Morpheus: Captain of the Nebuchadnezzar. Morpheus frees Neo from the Matrix, and helps him to become "The One."

Symbolism: (1) In Greek mythology Morpheus was the god of dreams. (2) Morpheus's role parallels that of John the Baptist, who paved the way for the coming of the Savior.

Mouse: A member of the Nebuchadnezzar crew, Mouse is the "digital pimp" who programmed the woman in red.

Symbolism: (1) A reference to a computer mouse. (2) A small rodent.

Neo: Thomas Anderson's hacker name. Neo is "The One," the prophesied rebirth of a man who can alter the Matrix at will. According to the Architect, Neo is the sixth One, or "anomaly."

Symbolism: (1) Neo is an anagram for "One." (2) Neo means new, and Neo represents a new beginning for both humans and machines. (3) The name "Neo" is concealed within Anderson.

Niobe: Captain of the Logos hovercraft. In *Reloaded* Niobe is with Commander Lock, but she dumps him for Morpheus in *Revolutions*. Niobe is also one of the two main characters in *Enter the Matrix*.

Symbolism: In Greek mythology Niobe was a mortal who compared herself to a Goddess. Because of her boastful arrogance, the Goddess Leto sent her sons Apollo and Artemis to kill Niobe's 12 children. After weeping for days, Niobe was transformed into a stone.

One, The: The title given to Neo. He is The One prophesied by the Oracle, who has returned to save humanity. Since the Architect tells us that this is the sixth version of the Matrix (counted from the emergence of each integral anomaly

– i.e., each "One"), we can surmise that Neo is the sixth version or reincarnation of The One.

Symbolism: (1) As "The One" to save humanity, Neo parallels Jesus in the Christian tradition. (2) As "the Awakened One" he parallels the Buddha. (3) As the reincarnation of a former "One" Neo parallels the Dalai Lama, who according to Tibetan Buddhists, is the fourteenth incarnation of former Dalai Lamas.

Oracle: A sentient program within the Matrix. The Oracle has the ability to see the future, and has prophesied the return of The One. Smith gains her ability to see the future when he overwrites his code onto hers in *Revolutions*.

Symbolism: Many aspects of the Oracle parallel the Oracle at Delphi, a cult of priestesses at the temple of Apollo in ancient Greece.

Persephone: She helps Neo rescue the Keymaker for the price of a kiss in *Reloaded*. Persephone thrives on experiencing the emotions of others. She is the wife of the Merovingian.

Symbolism: In Greek mythology Persephone was abducted by Hades and taken to the underworld, where she eventually fell in love with him.

Potentials: The children Neo meets in the Oracle's living room in *The Matrix*. They are all possible contenders for the role of "The One."

Symbolism: They are referred to as "potentials" because each may have the potential to be The One.

Priestess: The woman who answers the Oracle's door on Neo's first visit.

Symbolism: Priestesses served the Oracle at Delphi at the Temple of Apollo in Ancient Greece.

Q-ball Gang: The bald guards outside of Club Hel.

Symbolism: Q-ball is a fairly obvious reference to these thugs' bald heads.

Rama Kandra: Sati's father. He is first seen in the background when Neo, Trinity, and Morpheus enter the dining room of the Le Vrai Restaurant in *Reloaded*, but is featured primarily in *Revolutions*. He is the powerplant systems manager for recycling operations.

Symbolism: Rama Kandra (typically spelled Ramchandra) was the seventh incarnation of Vishnu in Hindu mythology. He returned to liberate the earth from evil.

Regan: See Cypher.

Symbolism: Mr. Regan wanted to be rich and famous – like an actor. Former US President Ronald Reagan also got his start as an actor.

Rhineheart: Thomas Anderson's boss at Metacortex.

Symbolism: A heart of stone.

Roland: Captain of the Hammer.

    Symbolism: The *Song of Roland* is the oldest surviving French poem. Roland was a knight for the Christian King Charlemagne. He dies when his temples burst from the force of sounding his horn to call Charlemagne to battle.

Sati: The little girl who finds Neo at the Train Station in *Revolutions*. She is the last exile – a program from the machine world who is hidden in the Matrix by her parents to spare her from deletion.

    Symbolism: (1) Sati means "virtuous woman" in the Hindu tradition. (2) Sati also refers to the Hindu practice in which a widow burns herself alive on the funeral pyre of her husband. The woman who committed sati was typically revered as a goddess, and shrines would be built in her memory.

Seraph: a.k.a. "Wingless." Guardian of the Oracle, Seraph is a program in the Matrix. He tests Neo before allowing him to see her.

    Symbolism: Seraphim are an order of angels described in the book of Isaiah 6:2. They have six wings, hence Seraph's nickname is "wingless."

Søren: Captain of the Vigilant hovercraft.

    Symbolism: His name pays homage to Søren Kierkegaard, the Danish existentialist whose philosophy of faith strongly influenced the Wachowskis' development of the character of Morpheus.

Sparks: The Operator of the Logos. Featured primarily in *Enter the Matrix* with Niobe and Ghost.

Spoon Boy: One of the Potentials. He teaches Neo to bend spoons with his mind. Spoon Boy was most likely freed from the Matrix, since Neo is given a hand-made spoon from one of the orphans in *Reloaded*.

    Symbolism: Spoon bending was popularized by alleged psychic Yuri Geller.

Switch: A member of the Nebuchadnezzar crew. Switch is the only character who appears in white inside the Matrix.

    Symbolism: Computers work essentially through "switching" by triggers of 1s and 0s.

Tank: A member of the Nebuchadnezzar crew in *The Matrix*. Tank thwarts Cypher's plan by blasting him with a plasma rifle, but not before Cypher kills Tank's brother Dozer, as well as Switch and Apoc.

    Symbolism: Like Dozer, Tank is a nickname given to large, slow computers.

Thaddeus: The Captain of the Osiris hovercraft. He and all his crew are killed by sentinels in *The Final Flight of the Osiris*, a computer-animated short from *The Animatrix*.

Symbolism: St. Jude Thaddeus, one of Jesus's 12 disciples. He is the patron saint of impossible causes.

Tirant: Captain of the Novalis hovercraft.
Symbolism: (1) A possible reference to *tyrant* – an oppressive ruler. (2) A possible reference to the epic Spanish novel *Tirant Lo Blanch.*

Trainman: The Trainman smuggles programs in and out of the Matrix. He wrote the Train Station program.
Symbolism: He first appeared in *Enter the Matrix*, when he told Niobe and Ghost that the last time Zion only lasted 72 hours against the machines.

Trinity: The second in command on the Nebuchadnezzar. The Oracle prophesied that she would fall in love with The One. In *The Matrix* her love resurrects Neo from death. In *Reloaded*, Neo returns the favor by removing a bullet from her chest.
Symbolism: (1) In Christianity the Trinity represents three in one: Father, Son, and Holy Spirit. In the films Morpheus plays the role of a father figure to Neo, the Son and Savior, and Trinity rounds out the triad akin to the Holy Spirit. (2) Trinity's key contribution is love. Only because of her love does Neo become The One and thereby make salvation possible for all.

Twins (The): a.k.a. E-2. The immaterializing dreadlocked henchmen of the Merovingian.

Vector: The first mate on the Vigilant hovercraft.
Symbolism: A vector is an object moving through space with magnitude and velocity.

Wingless: A nickname for Seraph. See Seraph.
Symbolism: Seraph gets his name from a six-winged angel. Since he lacks these wings, the Q-ball henchmen outside Club Hel call him Wingless.

Woman in Red: A program created by Mouse as part of the Agent training program.

Wurm: Most likely a member of the Gnosis hovercraft crew. He accompanies Corrupt when Smith delivers his earpiece in *Reloaded.*

Zee: Link's wife or girlfriend, and the sister of Tank and Dozer.

MATRIX GLOSSARY

01 (Zero One): The first machine civilization. It was developed by machines exiled from the human cities. This history is depicted in *The Second Renaissance Parts I and II* in *The Animatrix*.

    Symbolism: 01 refers to the binary code utilized by digital computers.

7 Males, 16 Females: The Architect tells Neo to choose this number of people to be spared in order to rebuild Zion in *Reloaded.*

    Symbolism: A likely reference to Genesis 7:16, "The animals going in were male and female of every living thing," as God had commanded Noah.

72 Hours: The amount of time it took the machines to destroy Zion the last time – according to the Trainman's cameo in *Enter the Matrix.*

101: The number of Neo's apartment and the floor on which the Merovingian's restaurant is located.

    Symbolism: The number references the fact that Neo is The One.

303: The room that Trinity is in at the Heart O' the City Hotel in the opening scene of the first film.

    Symbolism: The number references the fact that Trinity means three.

314 Seconds: The amount of time available to open the door to the Source. Only The One can open the door and only during that time can the door be opened.

    Symbolism: 3.14 is π.

250,000: The approximate population of Zion. Also, the approximate number of sentinels that descend on the underground city in *Revolutions*.

AI: Artificial Intelligence – computers that can think for themselves.

Animatrix (_The_): A collection of nine short animated films dealing with _Matrix_-inspired themes. Four of these stories were written by Andy and Larry Wachowski.

APU: Armored Personnel Unit, used in the battle to save Zion in _Revolutions_. According to The Second _Renaissance Part II_ in _The Animatrix_, these weapons were used by the humans in the original war against the machines.

Backdoors: Programmers' access routes into specific areas of the Matrix program. They are depicted as a series of green doors in a long white hallway.

Blue pill: (1) Take it and you wake up in your bed and believe whatever you want to believe. (2) A nickname for people still hooked into the Matrix from the power plant. (3) A euphemism for fear and complacency, e.g., "Are you red or blue?"

Brahma: A hovercraft in Zion's fleet captained by Kali.
Symbolism: Brahma is the Hindu god of creation, while Kali is a god of destruction.

Caduceus: A hovercraft in Zion's fleet captained by Ballard.
Symbolism: A staff in Greek mythology that is surmounted by two wings and entwined with snakes. It now serves as the symbol of the medical profession.

Cocoons: a.k.a. pods. The small structures in which the human crops at the powerplant lay as they sleep their lives away.

Coppertop: A person who is still hooked into the Matrix from the power plant.
Symbolism: Duracell batteries are known as coppertops. Human "coppertops" serve as the batteries of the machine world. See also: Blue pill.

Crops: Humans that are "grown" by the machines are referred to as crops: e.g., "With the failure of the first Matrix program entire crops were lost."

Déjà vu: A glitch in the Matrix. This occurs when the machines change something. Glitches are announced by the movements of a black cat in both _The Matrix_ and _Revolutions_.
Symbolism: From the French. The literal English translation is "already seen."

Double Destiny: The Oracle's brand of cigarette's in _Revolutions_.
Symbolism: Perhaps a hint that there are two ways the future may lead, depending upon whether Neo can defeat Agent Smith.

EMP: Electromagnetic pulse used to fry the circuitry of attacking sentinels. Use of an EMP also disables all other electronic equipment within its range.

Enter the Matrix: A home videogame with a story written by the Wachowskis. Completing game objectives unlocks a series of videoclips starring Niobe and Ghost.

Exiles: The exiles are of two types. They are either Matrix programs who refuse to accept their deletion, e.g. Agent Smith; or they are programs from the machine world who refuse to accept their deletion and have chosen to hide within the Matrix, e.g. Sati.

Franklin and Erie: The location of the exit at which Cypher kills Switch and Apoc. It also designates real streets from Chicago, where the Wachowskis grew up.

Gnosis: A hovercraft in Zion's fleet captained by Ice.
   Symbolism: "Gnosis" means knowledge. It is the root of Gnosticism, a religious movement in early Christianity. There are many Gnostic themes throughout the films.

Hammer: a.k.a. Mjolner. A hovercraft in Zion's fleet captained by Roland.
   Symbolism: A reference to the enchanted hammer of Thor, the god of thunder in Norse mythology.

Heart O' the City Hotel: The hotel in which we first meet Trinity. It is at this same hotel that Agents Smith, Brown, and Jones gun down Neo at the end of *The Matrix*.
   Symbolism: It is Trinity's heart — her love — that brings Neo back to life.

Hel: Club Hel is a nightclub that serves as the Merovingian's underground lair.
   Symbolism: Hell.

Hotel Lafayette: The location where Neo first meets Morpheus.

Icarus: A hovercraft in Zion's fleet captained by Ajax.
   Symbolism: In Greek mythology, Icarus made wings of wax and feathers. He flew too close to the sun and fell to his death.

IS 5416: Agent Smith's license plate in *Reloaded*.
   Symbolism: Isaiah 54:16; "Behold, I have created the smith who blows the coals in the fire, who brings forth an instrument for his work; and I have created the spoiler to destroy."

Jacking in/out: To enter and exit the Matrix by inserting a cable into a port in the back of one's head.

Know Thyself: The inscription (in Latin) in the Oracle's kitchen. It was also inscribed at the Temple of Apollo where the Oracle of Delphi made her prophecies.

Le Vrai: The restaurant in which we first meet the Merovingian in *Reloaded*.
   Symbolism: French for "the Truth."

Logos: A hovercraft in Zion's fleet captained by Niobe.
   Symbolism: (1) Logos means word or speech. (2) In the Christian tradition it can be used to refer to Jesus.

Machine City: The Machine City is on the earth's surface where it is too cold for humans to live. Neo travels to it at the end of *Revolutions*.

Mark III No. 11: The model number of the Nebuchadnezzar. Made in the USA Year 2069.
   Symbolism: Mark 3:11; "And unclean spirits, when they saw him, fell down before him, and cried, saying, Thou art the Son of God."

Mark VI No. 16: The model number of the Osiris. Made in the USA Year 2079.
   Symbolism: In Mark 6:16, King Herod says: "It is John whom I beheaded; he has risen from the dead."

Mark XIV No. 14: The model number of the Logos. Made in the USA Year 2101.
   Symbolism: Mark 14:14; Jesus tells his disciples, "And when you see the abomination of desolation standing where it ought not to stand – let him who reads understand – then let those who are in Judea flee to the mountains."

Mark XIV No. 62: The model number of the Hammer. Made in the USA Year 2111.
   Symbolism: Mark 14:62; "And Jesus said to him 'I am' and you shall see the son of man sitting at the right hand of power and coming with the clouds of heaven."

Matrix: A computer-generated dreamworld modeled after the height of human technology and culture as it was at the end of the twentieth century. According to the Architect, at the end of *Reloaded*, this is the sixth version.
   Symbolism: (1) Matrix literally means mother or womb. Humans now spend their entire lives lying in womb-like Matrix pods. (2) In mathematics, a matrix is a rectangular array of variables or constants arranged in rows or columns. The Architect describes the Matrix as a work of mathematical precision.

Metacortex: Thomas Anderson's employer. A major software firm in which it is imperative that every employee understands that they are part of a whole.
   Symbolism: "Cortex" refers to the outer layer of gray matter which covers most of the brain.

Mobil Ave.: The stop at the Train Station where Neo finds himself stranded in *Revolutions*. It exists "nowhere." See Train Station.
   Symbolism: (1) Mobil Ave. is analogous to limbo, for which its name is an anagram. (2) The symbol of the Mobil Corporation is Pegasus, the flying horse. In Greek myth, when Bellerophon tried to ride Pegasus to Mount Olympus in hopes of joining the gods, she cast him off and he fell to earth. Bellerophon

lived the rest of his days wandering the planet, shunned by both the gods and man. On Mobil Ave. Neo finds himself in a similar situation: he is unable to enter either of two worlds.

Monsters: In *Reloaded*, the Oracle tells Neo that every story he's ever heard about "vampires, werewolves, or aliens, is just the system assimilating some program that's not doing what it's supposed to be doing."

Nautilus: A cyclical shape that can be seen when the Matrix code is viewed from a great distance, as depicted in the opening credits of both *Reloaded* and *Revolutions*.
> *Symbolism*: Some believe that the nautilus shape holds the mathematical mysteries of the universe. See, for example, the film π (*Pi*).

Nebuchadnezzar: A hovercraft in Zion's fleet captained by Morpheus.
> *Symbolism*: Nebuchadnezzar was the King of Babylonia who captured Israel. He was plagued by disturbing dreams. Daniel was called upon to interpret the dreams, and he told Nebuchadnezzar that they were about the rise and fall of kingdoms. He said: "God of heaven will set up a kingdom which shall never be destroyed, nor shall its sovereignty be left to another people. It shall break in pieces all these kingdoms and bring them to an end, and it shall stand forever ..."

Night of Lepus: The horror film showing giant white rabbits that was playing on the television in the Oracle's living room in *The Matrix*.

Novalis: A hovercraft captained by Tirant.
> *Symbolism*: Novalis is a pseudonym of the German poet and philosopher Friedrich von Hardenberg.

Osiris: A hovercraft in Zion's fleet captained by Thaddeus.
> *Symbolism*: In Egyptian mythology, Osiris was the god of the dead and the judge of the underworld.

Pods: a.k.a. cocoons. The small structures in which the human crops at the powerplant lay as they sleep their lives away.

Pod-born: Anyone who was born at the powerplant, as opposed to the natural-born children of Zion.

Powerplant: Where humans are plugged into the Matrix and tapped for bioelectricity by the machines.

Rabbit Hole: Alice began her dream adventure by tumbling down the Rabbit hole in *Alice's Adventures in Wonderland*. Morpheus asks Neo if he feels a bit like Alice in *The Matrix*.

Red pill: (1) Take it and you find out what the Matrix is. Essentially the red pill is a trace program that enables the Zion rebels to pinpoint the location of your real body. (2) A nickname for people who have been unplugged from the Matrix powerplant. (3) A euphemism for courage and awareness, e.g., "Are you red or blue?"

Residual Self Image: The fact that people in the Matrix lack plugs and have hair is attributed to "residual self image."

Second Renaissance: *The Second Renaissance Parts I and II* are animated shorts featured in *The Animatrix*. They depict the events that precede the initial war against the machines, as well as the war itself and the development of the Matrix.

Sentient machines: While "sentience" typically refers to the ability to have sensations or feelings, the term "sentient machines" is used throughout the films to refer to artificial intelligence – machines that can think for themselves. Sentinels are the most commonly depicted sentient machines in the films.

Sentinels: a.k.a. squiddies, a.k.a. calamari. Sentinels are the sentient machines used to search the sewers for the hovercraft fleet. 250,000 of them are sent to destroy Zion in *Revolutions*.

***Simulacra and Simulation*:** In *The Matrix*, Neo pulls hidden software from inside this book to sell to Choi. *Simulacra and Simulation* was written by postmodern theorist Jean Baudrillard.

Source, The: Where programs are created and deleted. The Oracle tells Neo that this is where he must go in *Reloaded.*

Tastee Wheat: A brand of cereal within the Matrix. Mouse wondered how the machines knew what Tastee Wheat really tasted like, and whether they got it right.

Train Station: A program that enables programs to be smuggled between the machine world and the Matrix. According to Rama Kandra it is "nowhere."
  Symbolism: (1) Like the train stations of our world, this program is a boarding point to go from one destination to another. It links the machine city to the Matrix. (2) For Neo, the Train Station represents purgatory or limbo. See Mobil Ave.

Vigilant: A hovercraft in Zion's fleet captained by Søren. Bane blew its EMP, which allowed the sentinels to destroy it, along with several other ships.
  Symbolism: Vigilant means watchful, alert, or cautious.

VDTs: A virus of the brain. Most likely caused by a "bad hack" when jacking into the Matrix.

Wachowski Brothers: Andy and Larry Wachowski are the writers/directors of all three *Matrix* films. They wrote the screenplay for the 1995 film *Assassins* (but were disappointed with the execution of the film), and they wrote and directed the stylish 1996 thriller *Bound*.

White Rabbit: Neo follows DuJour's white rabbit tattoo in order to meet Trinity.
Symbolism: It was by following the White Rabbit that Alice tumbled down the rabbit hole toward paradox and discovery in *Alice's Adventures in Wonderland*.

Zion: The last human city, located deep beneath the Earth's surface.
Symbolism: Zion was the promised land of the ancient Israelites. Isaiah 14:32 states: "God has established Zion. Those in need and in trouble find refuge in her."

MATRIX GLOSSARY

CAST OF
PHILOSOPHERS

Bartky, Sandra: Professor of Philosophy and Women's Studies at University of Illinois at Chicago. Bartky has applied the philosophies of phenomenology, existentialism, and postmodernism to her analysis of feminist issues, as demonstrated in her 1990 book *Femininity and Domination: Studies in the Phenomenology of Oppression*.

Baker, Robert: Professor of Philosophy at Union College Schenectady, New York. While his analysis of sexism in language appeared in chapter 7 above, Baker is best known for his work in medical ethics. He is the director of the Center for Bioethics and Clinical Leadership of the Graduate College of Union University, and his most recent book is *The American Medical Ethics Revolution*.

Baudrillard, Jean: French sociologist born in 1929, Baudrillard is a cultural critic of contemporary Western society. He sees the West as dominated by technology, mass communication, and mass consumption. He argues that our lives are engrossed by simulated experiences such that the real and the unreal have come to lose all distinction. His book *Simulacra and Simulation* was one of the major influences on *The Matrix* screenplay.

Beauvoir, Simone de: (1908–86) French philosopher, novelist, essayist, and existentialist, de Beauvoir is often credited with launching the modern feminist movement through her seminal book *The Second Sex*. De Beauvoir argued that most of the differences between the sexes are socially and culturally imposed, rather than the result of biological differences. Women have been defined by men and shaped by men's desires, instead of defining themselves through their own freely chosen plans.

Berkeley, George: (1685–1753) An Irishman who became a bishop in 1734, Berkeley held the view called metaphysical idealism. He maintained that the only things in the world are finite minds, the infinite mind of God, and the thoughts, feelings, and sensations in these minds. There are no physical brains, nor physical objects of any kind. His major works include *Three Dialogues Between Hylas and Philonous* and *A Treatise Concerning the Principles of Human Knowledge*.

Bordo, Susan: Professor of English and Women's Studies at the University of Kentucky. Bordo's 1993 book, *The Unbearable Weight: Feminism, Western Culture, and the Body*, was nominated for a Pulitzer Prize.

Buddha: (563–483 BCE) "Buddha" means "the enlightened, or awakened one." This title was given to Siddhartha Gautama, the founder of Buddhism, after he achieved the enlightened state of nirvana. The essence of the Buddha's teaching is captured in his *four noble truths*: 1. Life is suffering. 2. Suffering is caused by desire or attachment. 3. Suffering can be overcome. 4. The path is the middle way. This "middle way" is further characterized as the *noble eightfold path*. It emphasizes honesty, compassion, and acute awareness.

Butler, Judith: Professor of Rhetoric at the University of California, Berkeley. Butler has been a leader within feminism, though she has often been critical of the feminist movement itself. One of her most significant works is *Gender Trouble: Feminism and the Subversion of Identity*.

Camus, Albert: (1913–60) Algerian-born French existentialist and novelist, Camus looked at the experience of "absurdity" or metaphysical nihilism. He won the 1957 Nobel Prize for Literature. His books include *The Stranger* and *The Plague*, and among his famous essays are *The Myth of Sisyphus* and *The Rebel*.

Churchland, Paul: Professor of philosophy at the University of California, San Diego. Churchland has written extensively in the philosophy of mind and cognitive sciences. In his 1988 book *Matter and Consciousness*, Churchland argued for a position he calls eliminative materialism, which maintains that folk-psychological states such as beliefs, desires, and emotions do not exist. The true causes of human behavior, he argued, are neurological events in the brain.

Clifford, William K.: (1845–79) A British mathematician with an intellectual interest in religious and philosophical topics. In an essay entitled *The Ethics of Belief*, he maintained that we should never believe anything upon insufficient evidence. By professing knowledge on insufficient grounds, he argued, we injure other people and society as a whole.

Dennett, Daniel: Professor of Philosophy at Tufts University. Dennett specializes in the philosophy of mind, and has emphasized how this area needs to be informed by work done in the sciences. His most influential books include *Consciousness Explained, Darwin's Dangerous Idea,* and *Freedom Evolves.*

Descartes, René: (1596–1650) A French philosopher, mathematician, and scientist, Descartes is often considered to be the father of modern philosophy. He is best known for his contributions to the theory of knowledge, and his famous *method of doubt.* Descartes is also known for his Cartesian dualism – his view that mind and body are separate and distinct substances. His major works include *Discourse on Method* and *Meditations on First Philosophy.*

Eckhart, Meister: (1260–1327) A German priest of the Dominican Order, Eckhart was one of the greatest Christian mystics. Similar to other mystics, he emphasized the experience of union with God in which the subject–object distinction is obliterated. Eckhart tells us, "My eye and God's eye are one and the same."

Frankfurt, Harry: Professor Emeritus at Princeton University. Frankfurt is an American philosopher best known for his work on Descartes's philosophy and on the problem of free will. Some of his most influential essays can be found in *The Importance of What We Care About: Collected Essays.*

Fromm, Erich: (1900–80) A renowned psychoanalyst, Fromm grew up in Germany, and came to the United States at the age of 34. His most popular book, *The Art of Loving,* has sold over 6 million copies and is a seminal work in the area of personal growth.

Hanh, Thich Nhat: A Vietnamese Buddhist Monk, Hanh tirelessly worked for peaceful reconciliation during the Vietnam War, and was nominated for the Nobel Peace Prize in 1967 by former recipient Dr. Martin Luther King, Jr. He championed "engaged Buddhism" which combined nonviolent civil disobedience and meditative practices. His numerous books include, *Joyfully Together: The Art of Building a Harmonious Community* and *Present Moment Wonderful Moment.*

Heidegger, Martin: (1889–1976) German phenomenologist, existentialist, and social critic. Heidegger lamented the fact that people are defined by others and society instead of being their authentic selves. He also criticized modernity and democracy, though his own support of the Nazi movement has made him the target of a great deal of criticism. Heidegger's most famous work is *Being and Time.*

Hui-neng: (7th–8th centuries) The sixth and last patriarch of the Chan Buddhist tradition in China. Hui-neng was an illiterate country boy who, based on his exceptional intuitive qualities, so impressed the fifth patriarch that he taught the boy about the Diamond Sutra. Hui-neng thereupon became enlightened. Chan Buddhism views meditation as the principle path to enlightenment. In Japan, the Chan School is known by the more familiar name of Zen Buddhism.

Hume, David: (1711–76) Hume, a Scottish philosopher, is considered by many to be the greatest philosopher to write in the English language. He was an empiricist, claiming that all of our knowledge is based on sense experience. Hume questioned whether we could ever be sure about much that we claim to know. He is famous for his skeptical views regarding the existence of the self, causality, God, and inductive inferences. His major works include *A Treatise of Human Nature, An Enquiry Concerning Human Understanding*, and *Dialogues Concerning Natural Religion*.

Kant, Immanuel: (1724–1804) Kant had an enormous impact on the three major areas of philosophy: epistemology, metaphysics, and ethics. In the *Critique of Pure Reason*, Kant argued that we can never really know about objects in the world as they are in themselves; we can only know how they *appear* to us. Space and time, he maintained, are manifolds of intuition within the mind and not a part of the world itself. In ethics, his *Groundwork of the Metaphysics of Morals* argued for a nonconsequentialist moral theory, centered upon a principle that he called the Categorical Imperative. This principle states that one must "act only on that maxim through which you can at the same time will that it should become a universal law."

Kierkegaard, Søren: (1813–55) A Danish philosopher and theologian, Kierkegaard is generally regarded as the first existentialist. He stressed that each individual needs to authentically choose his own way of life and he defended a radical view of faith that takes complete precedence over reason. His best-known works include *Either–Or, Fear and Trembling*, and *Concluding Unscientific Postscript*.

Lao Tzu: (6th century BCE) The reputed founder of Taoism, and the author of its primary text, the *Tao Te Ching*. Very little is known about Lao-Tzu's life, and some scholars doubt that he was the sole author of the *Tao Te Ching*. In contrast to Confucian formality and ritual, Taoism is the way of simplistic living in accordance with nature. The Taoist does not try to control or conquer nature, or other people, but instead acts through the natural action of *wu wei*. Lao Tzu tells us that when one lives the Taoist life, they will be quietly powerful, supremely happy, and at peace.

Laplace, Pierre Simon: (1749–1827) French astronomer, mathematician, and philosopher. Laplace argued for strict determinism in the mechanical operation of the universe in *On Celestial Mechanics*. He developed methods for calculating the probability of natural events in *Analytic Theory of Probabilities* and *Philosophical Essay on Probabilities*.

Lee, Bruce: (1940–73) Lee moved from Hong Kong to the United States at age 19 to study philosophy at the University of Washington. After graduation, he went to Hollywood, where he eventually became the world's top martial arts film star. Lee's most famous film, *Enter the Dragon*, was released the year that he died. His philosophical notes have been collected in *Striking Thoughts: Bruce Lee's Wisdom for Daily Living.* Lee's philosophical outlook is centered around the idea that "the creating individual . . . is more important than any style or system."

Lewis, David: (1941–2001) Philosophy Professor at Princeton. He has made major contributions in the areas of metaphysics, epistemology, and the philosophy of mind. In *Counterfactuals* Lewis introduced the now classic idea of "possible worlds" as an aid to metaphysical analysis.

MacKinnon, Catharine: Professor of Law at the University of Michigan Law School. MacKinnon has written 10 books and numerous articles on issues relating to sexual equality and the law. In 1986 the United States Supreme Court accepted MacKinnon's argument that sexual harassment in the workplace constitutes a violation of a woman's civil rights. In 2000 MacKinnon won a US$745 million damage award on behalf of Muslim women who were subject to sexual atrocities in Serbia.

Mill, John Stuart: (1806–73) An English philosopher and economist, Mill may well have been the most influential liberal thinker of the nineteenth century. He was the most vocal and thorough proponent of utilitarianism. Mill asserted that the foundation of morality is the Greatest Happiness Principle, which holds that "actions are right in proportion as they tend to promote happiness, wrong as they tend to produce the reverse of happiness." Mill's major works include *Utilitarianism, On Liberty, System of Logic, Principles of Political Economy*, and *The Subjection of Women.*

Nietzsche, Friedrich: (1844–1900) Perhaps the most famous philosopher of the nineteenth century, Nietzsche launched an assault on conventional morality in general and Christianity in particular. He argued that Christian morality honored weakness over strength, and prevented the strong from asserting their natural power and dominance, thus retarding any real human progress. Nietzsche's ideal, in contrast, favored change, growth, and experimentation. It embodied the notion of "will to power," which emphasizes becoming rather than being. Nietzsche espoused "perspectivism" – the view that there are no absolute truths, only truths from one perspective or another. His exploration of unconscious motivations predated Freud, and he is often considered the precursor to both existentialism and postmodernism. Nietzsche's major works include *Beyond Good and Evil, Human All to Human*, and *Thus Spake Zarathustra.*

Nozick, Robert: (1938–2002) Professor of Philosophy at Harvard University. Nozick's influential book, *Anarchy, State, and Utopia*, brought him instant notoriety as well as substantial criticism. In it, he argued that individual liberties are so important that only a minimal state is justified. Some of his other books include *The Examined Life*, *The Nature of Rationality*, and *Socratic Puzzles*.

Pike, Nelson: Professor Emeritus at University of California, Irvine. Pike specializes in the philosophy of religion. His best-known works include *God and Evil* and "Divine Omniscience and Voluntary Action." In the latter article, Pike argues that a God who possessed infallible foreknowledge would be incompatible with voluntary human actions.

Plato: (427–347 BCE) Plato was the star pupil of Socrates, and Aristotle's teacher. He was a gifted writer, and may have exerted more influence on Western philosophy than any other person. He founded the first university, called the Academy, and wrote numerous books in dialogue form. In most of Plato's dialogues, Socrates appears as the protagonist. In Plato's greatest work, *The Republic*, he argues for his original theory of justice and his conception of the ideal state under the "philosopher-king."

Ramakrishna: (1834–86) A Hindu priest from India, Ramakrishna practiced many of the other great religions, including Buddhism, Jainism, Islam, and Christianity, in order to better understand the many aspects of God. He concluded that all religions were different paths to the same ultimate truth. His writings are collected in *The Gospel of Sri Ramakrishna*.

Russell, Bertrand: (1872–1970) A British philosopher, Russell was not only one of the greatest philosophers of the twentieth century, he was also a brilliant mathematician and a committed political activist. His *Principia Mathematica* laid the foundations for modern logic. Russell's views on sexual morality were unconventional, and his book *Why I'm Not a Christian* made him a target of criticism. He was awarded the Nobel Prize for Literature in 1950.

Ruysbroeck, Jan van: (1293–1381) Born near Brussels, Ruysbroeck was foremost of the Flemish mystics. He loved to walk and meditate in the solitude of the forest. Some of the works in which he describes the mystical union with God include *The Adornment of the Spiritual Marriage* and *The Sparkling Stone*.

Sartre, Jean-Paul: (1905–80) French philosopher, novelist, and politician, Sartre became the leading proponent of existentialism. In his major work *Being and Nothingness*, Sartre denies that humans are born with a specified nature or essence, suggesting instead that we create our essence through our choices. Sartre was also the author of many plays including *No Exit*, *Nausea*, and *The Flies*.

Searle, John: An American philosopher at the University of California, Berkeley, Searle is one of the most famous living philosophers. He specializes in the philosophy of mind, and is a leading critic of the attempt to use computer programs as a model for understanding the human mind. He is best known for his "Chinese Room Argument" against Strong AI – the view that computers are capable of conscious thought. On Searle's view, understanding the particular biology of the brain is crucial to understanding consciousness. These ideas and many others are discussed in his now classic work *Minds, Brains, and Science.*

Stace, Walter: (1886–1967) Professor of Philosophy at Princeton University, Stace was one of the top Western scholars on the topic of mysticism. His most influential book is *Mysticism and Philosophy*, a classic in the field.

Suzuki, D. T.: (1870–1966) A Japanese Buddhist scholar, Suzuki was instrumental in spreading Zen Buddhism to the West through his translations of texts into English, and through his own books and lectures in America. His major works include *Studies in Zen Buddhism* and *Zen and Japanese Culture.*

Wasserstrom, Richard: Professor Emeritus of Philosophy at the University of California, Santa Cruz. Wasserstrom has written on a wide variety of ethical and legal issues including warfare, affirmative action, and sexism.

West, Cornel: Professor of Religion and African American Studies at Princeton University. West appears in the *Matrix* sequels as Councilor West. He has been a champion for racial justice, and his 1993 book *Race Matters* has sold over 400,000 copies.

INDEX

224

INDEX